BUSES
IN BRITAIN

STEWART J BROWN

Capital Transport

Foreword

BUSES IN BRITAIN covers all large operators and a sizeable number of small operators who have made some impact on their local transport scene. A large number of people have provided a lot of help in reading, correcting and updating my original drafts and they are listed below. Any errors are of course down to me, not to them. A large number of people also helped with photographs and these are individually credited.

A brief word on terminology seems necessary to molify purists who may take issue with styles of presentation. There is no clear agreement on the distinction between minibuses and midibuses. For the purpose of this volume, all truck-derived models are described as minibuses even though some, such as the Mercedes 811D, can carry as many as 33 seated passengers. The characteristics of this breed of relatively unsophisticated bus are such that I feel little compunction in lumping them all together.

By contrast, the term midibus is used to describe purpose-built bus chassis of smaller than standard size – which is to say less than 10m long. Two current production models fall into this category, the Dennis Dart and the Volvo B6.

I know some readers can become excited about errant apostrophes. When describing family firms I have tried to follow the style which the company uses on its vehicles (although even this is not always consistent), so if on one page you read about a company called Smith's Buses, but somewhere else there is a different operator described as Smiths Buses, it's not inconsistency in editorial presentation, but an attempt to stick to each operator's own style of describing himself.

The information contained in the pages which follow describes the situation in late-summer 1993. Readers seeking detailed information on individual fleets will find the series of regional Bus Handbooks an invaluable reference source. The northern and central parts of the country are dealt with by British Bus Publishing of Telford; while London and southern England are covered by Capital Transport. For those interested in keeping up with ever-changing events, Buses magazine, published monthly by Ian Allan, is the best way of doing so. And for readers interested in details of vehicle deliveries and withdrawals, of livery changes and depot allocations, the monthly News Sheets of the PSV Circle provide an unrivalled source of information compiled by a dedicated team of hard-working enthusiasts.

The kind assistance and helpful comments of the following are readily and gratefully acknowledged: John Aldridge, David Donati, Michael Fowler, Keith Grimes, Malcolm Keeley, David Little, Colin Lloyd, Alan MacFarlane, Iain MacGregor, Geoff Mills, Roy Marshall, Bill Potter and David Stewart.

I hope you enjoy the result.

Stewart J Brown MCIT
Framilode, September 1993

ISBN 185414 158 9

Published by Capital Transport Publishing
38 Long Elmes, Harrow Weald, Middlesex

Printed by The KPC Group, Ashford, Kent

© Capital Transport Publishing 1993

Title page photo:
Peter Rowlands

These pages:
Malcolm King, Mike Fowler, Tony Wilson

Cover:
Steve Warburton, Malc McDonald, Barry Spencer

Contents

INTRODUCTION
Page 4

SCOTLAND
Page 8

NORTH WEST ENGLAND
Page 32

NORTH EAST ENGLAND
Page 64

YORKSHIRE
Page 82

THE MIDLANDS
Page 106

EAST ANGLIA
Page 138

SOUTH EAST ENGLAND
Page 154

SOUTH WEST ENGLAND
Page 184

WALES
Page 208

Introduction: a time of change

The last few years have seen unprecedented upheaval in Britain's bus industry. It's been an exciting time as new operators have appeared to challenge long-established companies and, sadly, as some old-established operators have disappeared under intense competitive pressure.

The start point for the change was the 1985 Transport Act which abolished 50 years of tight licensing control of bus services and set in motion the privatisation of the National Bus Company (NBC), the Scottish Bus Group (SBG) and the bus companies owned by local authorities.

The privatisation process is nearing its completion. The NBC companies were sold off between July 1986 and April 1988; the SBG companies followed between August 1990 and October 1991. Of the seven bus operations which had been under the control of Passenger Transport Executives (PTEs), five had passed to the private sector by the summer of 1993, leaving only Greater Manchester Buses and South Yorkshire Transport under PTE ownership. Eleven erstwhile municipal operations – Chesterfield, Cleveland, Derby, Grampian, Hartlepool, Lincoln, Portsmouth, Preston, Rhymney Valley, Taff Ely and Tayside – have also been sold and it is the Government's intention that the rest will follow.

Privatisation of London Buses is expected to be completed during 1994, with deregulation in London planned to follow. However London Buses has not been immune from change. While there has been no competition on the capital's streets – apart from the short-lived first Docklands Transit operation – there has been competition for routes being put out to tender by London Regional Transport, with a number of private sector operators building up sizeable fleets to serve London.

One of the side effects of privatisation has been the emergence of new groups of bus companies. At the outset the rules governing the sale of NBC companies prohibited any one buyer acquiring more than three. But there was nothing to prevent the companies' new owners selling them on – which many have done.

The biggest of the 1990s bus groups is Stagecoach Holdings of Perth. Stagecoach started running express coaches when coach services were deregulated in 1980. It built up a network linking the main Scottish cities and connecting Scotland with London. These operations were later sold to National Express. The company operated a few buses on contracts and in 1985 took over the old-established McLennan of Spittalfield bus operation. Stagecoach started running local services in Glasgow in 1986, using the Magicbus name and a fleet of ex-London Routemasters. Such were its small beginnings.

When the privatisation of NBC got under way, Stagecoach soon built up a portfolio of English operators. During 1987 it bought Hampshire Bus and the associated Pilgrim Coaches business in April, Cumberland Motor Services in July and United Counties in November. Rationalisation soon followed as Pilgrim Coaches was closed and Stagecoach sold the urban Southampton operations of Hampshire Bus to Southern Vectis, which now runs them under the Solent Blue Line name.

Dramatic expansion of the Stagecoach business came in 1989, trebling the fleet from 800 to 2,400 vehicles. Its first acquisition was East Midland Motor Services, a former NBC company privatised in a management buy-out in February 1988. It was taken over by Stagecoach in April 1989. Weeks later Stagecoach took over Ribble Motor Services, another ex-NBC management buy-out operation whose territory adjoined that of Cumberland, making Stagecoach the major operator in north west England from Manchester to the Scottish border. No sooner had Stagecoach bought Ribble than Ribble acquired the operations of Barrow Borough Transport, which was in administrative receivership.

Another famous name was added to the Stagecoach empire in August 1989, when it took over Southdown Motor Services. This brought a half share in Top Line Buses of Hastings (the other half was owned by Eastbourne Buses) but by the end of the year Stagecoach not only owned all of Top Line, but had taken over the rival Hastings & District Transport business, another ex-NBC operation, as well.

Further south coast activity saw Stagecoach buy Portsmouth City Bus, although this attracted the attention of the Monopolies & Mergers Commission and Stagecoach's Portsmouth operations were sold to Transit Holdings in January 1991. At the other end of the country Stagecoach took over Inverness Traction in November 1989. It had been started 18 months earlier by a group of former Highland Scottish drivers.

Again there was some rationalisation. With East Midland had come Frontrunner South East, set up to run tendered services in Essex and London. The Essex business was sold to County Bus & Coach and the London operation to

Ensign Bus. In the north west there were also changes. Drawlane's North Western Road Car pulled out of Blackburn, leaving it to Ribble and Blackburn Transport, while Stagecoach effectively withdrew from Manchester, selling to Drawlane the Bee Line Buzz operations (acquired with Ribble) and Frontrunner North West, which had come with East Midland. Stagecoach took over Lancaster City Transport's operations in August 1993 and the sale of East Kent to the group was under way at the same time.

With a Scottish base it came as no surprise that Stagecoach was interested in acquiring SBG companies when they came up for sale. Here the rules stipulated that not more than two could be bought. Northern Scottish was taken over in March 1991 and subsequently united with Inverness Traction in Bluebird Northern, later renamed Bluebird Buses. Fife Scottish followed in July, after a wrangle over a rival bid by the company's management and employees.

Stagecoach is the only British-based group with international interests. In 1989 it took a 51 per cent share in United Transport Malawi. This was followed in 1990 by the purchase of Gray Coach Lines of Toronto (since sold again), in 1991 by a majority stake in Kenya Bus Services, and in 1992 by the takeover of the Wellington Transport Board in New Zealand.

The next biggest group is British Bus, or Drawlane as it was known until the end of 1992. Drawlane started in 1987 as a subsidiary of Endless Holdings, bidding for a number of NBC companies. This was happening against a background of accusations that Endless was trying to circumvent the rules restricting the number of companies it could buy by the use of another subsidiary, Allied Bus. Drawlane got Shamrock & Rambler Coaches of Bournemouth in July 1987 followed in 1988 by Midland Red North (January), London Country South West (February) and North Western Road Car (March). Drawlane also bought East Lancashire Coach Builders of Blackburn at the start of 1988. Bids by Endless Holdings for NBC subsidiaries North Devon, Southern National, East Midland and Lincolnshire Road Car were all accepted and then later rejected during 1987 as questions were asked about the links between Allied, Endless and Drawlane.

Like Stagecoach, Drawlane grew dramatically in 1989, doubling in size from just over 1,000 to just over 2,000 vehicles. Shamrock & Rambler was closed, after trying unsuccessfully to compete in Bournemouth. But in March Drawlane bought Crosville Motor Services from ATL Holdings (which had acquired it from NBC 12 months earlier). In September Drawlane expanded in Manchester, acquiring from Stagecoach its Ribble operations in south Manchester, along with the Bee Line Buzz business and the East Midland-owned Frontrunner North West. At the same time Drawlane purchased Midland Fox from its management.

This was followed in November by a redrawing of Crosville's operating territory, with part of it being added to an enlarged Bee Line (and then quickly being split off again to form a new C-Line), part going to Midland Red North, and another part going to North Western. This effectively halved the Crosville fleet and the remaining part of the business was sold to PMT in February 1990.

During 1991-92 Drawlane had a minority interest in National Express. This in turn gave it a stake in Crosville Wales and Amberline of Liverpool. Drawlane, through Midland Fox, has acquired a number of small companies. In 1993 the group purchased Southend Transport and Liverline of Liverpool.

Badgerline has perhaps been the most stable of the major new groups, expanding gradually since it was privatised in a management/employee buy-out from NBC in September 1986. In August 1987 Badgerline was involved with Plympton Coachlines of Plymouth in the purchase of Western National – and in 1988 took control. The company was also involved in short-lived joint ventures running buses in Poole (working with Southern Vectis as Badger Vectis) and in Portsmouth (linking up with Southampton City Bus in Red Admiral). In April 1988 Badgerline acquired Midland Red West and with it Bristol City Line. Bristol City Line and Badgerline had in fact been a single company – Bristol Omnibus – until January 1986 when NBC had split them in readiness for privatisation, as part of a policy of trying to ensure that none of the privatised companies would be so big as to stifle competition after deregulation came into effect.

The year of expansion for Badgerline was 1990. It took over South Wales Transport in February, Eastern National in April, and Wessex Coaches in June. All were former NBC subsidiaries. Eastern National was split into two companies in July, with its operations in south Essex and London passing to a new Thamesway operation.

The other 1990s groups are all considerably smaller. Transit Holdings runs Devon General and Bayline in Devon, Thames Transit and the Oxford Tube in Oxford and Red Admiral and Blue Admiral in Portsmouth – the operations taken over from Stagecoach in January 1991. It also has tendered routes in London, run by Docklands Transit. It did set up a Basingstoke Transit operation, but at the last minute decided not to proceed with it, leaving the town to Hampshire Bus.

Blazefield Holdings – previously the AJS Group – controls a clutch of operators who are the spiritual successors to West Yorkshire Road Car, namely Harrogate & District, Keighley & District and Yorkshire Coastliner, along with erstwhile competitor Harrogate Independent. The remainder of what was West Yorkshire Road Car territory is now in the hands of Rider Holdings. In the south Blazefield runs Sovereign Bus & Coach, formerly part of London Country North East. Most of the rest of the LCNE company is now with Lynton Travel's County Bus & Coach which, like Sovereign, was previously part of AJS.

Western Travel was created by a management buy-out from NBC of the Cheltenham & Gloucester Omnibus Co in October 1986. It bought Midland Red South in November 1987 and added to this the eastern area of National Welsh in January 1991. This was formed as a new company, Red & White. Western has also bought other smaller companies in the Midlands.

Q-Drive, which at its peak owned the Berks Bucks Bus Co (trading as the Bee Line) and Alder Valley South, has cut back considerably, selling parts of its business to Drawlane, City of Oxford Motor Services and Stagecoach. It has retained a part of the Bee Line business and at the start of 1993 bought Luton & District's Slough operations. Q-Drive also owns London Buslines, running LT tendered services in west London.

Caldaire Holdings controls West Riding, Yorkshire Woollen and Selby & District. It also owned United Auto, but in 1992 that was sold to Westcourt, created by former Caldaire directors, and with it went the associated Tees & District and Teesside businesses.

National Express, as well as running the long-distance coach network, controls Speedlink Airport Services. In May 1993 it acquired Scottish Citylink.

Proudmutual owns Northumbria Motor Services and Kentish Bus at opposite ends of England. Similarly Yorkshire Traction has a scattered empire, owning Lincolnshire Road Car and former SBG subsidiary Strathtay Scottish. It also acquired Lincoln City Transport at the start of 1993. Luton & District took over London Country North West in October 1991 and has gradually integrated the two operations. L&D also has a financial interest in Clydeside 2000 and Derby City Transport. Cambus, serving Cambridgeshire, spread westwards in 1992 by acquiring Milton Keynes City Bus.

The ownership of Scotland's buses has in part been covered with Stagecoach controlling Fife Scottish, Bluebird Buses and Inverness Traction. GRT Holdings, owners of Grampian Transport in Aberdeen, also own Midland Bluebird of Falkirk and have a share in Oban & District. Saltire Holdings, owners of Scottish Citylink Coaches, jointly owned Highland Scottish with Rapson of Alness. But when Saltire sold Scottish Citylink to National Express in May 1993 ownership of Highland passed totally to Rapson. Strathtay is owned by Yorkshire Traction, the only example of English ownership of a Scottish bus operator. The other SBG companies were privatised in management/employee buy-outs – Clydeside, Eastern (SMT), Kelvin, Lowland and Western. Luton & District has a minority stake in Clydeside.

Although the bulk of Britain's bus operations remains in the control of reasonably big companies or groups of companies, deregulation has encouraged the growth of small operators. Some are new companies which, ironically, have often been set up by redundant employees of major operators with whom they have then competed – examples of this include Liverline in Liverpool, the Buzz Co-operative in Harlow and Harrogate Independent Travel. Others have been established coach operators who have moved into bus operation.

These ventures have all met with varying degrees of success and it is this which has created some of the instability of deregulation as companies expand and, on occasion, fail – sometimes after only a few weeks of operation. With such rapid change it is impossible in a volume of this size to mention every operator providing local bus services in Britain. Some of the smallest only run one or two vehicles and these may not operate all day or every day – in many parts of the country it is becoming quite commonplace for one operator to run a service commercially during the day on weekdays, but for a different operator to provide the service on evenings and on Sundays, running under contract to a local authority.

This means that there are two levels of competition. Rival bus services on the streets, as happens in many of the conurbations in the north of England, is what most people think of when competition is mentioned. But there is also competition – which is no less intense – to win local authority and London Regional Transport tendered services. Bus companies can still be competing with each other even when their vehicles aren't jostling for position at city centre bus stops.

More changes are in the offing. As already mentioned, the Government wants to see London Buses privatised during 1994, and is pressing for the sale of the two remaining PTE-owned companies and of those which remain in municipal ownership.

The upheaval of the last few years is set to continue.

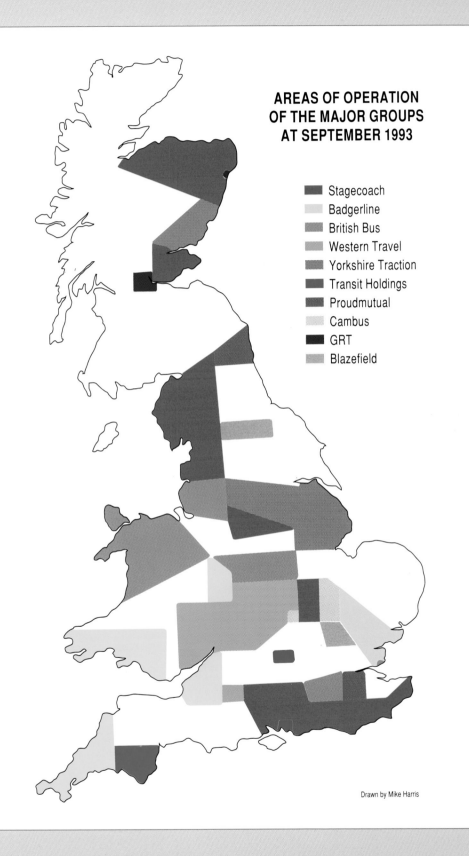

**AREAS OF OPERATION
OF THE MAJOR GROUPS
AT SEPTEMBER 1993**

- Stagecoach
- Badgerline
- British Bus
- Western Travel
- Yorkshire Traction
- Transit Holdings
- Proudmutual
- Cambus
- GRT
- Blazefield

Drawn by Mike Harris

SCOTLAND

One of Grampian's large fleet of Atlanteans seen at Marischal College. Donald MacRae

Scotland is a land of contrast — densely populated in the central region with its two great rivers, the Clyde and the Forth, yet almost uninhabited in the mountainous far North West. Chains of mountains and hills dictate patterns of settlement and patterns of transport — and all of this has influenced Scotland's bus operations.

With a population of 762,000, Glasgow is Scotland's biggest city — and it is served by three major and a number of minor operators. Biggest of the big names is Strathclyde Buses, which with nearly 800 vehicles is also Scotland's biggest bus company. It was until February 1993 owned by Strathclyde Regional Council when its management and employees finally concluded a successful buy-out of the company. Strathclyde Buses is the direct successor of the previous PTE and Corporation bus operations which served the city.

Glasgow Corporation and the PTE which followed standardised on the Leyland Atlantean for 20 years, during which time a total of 1,449 were purchased. Atlanteans still account for a fair proportion of the orange and black liveried fleet with around 370 still in use, the oldest dating back to 1973. Those bought new have Alexander bodies with detail differences between batches. However, bodywork variety was introduced to the company's Atlantean fleet after a fire at Larkfield garage in the summer of 1992 destroyed 60 buses. This saw Strathclyde Buses take the unprecedented step of acquiring a large fleet of second-hand vehicles — either by outright purchase or on long-term hire.

The most common modern type in the Strathclyde fleet is Volvo's Citybus with Alexander R-type body. A total of 95 were purchased in 1989-90 to give Strathclyde the country's biggest fleet of mid-engined double-deckers. The first G-registered example heads through George Square. Stewart J Brown

A Strathclyde Atlantean is seen against the backdrop of Glasgow's St Enoch Centre. Such vehicles once typified the standard Glasgow bus and are still the most common type in the fleet. Donald MacRae

These included Atlanteans from Nottingham City Transport, Grampian Transport, Busways Travel Services and Western Scottish. The Western vehicles were former Greater Manchester buses. The Nottingham buses were purchased; the Busways vehicles were originally on hire, but they too were purchased later in 1992 and painted in fleet colours. Hired buses were identified by being given fleet numbers in the C9XX series.

Apart from Atlanteans, Strathclyde's double-deck fleet also features Leyland Olympians, MCW Metrobuses and large numbers of Ailsas and Volvo Citybuses. A total of 95 Citybuses were purchased in 1989-90. These followed 133 Ailsas delivered earlier in the decade and make Strathclyde Britain's biggest buyer of both front-engined and underfloor-engined 'deckers. While Alexander won the lion's share of body orders on new-generation buses, there are also Olympians bodied by ECW and Roe, Metrobuses with MCW's own body, and a couple of what were dealer stock Ailsas (and the prototype Citybus) with unusual Marshall double-deck bodywork. The company's Ailsa fleet was increased after the fire by a batch of hired Tayside buses which, like many of the other hired buses, retain their original owners' liveries on the sides but with Strathclyde orange on the front and rear.

To replace buses lost in the fire Strathclyde ordered 52 Olympians with Alexander bodies for 1993 delivery. These are of lowheight layout which marks a change in policy. The only other lowheight buses in the fleet are a small number of Olympians which are used on a route south to East Kilbride which passes under a low railway bridge in Busby.

In August 1993 a low-cost subsidiary was set up by Strathclyde Buses to take over Kelvin Central's busy routes to Glasgow's huge municipal housing estates at Castlemilk and Easterhouse. This was part of an agreement on the re-drawing of boundaries between the two operators. GCT which uses the initials of Glasgow Corporation Transport has a mixed fleet including Atlanteans, Metroriders and ex-Kelvin Olympians.

Strathclyde launched its GCT low-cost unit in August 1993. Seen crossing Glasgow's Argyll Street is a former Nottingham Atlantean. Seven of these elderly vehicles were acquired in June 1993 and received extensive reconstruction including removal of the centre exit. Donald MacRae.

Three Leyland-bodied Olympians arrived in August 1991, one of which was subsequently destroyed by fire several months later. LO48 is one of the two survivors, seen on Victoria Road, Glasgow. Donald MacRae

Single-deckers play a comparatively small part in Strathclyde's operations. The great Larkfield fire saw the hire of five DAF SB220s with Hungarian-built Ikarus bodies and a pair of Scania N113s with Plaxton's Verde bodywork — the first examples of these types in Scotland. These operate in the company's harsh white, orange and black coach livery. They joined a mixed bag of odd single-deckers including three Volvo B10Ms with rare Caetano Stagecoach bus bodies, three B10M/Plaxton Derwent, and a bizarrely-rebuilt Ailsa which started life as a double-decker.

In PTE days, Glasgow was a pioneer in the operation of small buses. The first entered service in 1983, when the large scale NBC minibus conversion programme was but a glint in the planners' eyes (and which, no doubt, many enthusiasts still wish it had remained). After trying a variety of types, the MCW Metrorider was selected as the standard and 78 were bought between 1987 and 1991, including a few second-hand examples and two Optare-built demonstrators.

Most types of Strathclyde Buses' vehicles can be seen in or near Glasgow city centre, which is still the hub of the company's operations. The bus wars of the late 1980s which saw the city's traffic jams receive nationwide attention have abated but at peak times some city centre streets still get severely congested simply because of the number of buses using them.

Before deregulation in 1986 Strathclyde was spreading its tentacles beyond the city boundary with regular services stretching out to the East Kilbride, Paisley, Cumbernauld and Hamilton areas. Despite a vigorous competitive response from the Scottish Bus Group, Strathclyde quickly established itself as the major operator in East Kilbride (10 miles south-east of Glasgow city centre), ultimately forcing the withdrawal of SBG's Central Scottish subsidiary which had previously had a monopoly of East Kilbride services.

The company also has a strong presence in the Paisley area, with both large and small buses.

There are only three Plaxton Verdes in Scotland – a Dennis Lance at Tayside and two Scania N113s running for Strathclyde. The Scanias are part of the fleet hired in to replace buses lost in the 1992 Larkfield garage fire. This was the first Verde to be built and was originally a demonstrator. Donald MacRae

Two Plaxton Derwent bodied Volvo B10Ms were acquired by Strathclyde for a short lived tendered service into Central Region. Now fitted with coach seats, this one is seen in Glasgow's city centre on more local work. Donald MacRae

Five Ikarus-bodied DAF SB220s were hired in July 1992 to assist in the general vehicle shortage following on from the Larkfield depot fire. They are generally to be found on the lengthy service 66 and one is seen on Pollokshaws Road heading for East Kilbride. Donald MacRae

The other major operators around Glasgow are the former SBG subsidiaries Clydeside and Kelvin Central. Clydeside Scottish — now Clydeside 2000 — was created from the northern area of Kilmarnock-based Western Scottish in 1985 in the run up to deregulation. It immediately hit the headlines by buying a large fleet of ex-London Routemasters and reintroducing bus conductors to Glasgow. But the intense competition with Strathclyde seriously weakened Clydeside and it was rejoined with Western in 1989. Western was privatised in a management buy-out in 1991 and it immediately sold the former Clydeside operations to the Clydeside employees (with some help from Luton & District).

Clydeside 2000, in a bright red and yellow livery (although many buses are still in Western black, white and red or in an earlier version of Clydeside red and yellow) runs into Glasgow from the Paisley area, with additional services to the city's south-western and north-eastern suburbs. The company has its headquarters at its Thornliebank depot, in the south of the city, and has other garages at Greenock, Inchinnan, Johnstone and Largs making it the major operator in the area on the south side of the River Clyde to the west of Glasgow.

Its fleet is made up largely of vehicles bought in SBG days — lowheight Fleetlines and Dominators, highbridge Ailsas, a few examples of the short-lived Danish-built underfloor engined Leyland Lion and a large fleet of that old SBG workhorse, the Alexander-bodied Leyland Leopard. There are two Leyland Olympians in the fleet, one of which is an early B45 prototype and former NEC Motor Show exhibit. Clydeside 2000 also has a sizeable fleet of minibuses, mainly Dodges (or Renaults as they became known from 1987) including a number of former Merseybus examples with Northern Counties bodies which have joined the fleet since its privatisation. There are no longer any Clydeside Routemasters in regular service in Glasgow.

Clydeside 2000's busiest services outside the Glasgow and Paisley areas are in Greenock, where unbridled competition has seen the growth of small operators running ageing second-hand single-deckers (mainly Leyland Nationals) and minibuses. There are also small competitors in the Paisley area.

Clydeside 2000 operates 108 Leyland Leopards with Alexander Y-type bodies – indeed, these are the only full-size single-deck buses in its fleet. This livery layout, adopted when the company was privatised, is being simplified by the deletion of the thin red stripes ahead of the solid area of red at the rear. Stewart J Brown

Several applications of the Clydeside 2000 livery are carried by the collection of Fleetlines operated by the company. So far unique is this Alexander-bodied bus which has a much deeper red skirt. It is seen in Gauze Street, Paisley in June 1993. Donald MacRae

Clydeside 2000 has been selling Dominators and buying Leopards. A recent arrival from Cleveland Transit is this 1979 PSU3 with bus-seated Plaxton Supreme body. Donald MacRae

Kelvin Central is another former SBG subsidiary now in the ownership of its managers and employees. It was formed in 1989 to combine the interests of the Kelvin and Central companies, both weakened by the intense post-deregulation competition in Glasgow. It had a troubled start, with prolonged industrial strife, and its combined fleet of 492 buses in 1990 was no larger than the Central fleet alone only five years earlier.

Strikes at Central in 1989 saw the mushrooming of small operators, many of whom survived to compete with Kelvin Central until, after privatisation, it embarked on a programme of expansion by takeover which saw a number of businesses being absorbed in 1991 and 1992. Kelvin Central's biggest coup was the takeover in 1992 of the Glasgow area Magicbus operations of Stagecoach which, ironically, brought the first truly modern buses into its fleet in the shape of six Dennis Darts with Alexander Dash bodies. The former Magicbus services passed to Strathclyde's GCT operation in 1993.

Kelvin Central's fleet is gradually being repainted red and cream, but significant numbers of buses still run in the liveries of its two constituents — blue and yellow for ex-Kelvin buses and maroon and cream for former Central machines. Like Clydeside, Kelvin Central has bought no new buses since privatisation and its fleet is a mixture of generally ageing vehicles. Kelvin provided, among other things, Routemasters, Leyland Nationals, and Alexander-bodied Metrobuses. Central's contributions included Leopards, Dominators and Ailsas. Among its more modern single-deckers — 'modern' being a relative term — are comparatively rare Dennis Dorchesters and Leyland Tigers with Gardner engines; these all have Alexander T-type bodies. If they have lost their respective makers' badges they can be difficult to tell apart. The Gardner-powered Tiger was developed by Leyland specifically to counter Dennis's success in selling Dorchesters to Central, which in the early 1980s had a predominantly Leyland Leopard fleet.

Add to these such varied vehicles as second-hand Bristol VRTs and Leopard coaches (including two with ECW B51 bodies), more Nationals, and assorted minibuses taken into stock from acquired operators and you have some picture of the mix which makes up Kelvin Central. Most of the 24 buses taken over from Magicbus are still in corporate white Stagecoach group colours, although some VRTs are running in Ribble red livery, having been transferred north to Magicbus without being repainted. Kelvin Central's most recent major acquisition, John Morrow of Clydebank, was taken over in the autumn of 1992. Most of the former Morrow buses were running from Old Kilpatrick (where they helped oust Routemasters) but some are operating in the Motherwell area. With the Morrow business came the contract to run the inter-station service in Glasgow, operated by Leyland Nationals and linking Central and Queen Street stations, but that was lost on retendering to HAD of Shotts, running a minibus.

Kelvin Central's strength is north of the Clyde. It is the main operator westwards towards Dumbarton, north to Kirkintilloch and Cumbernauld, and east to

Coatbridge, Airdrie, Motherwell (its headquarters town) and Hamilton. In each of these areas it has networks of local services. It has depots in Airdrie, Cumbernauld, Kirkintilloch, Motherwell, Old Kilpatrick and Stepps.

Kelvin Central's fleet numbering system can appear a bit bewildering, with numbers ranging from 1001 to 3232 for a fleet of only 560 buses. The secret is that the first digit indicates the vehicle type — 1 is a bus, 2 is a dual-purpose coach and 3 is a full coach. Thus Tigers 3232 and 1233 were in fact consecutively numbered vehicles.

One of the most unusual vehicles in the Kelvin Fleet is 1100, a decapitated former Greater Manchester Fleetline which Kelvin acquired with the John Morrow business in 1992. The bodywork is by NCME. Donald MacRae

Kelvin Central runs a variety of double-deck types including 43 Dennis Dominators acquired from Central Scottish. They have lowheight Alexander bodies.
Malcolm King

Other former SBG subsidiaries run long-distance services into Glasgow — notably Eastern, Western, Fife and Midland. Old-established Barrhead independent, McGill, operates Leyland Nationals on a service into the city, while newer operators such as Bridge Coaches of Erskine and Henderson Travel of Hamilton run minibuses in and around the city. Henderson has been successful in winning a number of PTE contracts to run tendered services in Glasgow and also runs services in Lanarkshire. The fleet is based on Mercedes-Benz minibuses but there are also a few Leyland Leopards.

Competition for Kelvin Central outside Glasgow comes from some old-established operators. The biggest of these is Hutchison of Overtown, a company with a long tradition of buying new buses for its local services. Its current standard for both bus and coach operation is the Volvo B10M and its bus fleet includes 15 with the short-lived Duple 300-series body, making Hutchison the biggest user of the type. The last of these, with J-registrations, only entered service in 1992 — three years after being built. Hutchison was also the first Scottish Dennis Dart user, and runs an early Duple-bodied example — indeed Scotland's only example of the type.

Hutchison's services are concentrated in the Motherwell and Wishaw areas, and the latter is also served by Irvine of Law and Wilson of Carnwath, both running assorted second-hand vehicles. In Airdrie, Golden Eagle Coaches of Salsburgh runs to Shotts. Recent additions to the Golden Eagle bus fleet have been Volvo B10Ms, but three late 1970s AEC Reliances remain and are still in regular use. Further south, Stokes of Carstairs provides services in Lanark, and also runs to Hamilton and Peebles. Most of Stokes' vehicles have been purchased new and the front-line members of the bus fleet are four 1988 Leyland Tigers with Plaxton Derwent bodies. In 1990 the company won tendered minibus services and its newest buses are four Mercedes-Benz 811Ds with Carlyle bodies.

The Hutchison fleet was once an AEC stronghold but the Volvo B10M now typifies the fleet. Duple 300 bodywork is fitted to this example which carries the striking Hutchison 'H' logo on local services linking Motherwell and Wishaw. Donald MacRae

This Volvo B58 now operates for Irvine's of Law but originated with another Lanarkshire based operator, Hutchison of Overtown. It has Duple bodywork and was photographed in central Wishaw.
Donald MacRae

Golden Eagle of Salsburgh link Airdrie and Shotts. An Alexander-bodied Mercedes 709D is seen in Airdrie. Donald MacRae

Hamilton is also served by Whitelaw's Coaches of Stonehouse, whose bus operations expanded after the 1989 strikes by Central Scottish staff. Whitelaw's runs the second biggest fleet of Lynx IIs in Scotland (after Lothian) with five, including an ex-demonstrator. The company's bus fleet, in an unusual grey livery, also includes original-style Lynxes, a pair of Plaxton Derwent-bodied Volvo B10Ms, and assorted second-hand Leopards — mostly former SBG buses with Alexander bodies but including an ex-NBC machine with ECW's dual-purpose B51 body, a rare type north of the border.

To the west of Glasgow, Kelvin Central shares services in the Dumbarton area with Loch Lomond Coaches, running Leyland Leopards with Alexander T-type bodies which were new to NBC, and with some Willowbrook rebodied Leopards. Across the Clyde estuary is Dunoon, a town never served by SBG. Local services here are in the hands of two associated companies — Cowal Motor Services and Alexander Baird. Their fleets are made up mainly of former SBG Leopards and Seddons with Alexander Y-type bodies. Further down the west side of the Firth of Clyde, West Coast Motor Services with depots in Ardrishaig and Campbeltown provides services on the Cowal peninsula. The older vehicles in its fleet are Bedfords with Plaxton bus bodies and most services are in fact operated by coaches — including a through route to Glasgow run on behalf of Scottish Citylink. The company's newest bus is an Optare Vecta, based on the rear-engined MAN 11.190 underframe.

The steep gradient of Lanark High Street is the setting for one of four Plaxton Derwent bodied Tigers in the smart Stokes fleet. Donald MacRae

The first Optare Vecta in Scotland was purchased by West Coast Motors in 1992. It is a 41-seater built on a MAN underframe. The only other Scottish Vectas are two operated by Express Travel, a British Bus subsidiary, on airport services from Glasgow. Thomas Bryceland

Whitelaw's distinctive grey livery with coloured flashes has become commonplace in Lanarkshire since deregulation, and particularly since Central's retrenchment in 1989. This is one of several Lynx purchased and is seen in Hamilton Bus Station.
Donald MacRae

Lothian's current standard bus is the long-wheelbase Olympian with 81-seat two-door Alexander body with a distinctive short bay in mid-wheelbase which adds the extra length while maintaining standard bays. Roy Marshall

The Lothian Atlantean once reigned supreme in the Scottish Capital but is now overshadowed by more modern types. One of a batch of sixty bought in 1976 and 1977 is seen in Dalkeith town centre. Donald MacRae

Edinburgh is in the paradoxical situation of being both Scotland's first and second city — first insofar as it is the capital, second in that it is eclipsed by Glasgow in terms of its size. Where Glasgow experienced intense competition in the late 1980s, with frequent changes of operators and services, the situation in Edinburgh has been much more stable. Edinburgh's Princes Street in 1993 looks little different from 1983 (or even 1973 for that matter), with Lothian Region Transport's madder (deep maroon) and white double-deckers dominating local bus services, and the green and cream fleet of Eastern Scottish running most of the routes beyond the city boundary.

In fact, the situation is not really quite so clear cut. Under SBG ownership, Eastern Scottish stepped up its services in the city, introducing City Sprinter minibuses on high-frequency cross-town routes using Alexander-bodied Renaults. After privatisation (by a management-led employee buy-out in 1990) the company, which turned the clock back a quarter of a century by reviving the SMT fleet name, introduced more minibuses — although minibus services are not quite as intense or as fiercely competitive as they once were. LRT's response has been to open up new routes beyond the city boundary, and its double-deckers can now be seen as far west as Bathgate and Armadale, as well as in places like Dalkeith and Musselburgh which were once the exclusive preserve of Eastern Scottish.

LRT is now the only public sector bus operator in Scotland (unless you count the Scottish Postal Board's Post Buses) and there are no immediate plans for its privatisation.

The 600-strong Lothian fleet has carried on the tradition of its predecessor, Edinburgh Corporation Transport, with smartly turned-out buses. For nearly two decades the bus fleet has been 100 per cent Leyland (there were small numbers of Bedford coaches up to the mid-1980s), but Leyland's monopoly was broken at the end of 1992 with the delivery of Lothian's first Dennises, 12 Darts with Alexander Dash bodies which are used primarily on tendered services and do not generally penetrate the city centre.

Single-deck buses play but a small part in the Lothian operation, with one batch of Leyland Lynx IIs (the only production dual-door Lynxes) and small numbers of Leyland National 2s. Alexander-bodied Atlanteans were the standard choice in Scotland's capital city from 1966 until 1981, when orders were switched to long-wheelbase Olympians. The first two batches had ECW bodies; subsequent batches have been bodied by Alexander. Early vehicles had Leyland TL11 engines — a relatively unusual choice. When Leyland engine production ceased Lothian turned to the Cummins L10. Post-1988 buses (from the E-registered batch) have Cummins power.

The oldest Atlanteans in the fleet are L-registered open-toppers used on sightseeing tours. Lothian also runs a few closed top 'deckers in black and white coach livery and with coach seats, but most of its coaches are conventional Leyland Tigers with Duple or Plaxton bodies. As with the Olympians, the newest Tigers have Cummins L10 engines. Coach-liveried Olympians run the airport express service which has attracted competition from Guide Friday of Stratford-on-Avon running ageing ex-South Yorkshire Atlanteans. Guide Friday also competes on the busy city tours programme with open-top ex-Nottingham buses — a move which provoked retaliation by LRT which now runs city tours in Oxford, where Guide Friday has an established operation.

LRT continues to use dual-door buses, a type which now has a very limited following except in London. The centre exit costs seats, but is seen as improving passenger flow at busy stops. It is used in conjunction with a passenger-unfriendly exact-fare/no change system, also designed to cut boarding delays. This is a system which is also used by Scotland's three other major urban operators — Grampian, Strathclyde and Tayside.

Single-deckers play a small part in the Lothian fleet. The newest full-size examples are 12 dual-door Lynx IIs from 1991. Donald MacRae

The only non-Leyland buses in the Lothian fleet are 12 Dennis Darts with 35-seat Alexander Dash bodies. Donald MacRae

Lothian's black and white coach livery is carried by a handful of Olympians which are fitted with coach seats and usually operate on a service to the airport. Malcolm King

SMT covers Edinburgh and the surrounding areas with depots in Edinburgh, Bathgate, Dalkeith, Livingston and Musselburgh. Despite the intake of new minibuses in the 1990s — 30 Reeve Burgess-bodied Renaults followed by Optare's first Scottish fleet order, for 15 MetroRiders — the bulk of the fleet is still clearly an SBG legacy. ECW-bodied Fleetlines are the oldest buses in regular use with large numbers of Seddon Pennine 7s, a chassis developed specifically to meet SBG's need for a Gardner-powered single-decker. These, inevitably, have Alexander Y-type bodies for bus operation, but there are also Plaxton-bodied coaches. SMT is unusual for a former SBG company in having no Leyland Leopards. There are no rear-engined single-deckers in the SMT operation either — another legacy of SBG conservatism — and its more modern double-deckers can be rear-engined (Olympians), mid-engined (Citybuses and Lions) or front-engined (Ailsas). Which makes for plenty of variety. Big buses are dark green and cream; small buses are light green and cream. A few vehicles still carry a short-lived but attractive two-tone green and cream livery developed shortly before privatisation. SMT's coaches are dark red.

Small operators are noticeable by their virtual absence in Edinburgh, generally being kept out by the tight and efficient networks run by the two major companies. Edinburgh Transport, a trading name for Silver Coach Lines, runs a few tendered services with Leyland Nationals and a pair of former demonstrator Optare Deltas (the only ones in Scotland) in an unusual mid-blue and orange livery. Lothian Transit is an even smaller operation with a few former SBG Y-type Leopards which ran in competition with an LRT service. Now Lothian Transit has pulled out of Edinburgh but still runs in and around its home town of Dalkeith.

SMT's oldest double-deckers are Fleetlines. All have ECW bodywork, rather than Alexander which was the normal choice for SBG companies. A 1978 bus loads in Edinburgh's St Andrew Square. Malcolm King.

Optare's biggest Scottish order came from SMT and specified 15 MetroRider 25-seaters. This one is seen in Bathgate. Malcolm King

Silver Coach Lines runs buses under the Edinburgh Transport name. These include Scotland's only Optare Deltas. Malcolm King

Former SBG subsidiaries Lowland, Midland and Fife all have a presence in the capital with long-distance local bus services. Lowland, in 1990 the first SBG company to be privatised, serves the predominantly rural south-east, stretching down to the English border at Berwick upon Tweed, location of the company's southernmost depot. It also has bases at Galashiels (its headquarters), Dunbar, Haddington, Hawick, Kelso and Peebles. These were until 1985 part of the Eastern Scottish operation. The fleet is mainly single-decked — Pennine 7s and Tigers — but a small and varied double-deck fleet operates mainly on Edinburgh services and school contracts. These comprise Dennis Dominators, Daimler Fleetlines, Bristol VRTs, Leyland Olympians and a former Leyland Titan demonstrator acquired with the business of Ian Glass of Haddington. This is Scotland's only Titan. Glass ran a local service into Edinburgh which is now part of the Lowland operation; the Glass name is being retained for coaches.

Since privatisation Lowland has added new vehicles to its fleet: five Scania K113 coaches and a quartet of of unusual Volvo-powered Leyland Tigers with Alexander Belfast bodies, diverted from an Ulsterbus order and likely to be the only Volvo-engined Tigers to enter service in Scotland. They also look like being Scotland's last new Tigers.

Lowland's modern double-deckers are mainly Leyland Olympians with Leyland engines and Alexander bodies. This one was new in 1985 to Eastern Scottish. Geoff Morant

Alexander's T-type bodywork is normally associated with Seddons and Leyland Leopards in the former SBG fleets. However a few late variants were delivered on Tiger chassis including this Lowland vehicle, originally supplied to Eastern in 1982. Donald MacRae

Rarely seen outside Northern Ireland, Lowland purchased four Alexander Q-type bodies fitted to Leyland Tiger chassis in 1991. They are normally to be found on the lengthy Edinburgh Carlisle service. Donald MacRae

In Dundee, Tayside Public Transport is the main operator of local services with a fleet of 150 blue and cream-liveried buses, most of which are double-deckers. There is also a 30-strong coach fleet boosted in 1990 by the takeover of Greyhound Coaches and now marketed as Tayside Greyhound. Older vehicles are Ailsas (with a fine mix of bodies by Alexander, East Lancs and Northern Counties) while the newer examples are Volvo Citybuses. These operate an intensive network of services in the city. Dundee has seen little minibus operation; Tayside Buses only runs three in an otherwise double-deck fleet. However, the double-decker's supremacy is being challenged in 1993 as Tayside takes delivery of five Scania N113 single-deckers with East Lancs bodies. One of these will be an ultra-low-floor bus, the first in Scotland. The Tayside fleet can trace its origins back to Dundee Corporation Transport which was taken over by Tayside Regional Council in 1974 and was privatised in a management-led employee buy-out in 1991.

The Tayside fleet has a strong Scandinavian flavour with Volvo-powered Ailsas, Volvo Citybuses and orders in place for Scania N113s. There are 128 Ailsas in the fleet, 10 of which have Northern Counties bodies - not a common combination. They were new in 1983. The red lettering above the fleetname reads 'employee owned'. Malcolm King

Tayside runs this Plaxton Verde bodied Dennis Lance demonstrator which eventually settled with the Dundee based fleet in December 1992. Along with its NCME bodied sister, it can regularly be found on the lengthy services 13/14 to Ninewells Hospital. Donald MacRae

Tayside purchased two Plaxton bodied Dennis Darts in 1993 which are generally to be found on service 2. The second of the pair is awaiting departure to Dryburgh on Crichton Street, Dundee. Donald MacRae

The only other operator with a significant presence in Dundee is Strathtay Scottish, a former SBG company which since 1991 has been owned by Yorkshire Traction. Strathtay runs 150 buses in a distinctive blue, orange and white livery and is a comparatively young company, having been formed in 1985 by combining the Perthshire operations of Midland Scottish with the southern part of the Northern Scottish business. The fleet is a varied one. It inherited modern double-deckers from Midland (Metrobuses) and Northern (Olympians) to give it variety from the outset. Strathtay joined in the great Scottish Routemaster buying spree in the mid-1980s and a few are still in use in Dundee. To prolong the lives of some of its large fleet of Leyland Tigers, two were rebodied by East Lancs in 1992 — rebodying has not been widely practised by Scottish fleets in recent years.

Strathtay also runs a network of cross-country services and has depots at Arbroath, Blairgowrie, Dundee, Forfar and Montrose.

The Leyland Olympian is the most numerous double-deck model in the Strathtay fleet, with 21 in operation. The oldest are 1981 Alexander-bodied buses which were new to Northern Scottish. Geoff Morant

Routemasters are still in use on Strathtay services around Dundee. All have been re-registered; their original numbers have generally been transferred to coaches. Malcolm King

The Stagecoach name is used for services operated by Stagecoach Scotland in Tayside. A Willowbrook-bodied Leopard transferred from Cumberland loads in Perth for Dundee. It was new to United Counties. Stewart J Brown

The northernmost of Scotland's four major cities is Aberdeen. Grampian Transport — the inheritor of Aberdeen Corporation's operations — provides virtually all of the city's local services with the remainder being run by Bluebird Buses (formerly Northern Scottish), a Stagecoach subsidiary since its privatisation in 1991. Competition did flare up in the late 1980s with Northern Scottish stepping up its presence in the city and Grampian extending into the rural hinterland, hitherto served only by Northern. That has now largely died down with both operators concentrating on their traditional territories.

The Grampian fleet has until recently been predominantly double-decked — Atlanteans and Olympians, all with Alexander bodies. In 1983,

Grampian took delivery of the last new Atlantean for a Scottish fleet. Minibuses played a small part and single-deckers none at all. However that is now changing. Grampian runs Scotland's only articulated bus, an Alexander-bodied Mercedes which entered service at the end of 1992 as the company explored ways of improving the image of public transport in one of the few British cities never to have had parking meters. It was to be followed by 26 new single-deckers (20 Mercedes O405 and six Scania) and 18 Mercedes minibuses — deliveries which are radically altering the appearance of Grampian's services. Some of the new buses are for GRT's Midland Bluebird operation.

Grampian has two subsidiaries in the area, Mair and Kirkpatrick. Both are primarily coach operators.

Grampian 212 is numerically the oldest Atlantean in the fleet, many of its contemporaries having been transferred to Midland to replace Fleetlines. Donald MacRae

The most recent double-deck deliveries to Grampian Transport have been Alexander-bodied Olympians. The last 10, delivered in 1988, are long-wheelbase chassis with Cummins engines. John Boylett

Grampian acquired six Reeve Burgess bodied Mercedes-Benz 709Ds in 1991 and this example, No.36, was converted to run on fuel derived from oil seed rape in May 1993 in conjunction with the Robert Gordon Institute of Technology. It is seen here in Guild Street, Aberdeen on Circular Service 6, its usual haunt. Donald MacRae

The Alexander bodied Mercedes-Benz O405G articulated bus in Grampian's fleet is seen in College Bounds, Old Aberdeen. G Yuill

The attractive yellow and cream livery used by Northern Scottish is quickly being obliterated by the Stagecoach white paintbrush as the company assumes its new identity as Bluebird Buses. The double-deck fleet consists mainly of Leyland Olympians. Single-deckers are Leopards, Tigers and Nationals, although the unique Alexander-bodied Volvo B57 has survived the takeover by Stagecoach. The front-engined B57 was purchased for evaluation as a possible replacement for the large fleet of Fords which Northern used on rural services in the early 1980s. Since the company's acquisition by Stagecoach a number of new types have appeared — notably second-hand Bristol VRTs and new Alexander-bodied Mercedes 709D minibuses.

Although based in Aberdeen, Bluebird Buses is essentially a rural operator, serving the sizeable towns spread across the rich farming country which makes up the north-east corner of Scotland. It has depots in Aberdeen (since 1991 sharing that used by Grampian), Buckie, Elgin, Macduff, Peterhead and Stonehaven, as well as numerous outstations. As part of the complex evolution of Stagecoach in Scotland, Bluebird Buses also controls the Stagecoach services in and around Inverness, the former Inverness Traction business. IT has been owned by Stagecoach since 1989 and the town was the scene of a fierce bus battle in 1991 as IT clashed head on with newly-privatised Highland Scottish. The result was victory for IT as Highland cut back its established Inverness town services and concentrated on serving the sparsely-populated region to the north and east of Inverness. In terms of vehicles Invernessians found immediate benefit as Stagecoach drafted in new Leyland Olympians and Dennis Darts to consolidate its position as the town's premier operator.

The fast-disappearing cream, yellow and blue livery used by Northern Scottish before its sale to Stagecoach is seen on a 1980 Alexander-bodied Leopard in Gardenstown on the Buchan coast. Stewart J Brown

Corporate Stagecoach white is taking over in the north of Scotland. A former Northern Scottish Olympian in Aberdeen looks particularly smart after a repaint in its new livery. It is one of a minority of two-door buses in the Bluebird Buses fleet, bought for Aberdeen city services. Stewart J Brown

Bluebird Buses trades as Inverness Traction in the Inverness area. There are a dozen Dennis Darts in the fleet with 41-seat Alexander Dash bodies. Paul Gainsbury

Highland Scottish runs Alexander-bodied Leopards which started life with a variety of other SBG subsidiaries. This bus was new to Clydeside in 1980 and moved to Highland in 1988. The location is Inverness. Paul Gainsbury

Highland's minibuses in Inverness run under the Highland Terrier name - although in competition with Stagecoach the Terriers' bark was worse than their bite. This is a Renault S56 with Alexander body, new in 1988.
Paul Gainsbury

Highland, bought by a consortium formed by Scottish Citylink Coaches and Rapsons of Alness, is but a shadow of its former self. Its fleet has been cut to around 120 and many of its most modern vehicles have been sold, with comparatively modern Alexander-bodied Olympians finding new homes with English operators including Stagecoach's Ribble subsidiary — which is just a touch ironic since the sale of the buses was in part precipitated by Stagecoach's activities in the Highlands. The standard Highland bus in 1993 is the ubiquitous Leyland Leopard with Alexander Y-type body. These account for almost half the fleet and can be seen from Fort William in the south to Thurso in the north. Double-deckers are mainly Fleetlines with ECW or Alexander bodies. The company's operating area is enormous, with depots at Aviemore and Fort William in the south, Thurso and Wick in the north, Nairn and Inverness in the centre of its territory, and at Portree on the Isle of Skye. Fort William is almost 200 miles from Thurso, which is a fair span of territory to cover with a fleet of 120 buses. Rapsons became the sole owner of Highland in 1993 when Scottish Citylink was purchased by Northern Express

At one time, double deckers in Fort William seemed unthinkable but times have changed with both Gaelicbus and Highland operating deckers in the town. This VRT originated with United Counties and is seen leaving Fort William on a Gaelicbus service to Caol and Corpach. Donald MacRae

Gaelicbus is Scotland's biggest AEC Reliance operator, running seven with Duple Dominant bus bodies in the Fort William area. All were purchased from Hutchison. Donald MacRae

The local services around Oban have been in the hands of several operators over the years, the most recent being the Oban & District company. The fleet was inherited from the Midland allocation to the town. Bill Philip

Few small operators remain in the far north of the country. The last two decades have seen small bus companies give up — and Royal Mail Post Buses expand. The Post Bus fleet, which is scattered throughout the country, comprises Leyland DAF 200-series minibuses (derived from the venerable British Leyland Sherpa), Ford Sierra and Peugeot 405 estate cars, and a small number of Land Rovers.

At Fort William, Highland competes with Gaelicbus, a relatively new name for the old-established business of MacConnacher of Ball-achulish. The green Gaelicbus fleet is made up mainly of AEC Reliances with Duple bus bodies, although a second-hand Bristol VRT is operated too. Double-deckers in Fort William are largely a post-deregulation phenomenon.

South of Fort William, Oban is a town whose services have changed operators over the years. It was Highland's southern outpost but by the time of SBG privatisation had reverted to Midland Scottish who had previously served the town. Midland Scottish, based in Falkirk, was purchased by GRT Holdings (owners of Grampian Transport) in 1990. Oban is remote from the rest of Midland's operations which are based in Falkirk and Stirling in Scotland's Central region and at the end of 1992 GRT sold a stake in its Oban operation to a new company, Oban & District.

Midland — renamed Midland Bluebird by its new owners — runs a predominantly single-deck fleet: Leyland Nationals, Leopards and Tigers with a few Seddon Pennine 7s. Its double-deckers, used mainly in the Falkirk and Grangemouth areas, are Alexander-bodied Metrobuses.

Since the takeover by GRT, a number of former Grampian Atlanteans have appeared in the Midland Bluebird fleet — a type never previously operated. The company's urban depots are at Bannockburn, Larbert and Linlithgow and it has a rural outpost at Balfron. Livery is two-tone blue and cream, applied in a similar layout to that used by GRT for its Aberdeen fleet.

Midland Scottish has escaped major competition, although its services in both Stirling and Falkirk have attracted new operators. Old-established family firm Mackie of Alloa — one of the few Scottish operators with Leyland Lynxes — provides some local services around Alloa and in to Stirling.

To the north-east of Midland Bluebird's territory lies the Kingdom of Fife, served by Stagecoach subsidiary Fife Scottish — purchased from SBG in 1991 after some bitter wrangling as Stagecoach outbid a management/employee buy-out offer. One of the claims made by opponents of the Stagecoach takeover of Fife Scottish was that there would be no investment in new vehicles — a claim which was quickly proved to be false with the delivery in 1992 of Alexander-bodied Leyland Olympians, Fife's first new double-deckers since 1986.

They joined a fleet of Ailsas and Citybuses — Fife had previously operated Olympians too, but these were dispersed to other SBG subsidiaries in the late 1980s. Single-deckers are mainly Leopards and Tigers, but Fife also has a significant fleet of Renault and MCW minibuses, bought to counter competition in its two main urban centres, Dunfermline and Kirkcaldy. Fife Scottish has large depots in both these towns, as well as in Aberhill, Cowdenbeath, Glenrothes and St Andrews.

The nature of its operating territory varies widely. South Fife is predominantly industrial, with development based on coal mining. North Fife is largely rural.

All of the Leyland Tigers in the Midland Bluebird fleet have been re-registered with cherished numbers to disguise their ages. This one with Alexander T-type body was new in 1983 with a Y-suffix mark. It is seen in Glasgow. Stewart J Brown

Leyland Atlanteans are a recent phenomenon in the Midland Bluebird fleet which in SBG days was a Fleetline user. There are now 13 AN68s in use, all transferred from Grampian Transport. Midland Bluebird uses the same livery layout as Grampian, but with blue in place of green. Malcolm King

This Fife Scottish Leyland Leopard was new in 1982 to erstwhile sister SBG company Midland Scottish. Like many late model SBG Leopards it features a wide doorway, one of SBG's few concessions to easy passenger access. It is seen leaving Dundee. Malcolm King

The only sizeable competitor for Fife Scottish is Moffat & Williamson of Gauldry. This company runs second-hand double- and single-deckers on both tendered and an increasing number of commercial services which stretch out to Dundee, St Andrews, Glenrothes and Kirkcaldy. With around 25 Bristol VRTs in its fleet (including unusual MCW-bodied ex-West Midlands buses) it is Scotland's biggest user of the type. These run alongside Fleetlines, Atlanteans, Leopards and assorted minibuses and coaches in the 80-strong fleet. To combat Moffat & Williamson a number of small buses have been drafted into Fife from other Stagecoach companies and are competing in the Methil and St Andrews areas.

South-west of Glasgow in Renfrewshire and Ayrshire are two traditional pockets of independent bus operation. Of the old Renfrewshire operators only McGill remains, running Leyland Nationals and a solitary ex-demonstration Lynx II on services from Barrhead to Glasgow and Paisley and Renfrew. McGill's services have changed little since pre-deregulation days as the company has steered clear of the frequent confrontations between its two large neighbours, Strathclyde and Clydeside. Graham's Bus Service of Paisley has vanished without trace, one of the major Scottish victims of deregulation.

The established Ayrshire independents have fared rather better. The northernmost of these, Clyde Coast Services, runs between Largs and Saltcoats as it has done for decades, now with second-hand Nationals. Its services have expanded south to Irvine New Town and Clyde Coast also runs the Largs local minibus service and an express service to Glasgow.

A1 Service is the biggest of the three Ayrshire independents and the only one to survive as a co-operative. Ownership of the 100-strong fleet is divided between ten members. The only vehicles actually owned by A1 are its four minibuses, two Iveco Fords and two former Highland Scottish Renaults.

As might be expected with ten owners there is some variety in the fleet. The operation is predominantly double-decked with both new and second-hand buses. Most of the buses bought new date back to the late 1970s when A1's members enthusiastically took advantage of the government's new bus grant to keep their fleets up to date.

Moffat & Williamson is Scotland's biggest Bristol VRT user, with 26 in operation. This ECW-bodied bus was new to City of Oxford. David Harman

McGill runs one Leyland Lynx, an ex-demonstration Cummins-engined Lynx II. It was acquired in 1991 and is seen in Paisley with a Clydeside 2000 Ailsa. VL Bus & Coach

The Clyde Coast fleet has expanded again in recent years and several second hand Nationals have been purchased. One is seen at Garden City, Glengarnock. Donald MacRae

Atlanteans, Ailsas and Fleetlines joined the fleet, mostly bodied by Alexander.

Good second-hand buses have always figured in A1's vehicle policy and the current stock includes Ailsas acquired from Tayside and Maidstone & District, Fleetlines from London and West Midlands, Olympians from West Yorkshire and Atlanteans from South Yorkshire. Single-deck operation is in the hands of a few Tiger buses and Nationals.

The company's operations are centred on a corridor running from the Clyde coast at Ardrossan by way of Saltcoats, Stevenston and Irvine to Kilmarnock. A frequent through service is augmented by local services in each of the main towns served. A1 is unusual in never having totally dispensed with the services of conductors and a number of its buses are still two-person operated

The third of the established Ayrshire independents is AA Motor Services, which started as a co-operative similar to A1, but is now operated solely by Dodds of Troon. AA's standard bus is the Leyland National. There are 16 bought new, spanning the entire period of National production from an L-registered 1972 model to a C-registered 1985 example. A further 12 second-hand Nationals are operated, including buses from West Midlands. Double-deckers now play a small part in AA's business, being limited to three Fleetlines (bought new) and an unusual Marshall-bodied Scania which started life as a demonstrator with CIE in Dublin. AA also has four Scania single-deck buses bought new, two bodied by East Lancs and two by Alexander, and five Lynxes. It has recently added unusual second-hand Jonckheere-bodied Scania K92 buses to its fleet from the batch bought by Scancoaches of London in 1986 for operation on LRT tendered services. A 1951 Regent III remains and there is one Reliance surviving in the Dodds coach fleet, a 1979 Plaxton-bodied vehicle. The AA company takes its name from the terminal points of its original trunk service, running up the Clyde coast from Ayr to Ardrossan.

The closure of Graham's of Paisley in 1990 provided a number of operators with good second-hand buses. A1 got this Alexander-bodied Atlantean. Stewart J Brown

The A1 fleet has contained several demonstrators in the past and this Citybus maintains this tradition. Acquired by Docherty in 1988 from Volvo, this striking vehicle is seen in the outskirts of Irvine on the trunk service to Kilmarnock. Donald MacRae

East Lancs bodies are relatively unusual north of the border. AA bought two in 1987, mounted on Scania N112 chassis. More Scanias have been bought, but with other makers' bodywork. Malcolm King

Kilmarnock is the headquarters of Western Scottish which was the largest SBG company when it was privatised in 1991 in a management-led employee buy-out. Immediately after the sale the company's northern depots were sold to Clydeside 2000, leaving Western with a fleet of 360 buses and coaches based at depots in Ayr, Cumnock, Dumfries, Girvan, Kilmarnock, Rothesay and Stranraer.

The company's newest full-size single-deckers are W-registered National 2s, previously operated by Kelvin Scottish and acquired in 1988. Apart from four E-registered Volvo Citybuses, the most modern big buses actually delivered new to Western are V-registered Fleetlines, Leopards and Seddon Pennines. The Fleetlines are unusual in Scotland in that they have lowheight Northern Counties bodies; the single-deckers have of course, Alexander Y-type coachwork.

The late 1980s saw the company acquire Fleetlines from other SBG subsidiaries and invest in a substantial minibus fleet — all Alexander-bodied Dodges although these have since been joined by Talbot Freeway tri-axle minis with wheelchair lifts, and Mercedes-Benz van conversions displaced from Kelvin Scottish. More recently it purchased ten Dennis Darts for operation in Ayr. These have Alexander Dash bodies and were diverted from a Stagecoach order.

Western Scottish has routes as far south as Dumfries and as far north as Glasgow. The most modern double-deckers operated by the company are Volvo Citybuses with Alexander bodies, one of which is seen in Ayr. Malc McDonald

Western was unusual among SBG companies in specifying Northern Counties bodywork on batches of Fleetlines. A 1978 bus is seen at Little Lochans on a Stranraer Academy service. Donald MacRae

Until 1992 the company's only island operations were based at Rothesay, on Bute, but in the autumn of that year it moved on to the Isle of Arran when it won the tenders to operate most of the island's bus services — at the expense of the previous operator, Arran Coaches. There are no double-deckers on Arran or Bute.

Irvine, in many ways the hub of Ayrshire traditional independent operation, is also served by two new companies. Shuttle Buses started serving the town with Transit minibuses in 1990 and now operates a mixed fleet of new and second-hand small buses in and around Irvine and Kilmarnock in a white and yellow livery. Wynter-M also runs minibuses around Irvine.

Elsewhere in Scotland there are numbers of new and old small family firms providing bus services. Apart from Arran and Bute, served by Western Scottish, island operations are largely in the hands of family businesses running second-hand buses and coaches. A double-decker occasionally ventures to Skye in the shape of an ex-United Counties Bristol VRT operated by Clan Garage of Kyle who run from Kyleakin to Portree. Clan also trades as Skye-Ways, with coaches running from Skye to Glasgow. All other island operations are single-decked.

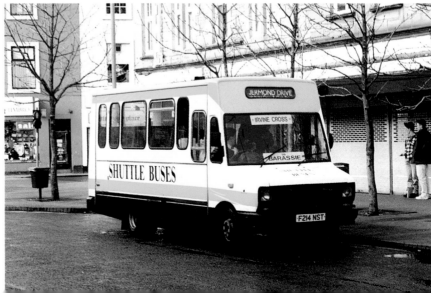

Early 1980s Duple bodies suffered from problems with corrosion and many in the Western fleet have been extensively rebuilt. This B10M at Rhubodach was originally a Dominant III with trapezoidal windows. Donald MacRae

Western started running on Arran in 1992 when it won tendered services. A one-time Highland National 2 is among the buses on the island. Arran Coaches, which lost routes, now competes with Western on Bute. Donald MacRae

An odd bus operated by Shuttle Buses is this Freight Rover Sherpa with bodywork by Aitken of Linlithgow. It was new to Inverness Traction. Stewart J Brown

NORTH WEST ENGLAND

Bolton, April 1993, with four different operators in view. G B Wise

GETS ROUND MORE BENDS THAN THIS BUS

The North West of England is an area of great contrast, ranging from the industrial centres in the south, to the remote grandeur of the Lake District in the north. It has a strong history of municipal transport operation — Lancashire alone boasted no fewer than 27 municipal bus fleets 30 years ago — and the legacy of this lives on despite the many changes which have taken place in the past few years.

Manchester is the commercial centre of the region, its heritage of Victorian architecture bearing witness to the wealth which it created in the latter part of the 19th century. It is also the home of what is now — but may not be for much longer — the region's biggest bus company. Greater Manchester Buses, the successor to the Greater Manchester PTE direct bus operation, has been at the centre of a political struggle which should see its demise before the end of 1993. Conservative central government wants GM Buses to be privatised, a move which local Labour politicians have been resisting. As a first step towards privatisation the government instructed at the end of 1992 that GM Buses be split up into smaller operating companies. Its current fleet strength is 2,138. The planned split should see two new companies emerge — one covering the north of the region and the other in the south.

One reason for doing this is to encourage competition — which suggests that London-based government is just a shade out of touch with events in the remote vastnesses of the North West. GM Buses faces more competition than any other major urban operator in Britain, claiming at one point that there were no fewer than 68 other operators in the area, though it has to be said that some were very small — and on occasion short-lived.

The company has suffered substantial setbacks. Its fleet was slashed when bus services were deregulated in 1986, and in the ensuing seven years there have been further fleet reductions and depot closures as the company has been forced to trim services and cut costs. Investment in new buses has suffered as a result, although 25 new 'deckers joined the fleet in 1991.

The bulk of GM Buses' operations are in the hands of so-called Manchester standards, a double-deck design which was evolved by the fledgling PTE back in 1971 and which has stood the test of time remarkably well. Originally fitted to Leyland Atlantean and Daimler Fleetline chassis — both of which are still much in evidence — it was later developed to fit other types and can be seen on Dennis Dominator, Leyland Olympian, MCW Metrobus, Scania BR112 and N113, and Volvo Citybus.

The Leyland Olympian with Northern Counties body has proved a popular combination in the GM Buses fleet, with over 300 having been purchased. A 1985 example of the type is seen in Manchester with City Central branding. The device above it incorporates the wording 'Safe, Reliable, Good Value' in the circle and the GM Buses logo underneath.
Alan Simpkins

The vast majority of the standards were built by Northern Counties of Wigan, which was owned by the PTE from 1985 to 1992, but there are still a number of Park Royal-bodied Atlanteans in operation from a batch of 160 delivered in the late 1970s. These are easily distinguished from Northern Counties-bodied buses by the shape of the front and rear domes. With few exceptions GM Buses Atlanteans and Fleetlines do not carry their makers' badges on the front — to spot a Fleetline (a type very much in the minority) you have to be sharp-eyed.

The least standard standards, if you follow the apparent contradiction, are those based on Scania and Volvo chassis. There are seven Scanias, which work from Hyde Road depot in Manchester, and 13 Volvos — three in Wigan, five in Bury and five in Oldham. The Dennis Dominators, 40 in number, are all allocated to Princess Road depot and run into central Manchester.

GM Buses runs the only MCW Metrobuses to have been bodied by Northern Counties, of which there are 30. These — and a few Olympians — have coach seats and a pale orange livery. They are used on a network of limited stop services. There is also a sizeable fleet of standard MCW-bodied Metrobuses.

Manchester was one of the centres singled out by United Transport for its ill-fated attack on the British bus business in 1987. In response to what appeared as the Bee Line Buzz Co, serving mainly south Manchester and Stockport, GM Buses built up a fleet of 360 minibuses — which has since been reduced to around 230. The first were Dodge S56s, many of which have now been sold. These were followed by Ivecos (all now withdrawn) and then by MCW Metroriders. Despite problems with the MCWs, they have all survived. The minibus operation was branded Little Gem (a subtle play on GM), with a bright livery to match. Since the end of 1991 the Little Gem name has been slowly disappearing and minibuses are now being repainted in fleet colours. Several MCW Metroriders acquired from West Midlands Travel were operated in WMT colours but these are now being repainted in fleet livery.

Fleetlines play a small part in the GM Buses fleet, with 124 remaining in service. A Bolton-based bus carries an intermediate livery with dark relief limited to the skirt. Stewart J Brown

With 208 in the fleet, GM Buses is the biggest user of Metrobuses north of Birmingham. An early MCW-bodied example is seen in Stockport. Mike Harris

Park Royal bodies are in a minority in the GM Buses fleet. This is an Atlantean, one of 93 similar Park Royal-bodied buses. The front dome outline is the main point of identification which distinguishes Park Royal from Northern Counties bodies. Malcolm King

The most interesting of Manchester's small buses are the unusual Dennis Dominos, most of which run on the Centreline service linking Victoria and Piccadilly stations by way of the city's business district. These have attractive Northern Counties bodies. The chassis is widely recognised as being over-engineered, using many Dominator parts in its construction — which made the Dominos particularly expensive. Greater Manchester was one of only two operators to buy Dominos and is the only one of the original buyers still running them; those owned by the other, South Yorkshire Transport, have been withdrawn from service.

Full-size single-deckers play a small part in the GM Buses fleet. Most are Leyland Nationals or ex-Lancashire United Plaxton-bodied Leyland Leopards. There are also four early (D-registered) Leyland Lynxes divided between Oldham and Bolton and, at Wigan (though liable to move), the company's sole Volvo single-deck bus. This entered service in 1992 with the first example of Northern Counties' new Countybus body. It was intended to be the first of five, but the other four were cancelled.

Manchester's buses have been orange since 1970, when the South East Lancashire North East Cheshire PTE adopted orange and white as the livery to be applied to the 2,504 buses which it took over from the region's 11 municipal fleets. The shades and layout have changed over the years, and GM Buses is currently in the throes of yet another change.

The current livery is deep orange relieved by white for the area around the windscreen and above the upper deck waist. Black — or more correctly a very dark shade of grey — is used for the skirt and window surrounds. This replaces the previous livery which used a brighter shade of orange and lacked the black relief. Some buses in the previous livery have received partial repaints, most notably with the application of black skirts.

GM Buses also operates a coach fleet under the Charterplan name, running Leyland Tigers, Volvo B10Ms, and Setra integrals.

The only surviving fleet of Dennis Dominos is that operated by GM Buses. New in 1985/6 they have stylish 24-seat bodies by Northern Counties. They are used mainly on the Centreline service in Manchester.
Stewart J Brown

Single-deckers are quite definitely in the minority in the GM Buses fleet. Only 15 Leyland Nationals survive, running alongside 19 Leopard buses, four Lynxes and a Volvo B10M. Stewart J Brown

Wheelchair-accessible buses are operated under the Localine name in various parts of Greater Manchester. The buses used are Renault S75s with Northern Counties bodies.
Malcolm King

A high proportion of the Bee Line fleet is made up of acquired Atlanteans. This Park Royal-bodied bus was new to Southdown but reached Bee Line by way of Ribble. Colin Lloyd

The Bee Line Buzz Co, now a subsidiary of British Bus, operates a 120-strong fleet which is concentrated to the south of Manchester, although it had routes in the north and east too, particularly around Rochdale. The Bee Line was conceived by United Transport and launched in 1987 as a high-quality high-frequency minibus operation. GM Buses responded with its own minibus fleet and ultimately United Transport conceded defeat. In the space of a few short months the Bee Line Buzz Co was sold to Ribble, which was bought by Stagecoach, who sold it to Drawlane (as British Bus was previously known) who reformed it as a more conventional bus operation with a mixture of minis and full-size buses. Bee Line's Rochdale area operations were inherited from Crosville when that was a Drawlane subsidiary, but were sold to Merseyside Transport in September 1993.

The Bee Line's double-deck fleet is made up entirely of what might loosely be described as second-hand buses — if the term can be extended to include third and fourth hand too. A number are one-time Greater Manchester Atlanteans, which came back home after a sojourn in the London area with Drawlane's London Country South West. There are also former Ribble Atlanteans and Crosville Olympians. Some G-registered London & Country Volvo Citybuses and Kentish Bus Olympians which added a much-needed touch of modernity to the company's big bus fleet for a brief period passed to Midland Red North in July 1993. Many of the original Bee Line Dodge S56s with Northern Counties bodies remain, and have been joined by new Carlyle-bodied Mercedes. The fleet livery is that originally adopted by United Transport — yellow with a black skirt and red roof. There is only one conventional single-deck bus in the Bee Line operation, a National acquired from Midland Red North. Management of Bee Line is being taken over by British Bus's North Western company.

Associated with Bee Line is C-Line of Macclesfield, which runs south from Manchester to Stockport, Macclesfield and Congleton. C-Line, also part of British Bus, runs a mixture of minis — mainly Mercedes — and full-size buses in the dark green and cream livery which was latterly used by Crosville. Part of what is now C-Line was previously Crosville. The big buses in the 50-strong C-Line fleet are mainly Bristol VRTs, although there are a few one-time Crosville Olympians and some Atlanteans. Since the start of 1993 C-Line's management has been integrated with that of Midland Red North, another British Bus subsidiary. A growing number of buses transferred from Midland Red North and running in Midland Red North's colours are appearing on C-Line operations with C-Line Midland Red fleetnames.

C-Line is in the throes of change. Most of the fleet retains the green and cream livery which was used prior to Midland Red North's involvement in the company from the start of 1993. The livery was inspired by that used by Crosville whose operations formed the core of C-Line when it was created at the start of 1990. This ECW-bodied VRT was new to Crosville. Steve Warburton

Some C-Line vehicles carry Midland Red North livery, including this Plaxton-bodied Scania K93. It is one of three K93s which were new in 1990 to Happy Days of Wood-seaves and passed to Midland Red North in 1991 with Happy Days' local services. Stewart J Brown

The oldest operator in Greater Manchester is Mayne, which started almost 75 years ago. Mayne ran for many years from Manchester to Droylsden, in co-operation with Manchester City Transport until 1969, and with the PTE until deregulation. Then Mayne entered into the new competitive environment, introducing routes in the Tameside and Droylsden areas and running out to Mossley, Oldham and Glossop — and expanding its fleet accordingly. The company has always bought new buses and has continued to do so despite the pressures of deregulation — although much of its fleet expansion has been with used vehicles. The newest buses in its fleet are three East Lancs-bodied Dennis Dominators diverted from Strathclyde Buses. Mayne has two of the first Marshall-bodied Dennis Darts and also runs five 1989 Scania N113s with Northern Counties bodies (one of which has an appropriate 113 registration).

These run alongside second-hand Fleetlines, from GM Buses, Clydeside 2000 and London, and a mixed bag of single-deckers which includes an assortment of rare Dennis Falcons (five from Chesterfield and one which started its life with Alder Valley) and a number of 20-year-old Leopards which have had their lives extended by the fitting of new Willowbrook Warrior bus bodies.

In 1990 four Mayne Leopards were rebodied with Willowbrook Warrior bodies and given dateless Ulster registration marks. This bus has a 1972 chassis. Roger Whitehead

Mayne also runs Dennis single deckers two Darts and six Falcons. This Falcon is one of five with Marshall bodywork which were new to Chesterfield Transport in 1984 and were bought by Mayne in 1991. Malcolm King

Mayne joined the small band of Dominator operators in the North West when it took three with East Lancs bodies at the start of 1993 and one more later in the year. Malcolm King

Citibus Tours of Chadderton started running buses shortly before deregulation, introducing services from Manchester to Middleton and Blackley which were operated by a fleet of one-time Preston and Bradford Corporation Leyland Panthers. An unusual blue and black livery was used; it has since been modified to an attractive two-tone blue. Citibus has expanded since 1986, consolidating its position as one of the major operators on the Manchester-Middleton corridor and extending out to Ashton and Oldham. Since 1988 the company has operated double-deckers and these, all second-hand Atlanteans, now dominate the fleet. The most common type are Roe-bodied buses acquired from South Yorkshire Transport — indeed no fewer than 39 of Citibus's 41 vehicles originated with SYT, including a pair of Leyland National 2s. In July 1993 Lynton Travel, owners of County Bus & Coach, purchased the Citibus business.

Timeline of Leigh runs one of the most modern fleets in the North West. Most of its 90 buses are less than six years old as a result of heavy investment by Shearings, the company's predecessor in the late 1980s. Holiday coach tour operator Shearings became heavily involved in local bus services at the time of deregulation. It started off with ageing Leyland Nationals, but recognising the benefits which modern buses would bring in reduced maintenance costs and improved service reliability, quickly started buying new vehicles. It adopted as its standard bodywork by Alexander (Belfast), initially on Leyland Tiger chassis and then on Volvo B10Ms. Timeline took over 40 Tigers and 16 B10Ms with Belfast-built bodies when Shearings decided in 1991 to pull out of bus operation.

Timeline has retained the late 1980s Shearing's livery — an unusual yellow, orange and cream — and operates primarily to the west and north of Manchester, with services from the city to Bolton and Bury, but it also has routes in the Eccles, Stockport and St Helens areas and a completely separate operation in Telford, Shropshire.

Stuarts of Hyde, like Citibus, is another operator which started running buses just before deregulation. The company runs from Manchester to Hyde and Marple and has a local service in Ashton. The fleet is made up mainly of second-hand Atlanteans and Fleetlines from a wide range of operators including Grampian, East Yorkshire and West Midlands, but in 1992 these were joined by the company's first new buses, a pair of DAF SB220s with Ikarus bodies—the first in the North West.

The Citibus fleet is made up mainly of ex-SYT Atlanteans with bodywork by Alexander, Roe and, as shown here, East Lancs. Colin Lloyd

Timeline, successor to Shearings' bus operations in the North West, has a fleet which is unusual insofar as most of its buses are bodied by Alexander (Belfast), a builder whose products are uncommon in Britain. There are 40 Leyland Tigers in operation which were new in 1988/9 and have 55-seat N-type bodies. More conventional are a pair of Mercedes minibuses ex-Kelvin. Mike Harris/Malcolm King

Stuarts of Hyde runs both Atlanteans and Fleetlines on services into Manchester. An example of the latter is this Roe-bodied bus purchased from Mayne in 1988. Mike Harris

The first new buses purchased by Stuarts were two Ikarus-bodied DAF SB220s, delivered in 1992.
David Harman

Following Stuart's success, another operator to the east of Manchester, Mybus of Hadfield, started running into the city. Mybus uses elderly buses which include two ex-Maidstone Boro'line Atlanteans (which were new to Nottingham), three ex-London DMSs and four Greater Manchester standard double-deckers — two Fleetlines and two Atlanteans. One-time DMS 1497 is one of the smarter buses in the fleet. Mybus ceased operations in the summer of 1993 but announced plans to restart in the autumn. Mike Harris

This smartly turned out Roe-bodied Fleetline is one of four purchased by Pennine Blue from Chesterfield in 1992. David Harman

Pennine Blue runs a varied fleet which includes this long-wheelbase AN68/2 Atlantean with Roe bodywork dating from 1974. It joined Pennine Blue from Yorkshire Rider in 1992 and is seen in Ashton bus station. Malcolm King

Pennine Blue of Denton operate around Ashton-under-Lyne and into Manchester. The fleet includes Bristol REs and VRTs, Fleetlines (including former London DMSs) and Atlanteans.

Wall's of Fallowfield is a coach operator which diversified into local bus operation in 1986 and has built up a strong presence on the Manchester to Didsbury road. The company started with a dozen ex-Greater Manchester Atlanteans, smartly repainted green and white and given so-called cherished registration numbers. The Atlanteans have subsequently been joined by Fleetlines from West Midlands Travel, 10 new and second-hand Optare Deltas and four standard NBC-style ECW-bodied VRTs from City of Oxford. There is also one Ikarus-bodied DAF SB220, previously operated by Pride of the Road of Royton, and an ex-East Kent Willowbrook-bodied VRT.

One other operator runs an Optare Delta into central Manchester, Dennis's Coaches of Ashton on a service from that town. It shares this duty with a selection of Mercedes and Sherpa minibuses.

Walls operate a mixture of modern DAF single-deckers and 1970s double-deckers. Many of the latter have been re-registered with dateless YSV-series numbers. This is a 1975 Fleetline with MCW body which came to Walls from West Midlands Travel in 1990. Malc McDonald

Dennis's Coaches of Ashton run one Optare Delta and a fleet of Mercedes minibuses, all purchased new, on a route into the centre of Manchester.
Mike Harris
Alan Simpkins

Another coach operator to have seized the opportunities presented by deregulation is Bullock of Cheadle, whose red-liveried double-deckers now penetrate the centre of Manchester on service from Stockport. These include some of the more unusual types to be seen in the city — four former SBG Alexander-bodied Metrobuses and four ex-Southampton Citybus East Lancs-bodied Dominators, although the company does also run other types, including the obligatory Greater Manchester standard Fleetlines, a few ex-London DMSs and Fleetlines from Derby, Yorkshire Rider and PMT. Despite the variety in the chassis, most have in common the use of Gardner engines. Bullock's only single-deck buses are a pair of Duple-bodied Tigers bought new in 1989. Bullock's use of

Gardner power also extends to coaches with Gardner-engined Dennis Dorchesters and a Leyland Tiger.

Finglands of Rusholme, since April 1992 a subsidiary of the Hull-based EYMS Group, runs buses south from Manchester to Stockport, Northenden and Didsbury. It is one of the few small operators in the area to have bought a new double-decker — an Alexander-bodied Volvo Citybus in 1989 — which runs alongside former Greater Manchester Fleetlines and Atlanteans and five recently acquired ex-London Buses Metrobus IIs. These were part of London's Harrow Buses fleet. Other Atlanteans in the fleet came from Lancaster and Hyndburn. The Finglands livery is white relieved by brown and orange. Finglands, like Bullock, runs a pair of Duple-bodied Tiger buses.

Bullock of Cheadle has been modernising its double-deck fleet by buying comparatively young second-hand buses. These include four C-registered Dennis Dominators with East Lancs bodies which came from Southampton Citybus in 1991. Alan Simpkins

Most of Finglands's bus fleet is made up of 1970s ex-Manchester double-deckers, but there are also five MCW Metrobus IIs which were new in 1987 to London Buses. These vehicles were part of a batch of 27 which were used on the Harrow Buses network and were disposed of after London Buses lost most of the Harrow area contracts in 1990. Malcolm King

Above: **Stotts operate local services in the Oldham area, mainly using second-hand Fleetlines and Atlanteans. This is one of four Roe-bodied Fleetlines.** Alan Simpkins

Below: **Pioneer run two Seddon Pennine 7s with Alexander bodies on services in the Rochdale area. New in 1978, this bus joined the Pioneer fleet in 1991.** Stewart J Brown

There is, of course, growing competitive activity for GM Buses outside Manchester. In Oldham, Stotts run local services using in the main former Greater Manchester Fleetlines and South Yorkshire Atlanteans in cream, red and black colours. The fleet also includes Fleetlines from South Yorkshire, Yorkshire Rider and West Midlands. Oldham and Middleton are reached by Iveco minibuses — 15 of them— operated by Bluebird of Moston, whose services reach down into Manchester. JP Executive Travel, trading as City Nippy, also runs minibuses between Middleton and Manchester. In Rochdale Bu-Val runs a fleet of predominantly Northern Counties-bodied minis, mostly Renaults and Ivecos bought from GM Buses, but including three Ivecos bought new in 1988. Pioneer of Littleborough also run in Rochdale. The Pioneer fleet has a strong Scottish flavour with three ex-Lothian Leyland Cubs and two former Western Scottish Seddon Pennine 7s.

Bolton is served by Timeline and by Blue Bus, which started up in 1990 and now runs a fleet of 30 generally elderly Leylands, mainly 1970s Atlanteans and Leopards. Modernity crept into the Blue Bus fleet in late 1992 when two Leopards were rebodied by East Lancs; a new East Lancs-bodied Dart (a rare combination) arrived in 1993. Both Timeline and Blue Bus also serve Wigan.

The Atherton Bus Company runs into Bolton, with a pair of former Strathclyde Atlanteans while Bolton Coachways serve the town with a fleet of small buses which includes Optare StarRiders in the dark green livery of their original owners, Athelstan of Chippenham. Evag Cannon runs locally in Bolton with ageing coaches and half-a-dozen Leyland Nationals. Heaton of Hindley Green has services to

Right: **Blue Bus operate a number of Alexander-bodied Leyland Atlanteans. This example was new to Greater Glasgow and is seen in Bolton.** P R Gainsbury

Above: **Bolton Coachways run a minibus service using three StarRiders which retain their previous owner's smart green livery.** Mike Harris

Above right: **Heatons Travel runs in the Wigan and Leigh area with a mixture of large and small vehicles. The company's only rear-engined bus is a National purchased from London & Country in 1992. It is seen in Bolton on a local service.** Malcolm King

Right: **The mid-1980s Leyland Tiger Cub is a rare beast indeed only two were built. They were manufactured in Denmark by Leyland DAB and it was Leyland's intention to compete in the midibus market using DAB-built vehicles which would be finished and trimmed by ECW. Jim Stones runs this former demonstrator which was originally registered A499MHG.** Malcolm King

Bolton, Leigh and Wigan, operated by minibuses (including two Optare MetroRiders) and Leopard coaches. One of the newest operators in Greater Manchester is the Wigan Bus Company. It runs four former Fife Scottish Leyland Nationals and four DMS Fleetlines in a maroon and white livery which is intended to evoke memories of Wigan Corporation's colours.

Jim Stones of Glazebury runs a small but tidy fleet of mini and midibuses in the Leigh area. Most are Mercedes-Benz with Reeve Burgess/Plaxton Beaver bodies, but there is also a Wadham Stringer-bodied Dennis Dart and a Leyland DAB Tiger Cub, one of only two imported to the UK when Leyland was looking at ways of providing operators with a bus which was smaller than the Tiger. Jim Stones' Tiger Cub was new in 1984 as a demonstrator. Many of Jim Stones' white and blue buses carry distinctive BUS or JYM registrations.

Another user of Plaxton-bodied small buses — Darts and Mercs — is South Lancashire Transport. SLT started in 1989, reviving the name of a long-vanished trolleybus operation in that part of the world. SLT runs in the St Helens area. Its full-size buses are second-hand Leyland Leopards and these include two consecutively-registered former Cleveland Transit buses which SLT has had rebodied by East Lancs and Willowbrook. There is also a unique rebodied Leopard which has a 1987 Cleveland Transit body built on a Northern Counties frame. The buses bought new in 1991 and 1992 — seven Plaxton-bodied Mercedes and two Darts —carry SLT registrations.

One of the smarter small operators to the south of the conurbation is Star Line Travel of Knutsford which serves Altrincham and parts of Cheshire. Star Line operates a fleet of Mercedes-Benz minibuses and two Plaxton-bodied Dennis Darts. Star Line started running buses in 1986 and now has 24 plus a few coaches. Stockport sees the buses of Pennine Blue and Tame Valley of Hyde, who also run to Ashton and Manchester. Tame Valley's livery is an attractive two-tone green and cream and its fleet includes second-hand Nationals and Atlanteans. There is also one Ailsa and a PD2 Titan.

Star Line has a very modern fleet of vehicles including two of these Plaxton bodied Darts which arrived in 1991 and 1992.
Ralph Oakes-Garrett

The Wigan Bus Company operates four Leyland Nationals on local services in the town. They came from Fife Scottish. Stewart J Brown

South Lancs run a mixed fleet of mini, midi and full-size buses. The big buses are all Leopards, with a variety of bodywork. New to Cleveland Transit in 1977 with Duple body, this Leopard now carries 1992 East Lancs EL2000 bus bodywork. Malcolm King

The Tame Valley fleet includes four Leyland Nationals, operating mainly in Ashton and Stockport. This bus was new in 1974 to West Yorkshire Road Car. Malcolm King

Left: **Leyland's Atlantean is the most common type in the Merseybus fleet with examples built between 1972 and 1984 still in all-day service. Most have Alexander bodywork. The current simplified livery is shown on this 1972 bus in central Liverpool. Buses in the previous livery have more cream relief.** Malcolm King

Below left: **Since deregulation Merseybus has bought 70 Leyland Olympians with bodywork by Alexander and Northern Counties. The last were delivered in 1989. This is a Northern Counties-bodied bus freshly repainted in the latest livery.** Malcolm King

Top right: **The standard Merseybus single-decker is the Leyland National, with both Marks 1 and 2 in operation. The former are in a minority and the oldest survivors were new in 1979. This is a 1980 National 2.** Malcolm King

Centre right: **The first of the new generation of ultra-low-floor buses to enter service in Britain did so in the summer of 1993. Owned by Merseytravel, it is a Neoplan N4014 and it runs on a contracted service across Liverpool. By the end of 1993 ultra-low-floor buses should be running in London and Dundee.** Malcolm King

Bottom right: **Mersey Rider is Merseyside Transport's low-cost subsidiary. It ran Atlanteans in drab unrelieved green at first but in 1993 changed to a maroon and grey livery and, just prior to the change of colour, added to its fleet five smart new Mercedes-Benz 811Ds with Marshall bodies.** Malcolm King

Liverpool is the North West's other great city. Like Manchester it is rich in symbols of Victorian prosperity — but unlike Manchester it has been ravaged by industrial decline. On Merseyside, as in Greater Manchester, the established operator faces strong competition. The area's major operator is Merseyside Transport which trades as Merseybus. This is the direct descendant of the former Merseyside PTE bus operation and it was privatised at the start of 1993 in a management/employee buy-out. Merseybus, with 937 vehicles, is the second-biggest operator in the region after GM Buses. Its headquarters are in Liverpool and as well as having depots in Liverpool it has one each in St Helens, Southport and Birkenhead on the Wirral peninsula. Merseybus routes operate as far inland as Bolton; equally GM Buses have a service which takes its vehicles to Liverpool.

It is a predominantly Leyland fleet. The oldest are L-registered Atlanteans. They are now 20 years old and over 70 still survive in all-day service. Merseybus Atlanteans come with a variety of bodies — Alexander, East Lancs, MCW and even a few Willowbrook — and the company is one of only three to run an Atlantean with a B-prefix registration. Its last, 1070, was one of the last built for a UK operator and entered service in 1984.

When Leyland announced the impending demise of the Atlantean, Merseyside tried some of the alternatives and a few of these still survive including ECW-bodied Olympians, and Alexander-bodied Olympians and Metrobuses. There are also 15 Alexander-bodied Ailsas which operate in the Wirral but do venture through the Mersey Tunnel and into Liverpool. New post-deregulation double-deckers in the fleet are 70 Olympians delivered in 1988-89 (one of which has been written off) with bodies by Alexander and Northern Counties, and 25 Mark II Metrobuses purchased in 1989 — and among the last to be built. The most recent additions to the Merseybus fleet have been ex-London Buses Leyland Titans which are now running in Liverpool. There are 120 in the fleet, making Merseybus the biggest operator of the type outside the capital.

The single-deck bus fleet is made up largely of Leyland Nationals, with both the original and the Mark 2 variant. These operate in Southport and St Helens, as well as in Liverpool. Of more interest are 10 Dennis Lancets with Duple Dominant bus bodies which are divided between St Helens, Southport and Birkenhead. These are neat 31-seaters, delivered in 1983 before midibuses became fashionable, and they make Merseybus the UK's biggest Lancet operator.

When deregulation came into effect Merseybus bought batches of Dodge S56s with Northern Counties and Alexander bodies. These were augmented in 1990 by 25 S56s from GM Buses, but minibuses have not played as significant a part in Merseyside's transport system as they have in other places and since then the minibus fleet has been cut back. It now numbers 50 vehicles. These include two survivors from the batch purchased from GM Buses and eight ex-Cambus Mercedes. The newest are five Optare StarRiders and a MetroRider delivered in 1993.

The current Merseybus livery of maroon and cream was introduced in 1988 (replacing a green-based colour scheme) and incorporated a swoop at the front so that the front panel below the windscreen was cream rather than maroon — this was allegedly to help distinguish Merseybus buses from Crosville buses at night when both liveries apparently looked similar under artificial light. Now Crosville has gone and from the end of 1992 Merseybus started to abandon the swept-down livery for a simpler (and more drab) layout with much more maroon and less cream. The simpler layout is cheaper to apply — and, sadly, it shows.

A low-cost subsidiary operation, Mersey Rider, runs ageing Atlanteans and new minibuses on tendered services.

Where Manchester has seen the growth of a large number of new but relatively small operators, Liverpool has experienced a smaller number of larger newcomers, with the three best-known being started by former Merseyside PTE employees.

Fareway started running from central Liverpool to Kirkby in 1986. Their original vehicles were former Merseyside PTE Bristol VRTs which were unusual in having East Lancs bodies. Seven are still in use. These were soon followed by former Greater Manchester Fleetlines, of which there are now around 30 in the fleet, including a number which came third-hand from Cambus. Further expansion of the Kirkby services led to the acquisition of former London DMSs, by which time Fareway's 50-strong fleet was made up entirely of second-hand double-deckers with Gardner engines. They were followed by new double-deckers in the shape of 10 long-wheelbase Olympians with Cummins engines and Northern Counties bodies. These were the first new buses for a Merseyside independent and entered service in 1988. They were joined in 1991 by four ex-London Buses Bexleybus Olympians. The Fareway livery is a distinctive blue and yellow and the fleet is now 67 strong. In a surprise move the business was sold to Merseyside Transport in April 1993 — but it remains a separate operating unit.

Liverline started up in 1988 and, like Fareway, was formed by redundant Merseyside PTE employees. The initial fleet comprised 10 former Strathclyde PTE Atlanteans which were acquired from Kentish Bus but, as with Fareway, Liverline quickly expanded its operations which are concentrated from Liverpool towards Speke. More second-hand Atlanteans were purchased, including some former Greater Manchester buses, along with vehicles from Ribble, Luton & District's London Country North West division, Hyndburn and Plymouth. All the Strathclyde and Greater Manchester Atlanteans have gone. New vehicles— ten Northern Counties-bodied Scanias — were purchased in 1990/91 and were followed by four DAF SB220s with Ikarus bodies in 1992. The DAFs

One-time Greater Manchester Fleetlines are the most numerous type in the Fareway fleet, with 30 in use. All but two have Northern Counties bodies as shown on this 1976 bus which came to Fareway by way of Cambus.
Mike Harris

Liverline's fleet is made up mainly of second-hand Atlanteans and new Scanias there are 30 of the former and ten of the latter. The Atlanteans include nine which were new to Ribble with bodywork by Park Royal.
Malcolm King

Odd vehicles in the Liverbus fleet are a pair of extended-wheelbase Olympians with ECW coach bodies. New to Eastern National in 1985, they joined Liverbus from Thamesway in 1991. They have Leyland engines. Mike Harris

are allocated to a PTE-sponsored service and carry a white and yellow livery. The rest of Liverline's buses are two-tone blue and grey. Liverline now runs 52 vehicles over half of which are Atlanteans. It also owns one Routemaster, which carries London red livery. Liverline was taken over by British Bus in July 1993 and is to be managed by North Western.

The third of the significant operators in Liverpool is Liverbus, which runs 33 former Greater Manchester Atlanteans. In 1992 it added three relatively modern C-registered Alexander-bodied Olympians to its fleet, when Highland Scottish introduced a major cutback in its services around Inverness. Its first new buses, four Northern Counties-bodied Volvo B10Bs, entered service in April 1993. Eight more are on order. Liverbus also runs Metroriders.

Also serving Liverpool are Amberline (a subsidiary of Crosville Wales) with Iveco and Mercedes minibuses and six ex-West Midlands Fleetlines painted in the same shades of green and white as the much larger parent fleet. Amberline's main business is the provision of coaches for National Express services and its bus operations are being taken over by North Western. Blue Triangle runs a variety of Bristol VRTs in the city, including one of the unusual Willowbrook-bodied buses originally owned by Northern General. It also has a one-time Alder Valley long-wheelbase Olympian coach. There are two 'deckers in the fleet which carry the AEC blue triangle badge, a Regent V which was new to East Kent and a former BEA forward-entrance Routemaster. The only new bus in the Blue Triangle fleet is a Dennis Dart with Plaxton Pointer body. Village Group Tours of Garston, like Blue Triangle, have a penchant for used VRTs and its fleet includes six East Lancs-bodied buses acquired from Burnley & Pendle. These run into central Liverpool and are backed up by assorted second-hand Fleetlines and Atlanteans and a Leyland-engined VRT.

Top: **Amberline is a subsidiary of Crosville Wales running Fleetlines and minibuses in Liverpool. Six of these ex-West Midland FE30AGR models make up the double-deck fleet. They carry Crosville-style HDG-prefixed fleet numbers indicating Highbridge, Daimler, Gardner. The 76-seat body is by MCW.** Stewart J Brown

Centre: **The Village group fleet includes a mix of Atlanteans, Fleetlines and VRTs. This Atlantean, new to the Selnec PTE in 1973, is one of the older buses in the fleet. It has Park Royal bodywork.** Stewart J Brown

Right: **Latest arrival on the streets of Liverpool is Mersey Line, running ex-West Midlands Fleetlines, smartly repainted in blue and cream.** Malcolm King

Merseybus does have competition from other small operators outside Liverpool and from two large ones. Ogdens Travel of St Helens runs services in and around the town. Leyland Nationals from a number of sources form the backbone of the fleet, but Ogdens have the distinction of running the only Optare Deltas in Merseyside, a pair bought new in 1989. These were joined in 1992 by a pair of Ikarus-bodied SB220s from OK Motor Services. The Deltas wear a white-based livery but older Ogdens buses, which include Leyland Leopards and Bristol REs, are in red and blue divided by a diagonal stripe, a combination of colours and livery layout which unashamedly copies that of North Western.

Town Flyer runs a selection of small buses in St Helens. These include Dodge S56s acquired from GM Buses, a Lex-bodied Bedford YMQ-S and, most unusually, two Optare-bodied Dennis Dominos which were new in 1986 to South Yorkshire but reached Town Flyer by way of Stevensons of Uttoxeter.

In Birkenhead and in Liverpool, Topping's Super Coaches runs local services. To launch these in 1987 the company bought ten Leyland Nationals from Greater Manchester. A blue skirt was applied to the GM orange and white colours to produce a livery not unlike that used by Strathtay Scottish. New buses arrived in 1988: four Leyland Lynxes. Some of Topping's buses carry Topp-Line fleetnames. The company also has double-deckers in its fleet, but these — ECW-bodied Bristol VRTs and a former GM Buses Fleetline — are restricted to contract operations. Also on the Wirral peninsula Avon Bus runs second-hand double-deckers which include two ex-London Buses Titans and an Ailsa. Avon Bus joined the small but growing band of East Lancs National Greenway users in 1993 with a T-registered bus which came from Rhondda.

To the north, ABC Travel of Ainsdale operates local services around Formby and in Liverpool using in the main Optare MetroRiders and Mercedes minis in a smart red and cream livery.

Ogdens run four DAF SB220s, two each bodied by Optare and Ikarus. The Optare-bodied buses were bought new in 1989. Mike Harris

The biggest bus operated by Town Flyer of St Helens is a 37-seat Bedford YMQ-S with unusual Lex Maxeta bodywork. It came from Hutchison of Overtown. Malcolm King

Topping's bus livery is a simple modification of that worn on a fleet of Nationals acquired from Greater Manchester on which blue has been substituted for brown at skirt level. Eight 1975 Nationals from Manchester survive in use on services in Merseyside. This one is in the Bootle area.
Stewart J Brown

ABC Travel operate in Liverpool, Formby and Southport. The fleet is composed primarily of minibuses. This Carlyle-bodied Freight Rover Sherpa was purchased new in 1989. Alan Simpkins

Avon Bus run an East Lancs Greenway rebuild of a Leyland National. New in 1978, the Greenway rebuild of the bus was carried out in 1993.
Malcolm King

The major operators competing with Merseybus are PMT and North Western. The latter is the successor to Ribble in Merseyside, being formed in 1986 to take over Ribble's depots in Aintree, Bootle, Skelmersdale, Southport and Wigan. North Western subsequently expanded into Blackburn (and then pulled out again) and Altrincham. As a Drawlane subsidiary the company found itself benefiting from the redrawing of Crosville's territory, taking over Crosville's operations in Runcorn, Northwich and Warrington in 1989.

The older buses in the 365-vehicle North Western fleet are of obvious Ribble parentage: Leyland Nationals, Atlanteans and Olympians; the oldest Nationals date back to 1972. The number of Nationals has been swollen by former Crosville examples, some of which retain Crosville's green and cream livery until due for a repaint in North Western's distinctive red and blue. The company has a fleet of around 40 minibuses. All are Mercedes-Benz 608D or 609D vans with Alexander or Reeve Burgess conversions. There are a few Tiger coaches for longer-distance routes including one with a Duple Laser body which has been rebuilt with shallow windscreens after a front-end collision. Under Drawlane ownership North Western has received numbers of new buses bodied by the group's coachbuilder, East Lancs. These comprise 18 Dennis Dominators, 14 Volvo Citybuses and eight Dennis Falcons, all delivered in 1989-90 and still the company's newest buses. It has also received Nationals and Atlanteans from London & Country. A red livery with Red Knight fleetnames is carried on a small number of Atlanteans in Liverpool.

Among the vehicles acquired from Ribble when the North Western company was formed were a number of Park Royal-bodied Atlanteans. New in 1974, they are now amongst the oldest buses in service. Stewart J Brown

New buses for North Western have included East Lancs-bodied Volvo Citybuses. With 88 seats, the Citybuses are the biggest vehicles in the fleet. Roy Marshall

PMT has since 1990 run what were the former Crosville services on the Wirral, largely using ex-Crosville buses most of which are now in PMT's bright red and yellow livery, but with Crosville or Red Rider fleetnames. The Crosville part of PMT's fleet is made up mainly of Bristol VRTs and Leyland Olympians, but there are small numbers of minibuses — primarily Mercedes and Metroriders — and new Dennis Darts with Plaxton Pointer bodies which run on the Wirral.

PMT's Crosville operation embraces Chester, where Chester City Transport provides the majority of local services, and has also expanded into surrounding districts. The Chester fleet is predominantly double-decked with Leyland Olympians, Dennis Dominators and Daimler Fleetlines. All three types have been bought new (the newest are a pair of 1989 long-wheelbase Olympians) but since deregulation the company has expanded by judicious second-hand buying. There are former Greater Manchester Fleetlines, and Olympians from Derby, West Yorkshire, Highland Scottish and A1 of Ardrossan. But it is in the Dennis Dominators that there is most variety, with around 20 second-hand examples which have come from the municipal fleets in Brighton, Eastbourne, Leicester, Hyndburn and Warrington, and from independent A1. The buses which came from Warrington started life with Blackburn while those from Brighton were new to Tayside.

Most of the recent new additions to Chester's fleet have been small buses with Northern Counties-bodied Dodges in 1987-88 being followed in the 1990s by Dennis Darts which have bodies by Reeve Burgess and Plaxton, both to the Reeve Burgess Pointer design. There are also Alexander-bodied Dodges in the fleet which came from Grimsby-Cleethorpes.

Recent new purchases for PMT's Crosville operation have been Dennis Darts with Plaxton Pointer bodies although this bus carries Reeve Burgess badging to the offside of the registration plate. PMT's warm bright livery suits the Pointer body well. Mike Harris

Chester also has been buying Pointer-bodied Darts and currently has nine in its fleet. Steve Warburton

Two other Cheshire towns boast municipally-owned bus operations: Warrington and Widnes. Like Chester, Warrington Borough Transport has expanded beyond its boundaries with services into Cheshire, Merseyside and Greater Manchester and, like Chester, much of this has been covered by the selective acquisition of good used vehicles. The older buses in the fleet are mainly Leyland Atlanteans, some bought new and some purchased second-hand from Eastbourne and Preston. Warrington's fleet livery is red and white.

The newest double-deckers are six F-registered long-wheelbase Dominators with East Lancs bodies, two of which have coach seats and are in the blue Coachlines livery used for Warrington's growing coach business. To combat competition from North Western, Warrington has added Dennis Darts to its fleet. These, too, are in the blue livery and the newest are unusual in having Northern Counties bodywork, as yet an uncommon choice for a Dart. The company's earlier Darts were bodied by Carlyle to the original Duple design.

But the real variety is in the second-hand fleet: former Greater Manchester Fleetlines, that staple of so many operators seeking to expand, Derby Olympians and Leicester Dominators. Warrington also has Olympians bought new, all high-capacity long-wheelbase models bodied by East Lancs. The older buses in the fleet include four 1975 Bristol REs with East Lancs bodies.

By contrast Halton Borough Transport, based in Widnes but with services stretching out to Runcorn, Warrington, Liverpool, St Helens and Prescot, has a highly-standardised fleet. There are no double-deckers. There are no small buses. The 55-strong fleet is made up entirely of Leyland Nationals and Lynxes, including both original and Mark 2 (or II in the case of the Lynx) versions. Halton's claim to fame is that it got the first and last municipally-owned National 2s and Lynxes. There is variety among the Nationals with second-hand acquisitions, given away only by their registrations. These have come from Crosville and Southern Vectis. The oldest surviving Nationals are 1976 R-registered buses. Halton was the main beneficiary when Crosville withdrew north of the Mersey, hence the large fleet compared with the former Widnes municipal operation.

Second-hand vehicles comprise about a third of the Warrington double-decker fleet. This Fleetline came from GM Buses in 1988.
T K Brookes

Warrington started buying Dennis Darts in 1991, taking 13 with Carlyle bodies. More recent deliveries have been bodied by Northern Counties. All carry MidiLines colours.
Steve Warburton

Halton is easily the North West's biggest Lynx user, with 36 in service. These include the comparatively uncommon Lynx II variant with its revised frontal styling. This is one of 14 delivered in 1992, equal to almost 25 per cent of Halton's fleet. G Mead

Moving north to the other end of the region, the main operators are both Stagecoach subsidiaries — Cumberland Motor Services and Ribble Motor Services. Stagecoach bought Cumberland from NBC in 1987 and added the neighbouring Ribble company in 1989, taking over from the management team which had bought Ribble from NBC in 1988.

Despite four years in Stagecoach ownership, not all of Cumberland's buses have succumbed to the corporate white paintbrush and a few still wear the short-lived dark red and beige livery adopted by Cumberland shortly before its privatisation. The recent histories of Cumberland and Ribble are closely intertwined, and under Stagecoach ownership this close relationship has continued.

Much of Cumberland's territory is rural, embracing as it does the Lake District with its scattered centres of population. Cumberland has depots at Barrow, Kendal, Millom, Penrith and Workington, as well as Carlisle — in none of these towns is there any significant competition.

The fleet is mixed. Original Cumberland buses, mainly standard NBC Leyland Nationals and Bristol VRTs, rub shoulders with similar ex-Ribble buses, as well as former Ribble Olympians. Some of the longer inter-town services are worked by Leopards, while one of Britain's most scenic long-distance services, the three-hour long 555 from Lancaster to Keswick through the Lakes, is worked by smart new Alexander-bodied long-wheelbase Olympians of the type to be found in most Stagecoach group companies.

Cumberland's Olympians are not all to Stagecoach's standard specification. A trio of former Northern Scottish examples runs at Barrow (where all traces of the failed municipal bus operation have vanished), and Cumberland also has two of the Stagecoach Group's three striking Megadekkers — tri-axle Olympians with Alexander bodywork seating a remarkable 96 passengers; the third is with United Counties.

Other new buses in the Cumberland fleet are five Alexander Dash-bodied Volvo B6s, part of a substantial Stagecoach group order for 1992 which was delayed by chassis production problems. The Cumberland five were built at the Steyr factory in Austria; future deliveries will be built at the Volvo truck plant in Irvine. At the end of 1992 delivery began of 100 new Alexander-bodied B10Ms. The first were allocated to Carlisle, the biggest town in Cumberland's area. These replaced the few remaining Routemasters in the city. Cumberland is the only Stagecoach subsidiary to have bought new Leyland Lynxes, with a trio taken into stock in 1989. These are accompanied by an ex-Leyland demonstrator and by a pre-production Lynx transferred from Ribble where it was non-standard.

The Lynx was, of course, built in Workington which is in the heart of Cumberland's territory. By a strange quirk of fate, part of Leyland's Workington factory is now a Cumberland depot. Workington's other claim to fame is that it has Britain's first covered bus station, opened in 1926.

A nice touch by Cumberland is the application of green and cream colours (copied from Southdown) to four convertible open-top Bristol VRTs and a former Portsmouth open-top Atlantean which operate the Lakeland Experience, serving the Windermere area in the summer. A similar livery is worn by the Borrowdale bus, a Leyland National which — surprise, surprise — runs down Borrowdale, from Keswick to Seatoller, and by three Mercedes-Benz minibuses which are named after local Lakeland worthies — though whether or not William Wordsworth would be impressed by the honour is hard to say.

Stars of the Cumberland fleet are the two three-axle Leyland Olympians with Gardner 6LXCT engines and 96 high-backed seats. Alan Simpkins

The first Volvo B6Rs for a British operator entered service with Cumberland in 1992. They have Alexander Dash bodies. Stagecoach ordered 100 of Volvo's midi model for 1993. G.B. Wise

A green livery copied from ex-Southdown Bristol VRT open-toppers is used by Cumberland on selected tourist routes in the Lake District, which may be tacit admission that the brash Stagecoach colours could be a shade intrusive. It is carried by a number of minibuses and by one B-series National. Stewart J Brown

Ribble is still a major force in the North West, although but a shadow of its former self. At one time its territory stretched from Carlisle to Liverpool; now it is centred on Preston and central Lancashire, although its Bolton operations reach into Greater Manchester, where some compete with GM Buses.

Many Ribble vehicles still carry the company's pre-Stagecoach livery, an attractive combination of NBC poppy red with grey and yellow relief. The big bus fleet is made up of Leyland Nationals, Atlanteans and Olympians (the last-named including 50 NBC and 29 standard Stagecoach types) and a few surviving Bristol VRTs. The Nationals include a unique prototype National 2, now in Stagecoach colours, which retained the rear-mounted radiator as used on the National 1. Only discreet National 2 badges and the sound of the 680 engine give the game away that it isn't just an ordinary National. Ribble was another operator to benefit from cuts at Highland Scottish and runs 13 former Highland Alexander-bodied Olympians.

Minibuses were introduced in 1986 and over 40 of the original D-registered Mercedes-Benz 608Ds with Reeve Burgess conversions remain in the fleet. Ribble took over United Transport's Preston operation — Zippy— in 1988 and a number of the Iveco 49.10s which came with Zippy are still in operation, although not necessarily in Preston. United Transport was one of the few major operators to buy minibuses with Portugese-built Elme bodywork (the Elme importer is based in St Annes, not far from United's Preston Zippy operation). Five were purchased and the three which remain with Ribble, on Iveco 49.10 chassis, run in Chorley.

Odd vehicles in the fleet include a solitary Leyland Tiger with Duple Dominant bus body and an early pre-production Leyland Olympian. Reminders of the Ribble takeover of Barrow Borough Transport's operations in 1989 are most visible in Preston, in the shape of three Atlanteans with Manchester-style Northern Counties bodies. These 1983 Y-registered buses are the newest Atlanteans in the fleet; Ribble had switched to Olympians in 1981 and is one of the few operators of W-registered examples. The only Dennises in a fleet long associated with Leyland products are 1989 Javelins with Duple 300-series bodies and 1993 Javelins with Plaxton bodies. The former had been purchased for evaluation by Stagecoach and spent the first two years of their lives with Hampshire Bus. Ribble has depots at Blackburn, Bolton, Chorley, Clitheroe, Fleetwood, Lancaster, Morecambe and Preston.

Ribble is one of three fleets in the North West which runs over 100 Leyland Nationals. A Mark 2, in corporate Stagecoach colours, is seen in Blackburn bus station. Steve Warburton

Ribble has 29 long-wheelbase Alexander-bodied Olympians of the type favoured by Stagecoach. This one is seen in Lancaster where Ribble's buses ousted those of Lancaster City Transport in August 1993. Malcolm King

Ribble's final livery lingers on, featuring grey and yellow relief added to the NBC poppy red and white. This VRT in Blackburn bus station is among the survivors. Stewart J Brown

The first style of Ribble fleetname applied after the Stagecoach takeover was similar to the NBC style. It is seen on an Olympian in Manchester Piccadilly. Kevin Lane

While Ribble operates town services and inter-urban services throughout Lancashire, many of the main towns in the area have their own sizeable municipal fleets, giving the company much more competition than its northern neighbour in Cumbria. Only one—Preston—has been privatised, although government pressure for sell-offs is mounting and others are likely to follow Preston's lead. One of Ribble's longest routes, that from Blackpool to Accrington, runs through towns served by four municipal companies — Blackpool, Fylde, Blackburn and Hyndburn.

After the failure of Barrow in 1989, Lancaster City Transport was the northernmost of the Lancashire municipals. It was offered for sale by the city council in 1993 but, once the sale process was under way, Ribble registered a number of competing services in the town, weakening the municipality's position. The City then decided to close down the operation in August and the depot and part of the fleet were sold to Stagecoach.

In Ribble's headquarters town, Preston Borough Transport — sold to its employees in March 1993 — provides most of the local services. Preston bought 52 Dodge S56 minibuses to counter the challenge of United Transport's Zippy operation and these are still in use. All have Northern Counties bodies. The newer ones have Renault badges and a front end designed by Northern Counties which takes the place of the S56's protruding bonnet. This was Northern Counties' answer to the new breed of minibus being manufactured by Optare and MCW, but it is an option which added to the cost of the vehicle and which few operators specified.

For the best part of the last two decades, the typical Preston bus has been the long-wheelbase Leyland Atlantean with dual-door bodywork by Alexander or East Lancs. The oldest examples have now been withdrawn, but Preston is still very much an Atlantean town. Almost 40 survive, but all rebuilt to one-door layout.

Single-deck operation was reintroduced in 1986 with three ex-Merseyside Nationals. These have gone (they now run for North Western), but Preston now runs 15 Leyland Lynxes, while the newest buses in the fleet are eight Leyland Olympians with Leyland bodies, delivered in 1991-92, and including a former demonstrator. Preston also has batches of Olympians bodied by ECW and by Northern Counties. There are two odd long-wheelbase Olympians: an ECW-bodied version with 74 coach seats, originally used as a demonstrator by Leyland, and a one-off Northern Counties 85-seater.

The old-established business of John Fishwick & Sons of Leyland (its roots go back to the early 1900s) runs services into Preston from Leyland and Chorley. These are operated by Leyland Nationals or Lynxes. Fishwick's few double-deckers are now restricted largely to school journeys and include East Lancs-bodied AN68 Atlanteans and two rare AN69 prototypes (with turbocharged Leyland 690 engines). One has a standard old-style ECW body as fitted to AN68s for NBC, while the other has an ECW body based on the style fitted to the Olympian. Fishwick's bus livery is a dark two-tone green, but a brighter white and green livery is used on coaches and for the small fleet of FishKwick Mercedes minibuses which run local services in Leyland.

Leyland is the location of this view of a Lynx II in the smart livery of John Fishwick & Sons. The JFS script above the doors is matched by the registration letters. David Stewart

The most numerous type in the Fishwick fleet is the Leyland National. This 1979 bus is one of the older examples. It is seen in Chorley. Stewart J Brown

To the west of Preston there are two municipally-owned bus companies, Fylde Borough Transport and Blackpool Transport Services. In the days before 1986 they operated in co-ordinated harmony. Deregulation brought that to an end, although the intense competition which characterised Blackpool in the late 1980s has now eased.

Blackpool, with just over 130 buses, is the bigger fleet. It standardised on East Lancs-bodied Atlanteans in the late 1970s and early 1980s and its last are a pair with B-suffix registrations. Blackpool's other 'deckers are Olympians and Routemasters. The Olympians are three with Roe bodies purchased from West Yorkshire PTE in 1986, followed in 1989 by six new examples with East Lancs bodies built to Alexander's R-type design.

The Routemasters, of which there are 13, were purchased from London Buses in 1986-87 and are used on a summer season seafront service. They wear a dark red and white livery; the rest of the big bus fleet is green and cream.

The fleet's full-size single-deckers are 29 stylish new Optare Deltas, delivered between 1990 and 1993 and the biggest fleet of the type in the area. The Deltas followed on from a fleet of 35 of Optare's eye-catching CityPacer minibuses which run in black and yellow HandyBus livery. The Deltas are based on DAF SB220 chassis; the CityPacers are on MAN-VW LT55s.

The current standard Blackpool bus is the Optare Delta, based on the DAF SB220 underframe. Blackpool runs 29, giving it the largest fleet in the North West and one of the largest in the country. Colin Lloyd

Blackpool's newest double-deckers are Leyland Olympians with East Lancs bodies to Alexander designs. Six were delivered in 1989. They have Cummins L10 engines, the only ones in the Blackpool fleet. K R Crawley

Fylde Borough Transport runs from Blackpool to Lytham and St Annes, as well as providing comprehensive services in the two last named resorts. It has perhaps fared less well under deregulation than its larger neighbour and 18 buses in its 90-strong fleet are 20-year-old second-hand Atlanteans purchased in 1987 when competition was at its peak. These have Roe bodies and came from Hull and are all PDR1A/1 models, making Fylde one of the country's largest user of first-generation Atlanteans.

Before this Fylde had standardised on AN68 Atlanteans, buying 18 between 1975 and 1984. Its last is B-registered, putting Fylde with Blackpool and Merseybus as the only operators of B-registered Atlanteans. Some of the Atlanteans have been refurbished by Northern Counties, with new front ends, while others have had new Paladin style single-deck bodies fitted.

The company's single-deck fleet is varied and includes five ECW-bodied Bristol REs, a Leyland Tiger with a Duple Dominant bus body and, no doubt with an eye to events in Blackpool, three Optare Deltas which entered service in 1991 with distinctive FBT registration marks. Fylde's 22 minibuses, whimsically marketed as Baby Blues, are all Northern Counties-bodied Dodges.

The company's livery is two shades of blue, and it trades as Blue Buses. In 1987 Fylde acquired Seagull Coaches of Blackpool and now uses the Seagull name for its coach fleet.

Moving to the other side of Preston, there are four municipal fleets in East Lancashire — Blackburn Borough Transport, Burnley & Pendle Transport, Hyndburn Transport and Rossendale Transport. Blackburn's double-deck fleet is standardised on East Lancs-bodied Atlanteans, the newest dating from 1983. New bus purchases since then have been limited to 25 MCW Metroriders in 1987-88, and five Volvo B10Ms with East Lancs EL2000 bodies in 1991. Other single-deck buses include an unusual type for a municipally-owned fleet — four ex-SBG Leopards with Alexander Y-type bus bodies. New in 1981, they were acquired from Kelvin Scottish in 1987. Also unusual are four ECW bodied Tigers which have been rebuilt at each end by East Lancs, who received another order from Blackburn in 1993 for Greenway rebuilt Nationals. East Lancs National Greenway rebuilds are being delivered during 1993 and are Blackburn's first Nationals of any description.

While the bulk of the company's operations are centred on Blackburn, it does run services to and in Accrington and Darwen, and has limited stop operations from Blackburn and Clitheroe to Bury and Manchester.

Unusual single-deckers operated by Blackburn are four ECW-bodied Tigers which were new in 1982 as Green Line coaches and came north from Kentish Bus in 1988. They have been rebuilt as 51-seat buses by East Lancs and fitted with new front and rear ends which transform the appearance of the rather awkwardly-styled ECW body. Steve Warburton

Fylde followed Blackpool's lead and added three Optare Deltas to its fleet in 1991, its first new full-size buses since 1984. The first picks up passengers outside Blackpool's famous Tower. Malcolm King

Blackburn's latest livery retains green and cream, but in revised proportions and with an italicised fleetname at upper deck floor level. There are 61 East Lancs-bodied Atlanteans in the fleet. This one dates from 1982. Malcolm King

In Accrington, Hyndburn has one of the most unusual liveries of any major operator, a striking combination of dark blue, red and grey. This is a modification of the even more unusual blue, black and red once used by Accrington Corporation Transport. The double-deck bus fleet is made up of a few Atlanteans bought new in the late 1970s, augmented by a variety of second-hand examples which are also made available for short-term hire to other operators. A few East Lancs-bodied Leopards survive in the single-deck fleet, along with a pair of Dennis Falcons purchased in 1984-85. Hyndburn's services run west to Blackburn and south to Bacup.

Since 1985 new vehicles have been minibuses and midibuses — Ford Transits, followed by MCW Metroriders, Iveco 49.10s (all marketed under the HyRider name and in a mainly grey livery) and finally Leyland Swifts. Each type was bigger than its predecessor. The seven Swifts, with 39-seat Reeve Burgess Harrier bodies, are an unusual choice for a municipal fleet. Hyndburn has also built up a large fleet of second-hand Leopard coaches, most of which have Duple Dominant bodies. These are used on longer-distance routes which take them as far south as Altrincham and Manchester Airport on a service which runs from Accrington via Bolton, although this route is also served by double-deckers.

Burnley & Pendle has invested more in updating its bus fleet than have some of its neighbours. Since 1988 it has standardised on Volvo with 34 B10M and Citybus single- and double-deckers joining the fleet. The single-deckers have been bodied by Alexander and East Lancs, the double-deckers by Alexander. The only other double-deckers in what is a predominantly single-decked fleet are a few surviving Bristol VRTs, including four former Tayside buses with Alexander bodies. Older single-deckers are Leyland Nationals and Leopards, the former including second-hand National 2s. There are 22 Mercedes minibuses and two Optare MetroRiders in a yellow and red livery operating under the Whizzard name, and the company also runs a coach fleet under the Viscount Central banner. This includes two examples of the rare Volvo C10M integral, purchased from Park of Hamilton. Only ten C10Ms were sold in the UK.

There are two Dennis Falcons with East Lancs bodies in the Hyndburn fleet. New in 1985, this one has 40 high-backed seats. Malcolm King

Hyndburn runs both new and second-hand East Lancs-bodied Atlanteans. The latter are five former Ipswich buses which were acquired in 1991. They are regular performers on the Manchester Airport run. Malcolm King

Burnley & Pendle's minibuses run under the Whizzard name, a loose reference to the witches of nearby Pendle Hill. This is an Optare MetroRider. Malcolm King

The last of the Lancashire municipalities lies to the south. Rossendale Transport was a late buyer of Bristol REs and its newest, three P-registered buses dating from 1975 with East Lancs bodies are still in use. These were not the fleet's last Bristols: in 1982 it purchased two little LHSs with 28-seat East Lancs bodies — a unique combination — for a service to Waterfoot and Cowpe and these are still owned. Its newest full-size single-deckers are four East Lancs-bodied Tigers delivered in 1989. Rossendale, like Blackburn, has ex-Kelvin Scottish Leopards. Other second-hand single-deckers include Duple Dominant-bodied Tiger buses from Hutchison of Overtown and Trimdon Motor Services. Single-deckers feature on the services which run out of the immediate Rossendale area — notably to Burnley, Bury, Rochdale (where Rossendale runs local services), Manchester and Accrington.

The company's original double-deckers are 14 East Lancs-bodied Atlanteans purchased between 1977 and 1982, but since deregulation it has expanded its double-deck fleet with former Greater Manchester, South Yorkshire and Hastings Top Line Atlanteans, 19 of which remain in service. Its last new double-decker, in 1987, was a solitary long-wheelbase Olympian with East Lancs 78-seat coach body. Minibuses — mainly MCW Metroriders — play a small part in the company's operations around Rawtenstall and it also has five Dennis Dart midibuses.

In 1991 Rossendale took over the old-established Ellen Smith Coaches business in Rochdale and the Ellen Smith name survives on some coaches.

There are, of course, other small operators spread throughout the North West who operate local services either commercially or on tender to Lancashire, Cheshire or Cumbria county councils or to the PTEs in Greater Manchester and Merseyside. None have substantial fleets, and none have bought new full-sized buses. Few operate frequent all-day services. The diligent observer may find such operators in Accrington (Pilkingtons), Burnley (Border Tours), Chester (Loftys and AIA Travel), Clitheroe (Lakelands) and Lancaster (Heysham Travel). All have just a handful of vehicles.

For a time Burnley & Pendle was buying both rear-engined National and mid-engined Leopards. The latter type is represented by one of the last batch, delivered in 1980 and bodied by East Lancs. It is a 47-seater based on the short-wheelbase PSU4 model. Stewart J Brown

Burnley & Pendle's oldest double-deckers are Bristol VRTs, including a small number of Alexander-bodied buses which were new to Tayside in 1977 and moved south to Lancashire in 1982. Steve Warburton

Most of Rossendale's double-deckers are second-hand acquisitions. This 1979 Roe-bodied Atlantean came from South Yorkshire Transport in 1991. Steve Warburton

NORTH EAST ENGLAND

A Sunderland Busways Alexander bodied Dart in the City Centre. Steve Warburton

The North East of England has long been good bus operating territory — or at least parts of it have. The densely-populated urban areas around Tyneside and Wearside have supported thriving networks of bus services, and still do. Inland, former colliery towns support frequent inter-urban services with a long tradition of a multiplicity of colourful operators. It is only in the rural hinterland, particularly in Northumberland, that services are sparse.

In some parts of the North East it's almost possible to imagine that deregulation has not really happened. The big operators have managed to avoid major confrontations and in so doing have not only preserved much of their own networks — but managed quite effectively to stifle competition.

Newcastle with its spectacular cross-Tyne bridges is the region's commercial centre and it is served by three major operators — Busways Travel Services, the Go-Ahead Northern group and Northumbria Motor Services. Busways is the former PTE-owned operation; the other two are former NBC subsidiaries.

The Busways livery is yellow, an inheritance from the Newcastle Corporation fleet which was absorbed by the PTE in 1970. But since its formation in 1986, the company's three main operating divisions have adopted different relief colours. Buses in Newcastle — which operate as Newcastle Busways, have maroon relief. Sunderland Busways' buses have green relief, while those of South Shields Busways have blue — in both cases using the colours of long-vanished municipal buses.

Busways' predecessor, the Tyne & Wear PTE, maintained its vehicles to a high standard — a tradition which has been carried on since the company's move into the private sector in May 1989. The standard PTE vehicle in the 1970s, and a type still much in evidence, was the long-wheelbase Atlantean with Alexander body. Some of the oldest survivors, R-registered vehicles numbered in the 500s, started life as dual-door buses with nearside staircases — the only Atlanteans to have this unusual layout. The centre doors have gone, but the nearside staircases remain, an identifying feature of an ex-Newcastle Atlantean wherever it goes. The Alexander bodies have panoramic windows of the style pioneered by Edinburgh Corporation in the mid-1960s.

Busways also inherited Fleetlines from the PTE and these are all allocated to Sunderland. There are two batches of 40, one bodied by Alexander and the other by MCW. Delivered in 1979, the MCW-bodied buses were among the last body-on-chassis vehicles built by the Birmingham manufacturer before it turned production over entirely to complete Metrobuses.

The fleet's more modern buses are a mixture of Leylands and Scanias. Two early Scania double-deckers, 1982 X-registered buses with Alexander R-type bodies, have been joined more recently by further batches of Scania double- and single-deckers, all bodied by Alexander. These operate in and around Newcastle. A batch of 65 Alexander-bodied Olympians was delivered to the PTE in 1986 and while most operate in Newcastle, there are some in

Busways has added both Leyland Lynxes and Scania N113s to its single-deck fleet. The Scanias have Alexander PS-type bodywork. Geoff Morant

both Sunderland and South Shields. The newest Olympians, Northern Counties-bodied buses of 1991 vintage, are at Sunderland. The new Olympians have Cummins engines; the earlier batch have Gardner power. Leyland also supplied Lynxes to Busways. Most are in Sunderland, but there are smaller numbers elsewhere. Busways' newest buses are Dennis Darts with Alexander Dash bodies allocated to the Newcastle and Sunderland divisions.

Busways and its predecessors have in fact been good customers for Alexander over a long period of time. Older Alexander-bodied buses in the fleet are a mixture of Atlanteans and Fleetlines, all with panoramic windows. The basic yellow and white livery is relieved by blue on this South Shields Busways vehicle. M Fowler

Parts of Busways' operations use vehicles in liveries which belie their ownership by a major operator. The Blue Bus fleetname and an appropriate livery adorn some 20 buses in Newcastle. All are single-decked and include ECW-bodied Bristol REs, one-time Lancashire United Transport Leopard buses, and a pair of Dennis Darts with Plaxton Pointer bodies which entered service in 1992 and are 15 years younger than most of the rest of the Blue Bus fleet. The Blue Bus name and livery are a nostalgic revival of prewar Newcastle, when the city's municipal buses were blue.

The Economic fleetname and dark red livery is worn by 11 Olympians, some of which operate on the erstwhile Economic service between Sunderland and South Shields. Economic was taken over by the PTE in 1975 and provided it with its first service between the two towns. Also in Economic livery are four Lynxes and three Atlanteans.

Another former independent's name used by Busways is Favourite, running in the white, orange and brown livery which was worn by the ex-Greater Manchester Leopards acquired in 1987 to launch the operation to compete with Trimdon Motor Services in County Durham. The Favourite colours are also carried by some minibuses and a small number of Atlanteans. The irony in Busways' use of the Favourite name is that Favourite was a company taken over by TMS in the early 1970s. Now TMS has gone, and Busways' Favourite fleet runs into Sunderland and on contracted services in Durham.

The competition with TMS in County Durham was prompted by TMS setting up an operation in Newcastle, the Tyne & Wear Omnibus Co. This proved to be a thorn in Busways' side but in a series of rapid and surprising moves, TWOC was taken over by Go-Ahead Northern in 1989 and immediately resold to Busways who effectively closed it down. Competition or collusion, one might well ask. However the TWOC name has been retained and is used on minibuses in Sunderland.

Blue Bus Services is a post-deregulation operation set up by Busways. Its fleet is made up largely of second-hand single-deckers, but in 1992 it got its first new buses. These were a pair of Dennis Darts with Plaxton Pointer bodies. Michael Fowler

Ten Northern Counties-bodied Leyland Olympians joined the Busways fleet in 1991. This one in South Shields carries Economic livery. Mike Harris

An ex-Greater Manchester Plaxton-bodied Leopard in the Favourite fleet, another of Busways' identities. The livery is that which was worn by the buses when they were purchased in 1987. Malcolm King

Northumbria Motor Services is owned by Proudmutual, set up as a management buy-out from NBC in 1987 — when the company was but a year old. It was created in 1986 to take over the operations of United Automobile Services north of the Tyne. United had at that time almost 800 buses and was considered too big to be privatised as a single entity. Northumbria now runs just under 400 buses and its operating territory stretches from the Tyne to the Scottish border. The company has depots on Tyneside at Newcastle and Whitley Bay, inland at Hexham, and further up country at Ashington, Blyth, Morpeth, Alnwick and, finally, Berwick.

The most striking feature of Northumbria buses is the livery — white, red and grey in an unusual diagonal layout which was designed by the consultants who developed North Western Road Car's equally distinctive colour scheme. This is carried by such disparate vehicles as diminutive Freight Rover Sherpas and huge Leyland Olympian coaches. The fleetname is applied in reflective lettering, a feature which can only be appreciated after dark.

Northumbria's single-deck fleet comprises elderly Nationals and a decreasing number of Bristol LHs, all inherited from United. To this it has added Optare Deltas. For longer services it has a variety of former United Leopard coaches. Most interesting of these are five which were rebodied by Duple in 1987 with 55-seat 320 bodies — an unusually (and perhaps uncomfortably) high capacity for an 11m coach.

The standard NBC-style double-deckers — ECW-bodied VRTs and Olympians — run in the company of a few rather more interesting Olympian variants. Northumbria's only new double-deckers are ten long Olympians with Alexander bodies to a high specification with 76 coach seats. These were purchased in 1988. Even longer Olympians operate to and from Newcastle, in the shape of ex-Green Line and Invictaway coaches with ECW bodies based on a chassis with a specially extended wheelbase. These have fixed tinted windows and feature the double curvature BET lower-deck windscreen and unusually deep flat-glass upper deck screens. The overall effect is impressive, rather than harmonious. Most of these unusual machines came from Kentish Bus, a sister company of Northumbria within the Proudmutual group. The most recent double-deck addition is a another ex-Green Line Olympian coach which was rebodied as a bus by Northern Counties in 1992.

Proudmutual also owns two small operators in the North East, Moor Dale Coaches of Newcastle and the associated Rochester & Marshall of Hexham. The latter now operates from Northumbria's Hexham depot. Both were acquired in 1989. Moor Dale runs services from Four Lane Ends station on the Tyne & Wear Metro. These are operated by a pair of Leyland Lynxes bought new in 1987, although some of the company's older coaches are also used on service. Moor Dale's double-deckers are normally confined to contract work.

The only new double-deckers purchased by Northumbria since its privatisation have been 10 Leyland Olympians. These have Cummins engines and Alexander bodies, whereas in NBC days Gardner engines and ECW bodies were the norm.
Richard Eversden

For new single deck buses, Northumbria has chosen the Optare Delta, on which the livery sits particularly well. Mike Harris

The Tyne & Wear PTE specifies an orange and yellow livery for buses operating on Carebus services for travellers with impaired mobility. This East Lancs National Greenway rebuild in the Northumbria fleet is based on a 1984 National 2. Malcolm King

VFM Buses is the brand name of the Tyneside Omnibus Co, part of the Go-Ahead Northern group. The group runs 89 Dennis Darts with Wright Handybus bodies to give it the biggest fleet of Wright bodies outside London. Malcolm King

The area to the south of Newcastle is dominated by the Go-Ahead Northern group which has spent the early 1990s evolving a series of new local images. The bright but traditional-looking red and white Go-Ahead Northern livery is gradually disappearing from much of the company's area as new subsidiaries establish their identities — but is being retained for operations in Chester-le-Street, Stanley and Consett, with the fleetname Northern. The group runs almost 700 vehicles, making it the region's biggest operator.

The first of the new identities appeared in South Shields at the start of 1992 when the Tyneside Omnibus Co relaunched its services with a two-tone blue livery and the fleetname VFM Buses: VFM stands for Value For Money. VFM operates around 60 vehicles including 13 Dennis Darts with Wright Handybus bodies from 89 delivered to the Go-Ahead Northern group in 1992-93. Most of the remainder of the VFM fleet is made up of Leyland Atlanteans with bodies by Roe and ECW.

The newest double deckers in the VFM fleet are some ECW-bodied Olympians dating from 1985. Atlanteans, like the ECW-bodied example in the background, are more common. Mike Harris

Next came Go-Ahead Gateshead, which started in February 1992, also with some of the new Wright-bodied Darts. Its livery is red, blue and white. This is a much bigger fleet—around the 160 mark—and it contains just over half of the group's MCW Metrobuses, which number almost 100. Go-Ahead Northern was one of the few NBC operators to obtain authority to buy non-Leyland buses in the 1980s. The Gateshead fleet has 11 of the group's Optare Deltas. Five of these are used on a link to the Gateshead Metrocentre which, somewhat confusingly, is nowhere near the Metro. Go-Ahead Gateshead also runs Optare MetroRiders.

Northern was launched in March 1992, again with a batch of Darts. These joined a fleet which includes 17 Bristol VRTs (all of the group's VRT fleet), along with more of the Metrobuses and 14 Optare Deltas.

Above left: **Go-Ahead Gateshead appeared at the start of 1992 as a new livery for Gateshead & District. An ECW-bodied Olympian from the Go-Ahead Gateshead fleet passes Newcastle Central station.** Geoff Morant

Above right: **The Northern name is used with a conventional red and white livery. The application of the Northern livery to single deckers is shown on a Dennis Dart.** Geoff Morant

Centre: **Wear Buses is based in Sunderland and uses a green livery. Its first new buses were more of the group's Dennis Darts.** Geoff Morant

Right: **A number of coach-seated MkII Metrobuses are in a modified livery for express services from Newcastle.** D J Little

Wear Buses is the trading name for Sunderland & District and it adopted a green and grey livery in the autumn of 1992. Here again the new identity appeared at the same time as a fleet of Wright Handybuses. Wear Buses operates from depots in Sunderland and in the rather exotic-sounding towns of Philadelphia and Washington. It has 175 buses including a large number of the group's Alexander-bodied Renault S56 minibuses and the earlier Alexander conversions of Mercedes vans.

Coastline, based in North Shields, is running in dark red and cream, announcing its fresh image at the start of 1993. Its fleet is predominantly Atlanteans and Olympians — with eight of the ubiquitous Darts and a few minibuses for variety. The Atlanteans include some long-wheelbase AN68/2s with MCW bodies which were purchased from the Tyne & Wear PTE in 1982 when they were only three years old. At that time co-ordination was the name of the game and most of the Go-Ahead Northern fleet (or Northern General as it was then known) wore the PTE yellow and white livery.

Gypsy Queen, running between Langley Park and Durham, has been a Go-Ahead Northern subsidiary since 1989, although with no outward change to the company's operations. Its small fleet includes a Carlyle-bodied Dennis Dart, delivered in 1991 and the first production example of Duple's short-lived 300-series bus body, on a Volvo B10M chassis. This was new in 1987. The Gypsy Queen colours are cream with deep red and blue relief. A more recent acquisition by Go-Ahead Northern is Low Fell Coaches who hit the headlines in the early 1980s when it won a licence to operate a cross-Tyne service between Gateshead and Newcastle, despite opposition from the PTE which was trying to encourage cross-river travellers to use the new Metro. The cross-Tyne service continues, normally operated by a Leyland Tiger or Dennis Javelin with Duple 300-series bus body. Low Fell continues as a separate subsidiary rather like Gypsy Queen and the most recent addition to its fleet is the prototype Alexander-bodied Dennis Lance which was exhibited at Coach & Bus 91 in the colours of SMT.

Go-Ahead Northern's small fleet of coaches trades under the Voyager name and wears an unrelieved dark red livery; most are Plaxton-bodied Tigers.

Coastline operates on the north bank of the Tyne and its fleet is mostly double-deck. This Olympian is seen at Whitley Bay. D J Little

Gypsy Queen shows no outward sign of its ownership by Go-Ahead Northern. The only Dennis Dart in the small fleet has Carlyle bodywork and is seen in Durham. Malcolm King

Low Fell Coaches runs this Bedford YMT with Plaxton Derwent bus body on its cross-Tyne service. Geoff Morant

Parts of the North East have a long tradition of independent bus operation, particularly in County Durham where many of the current small — and not so small — businesses have long histories. There are fewer small operators in Northumberland, which has a farming rather than an industrial background. Three are worth singling out: Raisbeck, Tyne Valley and Hunter.

Raisbeck's claim to fame is a unique bus, the only Volvo B7M in Britain. This has a mid-mounted Volvo 7-litre engine and an angular 53-seat East Lancs body which can best be described as serviceable rather than beautiful, its design owing a little to the garden shed school of aesthetics. New in 1985, it was a product of Volvo toying with the idea of competing in the lightweight bus market, an idea which it quickly abandoned, realising that if there was a demand for a lightweight bus, the B7M wasn't quite the beast to cater for it. Raisbeck operate a town service in Bedlington. A Bedford coach acts as a relief for the B7M.

Tyne Valley Coaches of Acomb provides links from Hexham to Bellingham, Colwell and Haltwhistle and goes back 25 years. Its services are generally operated by Leyland Leopards, with a choice of Duple and Plaxton coach bodied examples and a pair with Plaxton bus bodies.

Hunter's of Seaton Delaval operate between North Shields and Whitley Bay and on to Cramlington where they run a local service. The company used to buy new double-deckers, but its current fleet is made up of second-hand ones: Atlanteans from Greater Manchester and from Go-Ahead Northern. Hunter's also run three Leopards and a pair of Transit minibuses.

The most visible new competition for Busways in Newcastle came from Welcome Passenger Services, formed in October 1991 amidst a welter of legal threats from Busways over its mainly yellow livery and its use of Busways route numbers. Welcome started up with 20 new minibuses — ten Optare MetroRiders and ten Renaults with Reeve Burgess Beaver bodies. The company's livery is now red and yellow and its initial fleet has been increased with repeat orders for both types of vehicle. Its newest Renaults, S75s delivered in the autumn of 1992, are among the last Renault minibuses to enter service. In August 1993 Busways took over Welcome but is retaining the company's identity.

Raisbeck runs the country's only Volvo B7M. It has a 53-seat East Lancs body. Malcolm King

Hunter's of Seaton Delaval run Atlanteans in the North Shields and Cramlington areas. New to Greater Manchester in 1978, the Park Royal-bodied AN68 joined Hunter's fleet in 1990.
Mike Harris

Welcome Passenger Services runs Renault S56s and Optare MetroRiders on services in Newcastle. This is a long-wheelbase MetroRider. Malcolm King

Catch A Bus runs
Bristol REs,
although these
are now being
replaced by
rebodied buses.
This 1974
RELL6G came
from Cambus in
1989. It has an
ECW body.
Peter Rowlands

South of the Tyne, Catch A Bus, the name coined by Hylton Castle Motors for its post-deregulation venture into local bus operation, runs town services in South Shields and in Sunderland. The standard Catch A Bus bus is the ECW-bodied Bristol RE, although RE afficionados will note that there are RELL (low frame) and RELH (high frame) models, and also a couple of short RESLs. Most of the fleet's REs date from the mid-1970s and were new to various NBC subsidiaries. Catch A Bus also has one AEC Reliance — an increasingly rare breed in the 1990s — with Duple Dominant bus body which was new in 1980 to Hutchison of Overtown, and a similarly-bodied Leopard which came from Merthyr Tydfil Transport. The most recent additions to the fleet are two single-deck Atlanteans, rebodied by East Lancs. The company's coaches retain the Hylton Castle name.

Sunderland is also served by W H Jolly of South Hylton, a company which seems to have been untouched by deregulation. Its five buses are all Duple-bodied Bedford YMTs, delivered between 1977 and 1981 — and these run from South Hylton to Sunderland much as they have always done. By contrast, Redby Travel is a post-deregulation bus operator although it has been running coaches since the 1940s. Its fleet is distinguished by eight Dennis Lancets – four ex-Blackpool buses with Marshall Camair 80 bodies and four former Northern Scottish machines with Alexander P-type bodywork. There are also ECW-bodied Tigers, former Green Line coaches bought from Luton & District in 1992, and four Leyland Nationals. Redby runs local services around Sunderland.

The W H Jolly
fleet has
remained
unchanged since
the start of the
1980s. The last
buses to be
added to it were
a pair of X-
registered
Bedford YMTs
with 53-seat
Duple bus
bodies. D J Little

Redby Travel
runs into
Sunderland and
South Shields.
Recent arrivals
have been
former NBC
Tigers with ECW
bodies. Malcolm
King

The cathedral city of Durham is served by United and Northern, as well as by smaller operators. Bob Smith Travel of Langley Park runs a pair of Freight Rover Sherpa minibuses in the city and up to the cathedral, as well as operating between Langley Park and Durham, normally with a 1980 Leyland Leopard which was rebodied as a bus by Willowbrook in 1990. Diamond Bus Service of Stanley operates in a distinctive two-tone grey and red livery. For many years Diamond standardised on Bedfords and a number remain with both Duple and Plaxton bus bodies. Following the demise of Bedford, Diamond switched to the Dennis Javelin. The first two had Duple 300 bus bodies but since Duple has followed Bedford into oblivion, Diamond's newest Javelin bus has a Plaxton Derwent body.

Diamond's services link Durham and Stanley, from where Hunter's of Tantobie operate a pair of late 1970s Bedford Y-series with Duple bus bodies in a smart black and white livery. Hunter's also run Bedford coaches. Star Travel, a relative newcomer to the bus business (it dates back to 1983) links Stanley with Flint Hill (also served by Hunter's) and the quaintly-named Quaking Houses. Rare Optare-bodied Dennis Dominos are used.

A few miles east lies Consett which is served by another long-established company, Armstrongs of Ebchester, running local services in and from the town. Some of the company's older coaches are used on service, but of more interest is a Scania K93 with Plaxton Derwent bus body which was bought new in 1990. Mercedes-Benz minibuses are also operated.

Gardiners of Spennymoor operate north to Durham and south to Bishop Auckland. There are no buses in the fleet, and the services are operated by coaches. The full-size vehicles in the Gardiners fleet are mainly Volvo B10M coaches and these, too, are used on service as are Volvo B58s and Leyland Leopards.

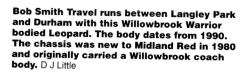

Bob Smith Travel runs between Langley Park and Durham with this Willowbrook Warrior bodied Leopard. The body dates from 1990. The chassis was new to Midland Red in 1980 and originally carried a Willowbrook coach body. D J Little

The newest bus operated by Diamond Bus Service of Stanley is a Dennis Javelin with Plaxton body. It entered service in 1991. Malcolm King

Classic of West Pelton runs competitive services with second-hand buses, including this ex-GM Buses Atlantean. Steve Warburton

Bishop Auckland has long been a centre of independent bus operation. Most famous of the companies serving the town is OK Motor Services, set up 80 years ago and quick to seize the new business opportunities which deregulation offered. Ten years ago OK ran 70 buses and coaches; it now runs nearly 200, which represents significant expansion by any standards. Its routes reach north to Newcastle and south into Cleveland, but the heartland of its operations remains in County Durham. The fleet is a varied one, even if that good old workhorse, the Leyland Leopard, accounts for almost half of it. A number of the Leopards were bought new in the 1970s, but good used examples have played a key role in OK's expansion. The company has Leopards from Crosville Wales, Kelvin Scottish, National Welsh and Rhymney Valley amongst others. OK has a small number of Bristol LH buses which were new to London Transport. The newest single-deckers are DAF SB220s with bodies by Optare; DAF coaches are operated too.

Leylands feature strongly in the double-deck fleet, with Atlanteans bought new and second-hand, and two small batches of long-wheelbase Leyland Olympians bodied by Northern Counties.

OK continues to buy new double-deckers, its post-deregulation standard being the Northern Counties-bodied Leyland Olympian. Three were delivered in 1992. Malc McDonald

OK Travel's fleet is predominantly Leyland. This Alexander-bodied Atlantean was new to South Yorkshire Transport in 1981. Mike Harris

Leyland Leopards figure strongly in the OK fleet. They include 12 with East Lancs bodies purchased from Inter Valley Link in 1989. These are 10m PSU4s and 11m PSU3s. This is a PSU4 in South Shields. Malc McDonald

Weardale Motor Services of Stanhope, in north-west County Durham, operate from there down to Bishop Auckland in a red, maroon and white livery not dissimilar to OK's maroon, red and cream. Weardale used to buy the occasional new double-decker and its last, a 1970 long-wheelbase Leyland Atlantean PDR2, still survives. It has Roe dual-door bodywork of a design developed for Leeds City Transport. The other double-deckers in the fleet are front-engined Leyland Titans, the oldest of which, a 1959 Alexander-bodied PD3, was also new to the company. The double-deckers are now used principally on school services. Buses in the single-deck fleet are notable for their high capacity, achieved by two-plus-three seating. Two 1974 Plaxton coach-bodied Volvos now have 68 bus seats.

One of the smaller operators serving Bishop Auckland is Bond Bros, with a route from Willington, where the operation is based. This can be operated by one of the company's second-hand coaches or, more interestingly, by an ECW-bodied Bristol LH which came from Lincolnshire Road Car.

The Eden Bus Services runs from Bishop Auckland to Darlington, among other places, and it is another operator whose fleet bears witness to the virtues of the Leyland Leopard: 13 of its 16 full-size vehicles are Leopards. Most have coach bodies but there are two with Plaxton bus bodies (bought new in 1976) and one with an Alexander Y-type body (acquired, used, in 1984). Minibuses — MCW Metroriders — joined the fleet in 1988 for a local service in Birtley.

To the east of Bishop Auckland two small operators serve Ferryhill. Based in the town, Martindales is primarily a coach operator, but the fleet includes some elderly ex-SBG Leopard buses for contracts and a local service. Similar buses are operated by Scarlet Band of West Cornforth, again on contract work as well as on a service linking Ferryhill with Bowburn.

The southernmost town in County Durham is Darlington, home of Darlington Transport, owned by the local council, and United Automobile Services. The Darlington fleet has suffered from a lack of investment in recent times — and some of the buses which it bought when it was investing have been just a bit off-beat. The only new additions to the fleet since deregulation have been six MCW Metroriders, which run local services in the town. Its newest big buses are six Ward Dalesmans (or Dalesmen?), now ten years old. The unusual rear-engined Wards — unique to Darlington — have almost equally unusual Wadham Stringer Vanguard dual-door bodies. The Ward chassis were built near Huddersfield by an offshoot of a Yorkshire coach operator.

Before buying Wards, Darlington backed another odd design, the long-wheelbase single-deck Dennis Dominator. Darlington's eight have two-door Marshall Camair 80 bodies and were new in 1980. These followed a small batch of Leopards, distinctive only in sticking to Darlington's favoured two-door body (this time by Duple), a style which it has to be said is ill-suited to a high-frame mid-engined chassis. Previous generations of bus still in service, and not to be found elsewhere in Britain in any significant numbers, are single-deck 36ft-long Daimler Fleetlines with Roe bodies.

Rear-engined double-deckers made their first-appearance in the Darlington fleet as recently as 1990, with the purchase of Fleetlines from Nottingham City Transport. These buses, new in 1976, have Nottingham's quirky style of Northern Counties bodywork. Since 1986 Darlington Transport has branched out into coaching, taking over two local operators — one of which gave the company a base in the attractive market town of Richmond, where it now runs a local service. From May 1993 Darlington has faced competition from South Durham Buses using second-hand Ivecos. This company, set up by a former United manager, trades as Your Bus.

An Alexander-bodied Leyland Leopard is seen in Spennymoor on one of Scarlet Band's Durham County Council contracts. G R Mills

Darlington Transport is the only operator of the rear-engined Ward Dalesman GRXI. Six were delivered in 1983 with dual-door Wadham Stringer Vanguard bodywork. The model code indicates Gardner, Rear engine and 11m (Roman XI) long. D J Little

Double-deckers reappeared in the Darlington fleet in 1990 in the shape of 1976 Daimler Fleetlines purchased from Nottingham. They have Northern Counties bodies. Mike Harris

United is a former NBC company. In its postwar heyday its territory stretched from Scarborough in the south to Berwick-on-Tweed in the north, but in the 1980s it was cut back to its present operating area with depots in Bishop Auckland, Darlington, Durham, Peterlee, Richmond and Ripon which are supported by outstations in smaller towns.

United was privatised in December 1987 when it was purchased by Caldaire Holdings, owner of West Riding. When Caldaire took it over it had 490 buses, but even this was deemed too large by its new owners and United's Cleveland operations were transferred in February 1990 to a new Tees & District company set up by Caldaire. Caldaire itself has since had its own divisions and United, along with Tees & District and Teesside Motor Services — all previously part of Caldaire North East — are now part of the Westcourt group, owned by a group of former Caldaire directors.

Back to United. Double-deckers are in a minority in the United fleet. There are 50, a mix of NBC-style Bristol VRTs and Leyland Olympians, mostly Gardner-engined and ECW-bodied. There is more interest in the single-deck fleet. United's NBC heritage includes the inevitable Leyland Nationals — whose ranks have increased with the arrival of ex-Blackpool Transport National 2s — and a sizeable fleet of Bristol LHs whose days are numbered. Minibuses are a mixture of Mercedes van conversions (by Reeve Burgess) and Alexander-bodied Dodge S56s. There are a lot of Leopards, mostly with coach bodies for use on longer-distance services but including some with Duple Dominant bus bodies which originated with Trimdon Motor Services, acquired by Caldaire and absorbed by United in 1990. Trimdon also provided some Duple bus-bodied Tigers.

Caldaire's avowed policy — and one which looks set to be continued by Westcourt — was that it was essential to maintain investment in new buses. The first for United since its privatisation arrived in 1990 — five Leyland Lynx, five Optare Delta, and two unusual Leyland Tigers with Alexander (Belfast) Q-type bodies. Caldaire's aim was to evaluate different types for possible future fleet replacement. In some respects the decision was eventually made for them. Neither the Lynx nor the Tiger are now available and Westcourt ordered for 1993 a fleet of 15 Optare Deltas and 41 Optare Vectas divided between its three subsidiary companies.

United's latest livery is shown on a Bristol VRT which was new to West Riding. The bus was photographed in Darlington. Keith Grimes

The acquisition of Trimdon Motor Services in 1990 added an assortment of Leyland Leopard and Tiger buses to the United fleet. This is a Duple-bodied Leopard, seen in Hawes.
Malcolm Keeley

In its search for a simple vehicle for rural operation United purchased a pair of Leyland Tigers with Alexander (Belfast) Q-type bodies for evaluation. They entered service in 1990.
Malcolm King

The Vectas will replace LHs and were ordered after a trial of two in the Teesside fleet during 1992. These are smaller and lighter than the Delta and are based on the MAN 11.190 underframe — giving Westcourt the distinction of being the first UK bus operator to run a fleet of MANs. Teesside's 60-strong fleet currently comprises the two original Vectas and 44 Bristol LHs built between 1974 and 1980. The company is a child of deregulation, set up by Trimdon Motor Services to operate in Cleveland — particularly in the busy towns of Stockton, where the company is based, and Middlesbrough. Teesside was acquired by Caldaire in April 1990 and the livery changed from white with two shades of blue as relief, to a darker overall blue relieved by white window surrounds. This was further modified — and improved — on the first two Vectas, with the blue being relieved by a broad diagonal cream band in mid-wheelbase.

The third Westcourt company is Tees & District with its headquarters in Middlesbrough and depots in Hartlepool, Loftus, Redcar, Stokesley and Whitby. Tees & District runs 200 buses — including over 50 of the LHs of which United was so fond. As with United, the bulk of Tees & District's buses are of obvious NBC origin and a minority – 37 – are double-deckers. It comes as no surprise to find the same fleet mix too — VRTs, Olympians, Nationals and Leopards, and a small number of minibuses. National 2s have come from a number of sources to replace older Mark 1 Nationals — and a few National 1s have been given a new lease of life by the fitment of DAF engines in place of their original Leyland 500-series units.

Tees & District adopted a simple way of applying a bright new identity to its buses by adding a broad area of rich yellow to United's poppy red and white colour scheme. This enabled the entire fleet to be given a new look in a short space of time without the expense of a complete repaint for every bus. The company's longer routes take its buses as far north as Newcastle and as far south as Scarborough.

Teesside runs both Optare Deltas and Vectas. One of their Deltas is seen at Middlesbrough Michael Fowler

Tees & District added a broad swathe of yellow to United's red and white colour scheme, radically altering the appearance of its fleet. This Leyland National 2 was new to Ribble. It is seen in Hartlepool bus station. Stewart J Brown

Optare Vectas for Westcourt subsidiaries were delivered in 1993. Tees & District was one of the recipients. Westcourt have 41 Vectas on order. Steve Warburton

78

The main operator of local bus services in the Middlesbrough/Stockton conurbation is Cleveland Transit. This former local authority bus fleet was sold to its management and employees in May 1991. Its fleet numbers 150 vehicles, including those owned by its Cleveland Coaches subsidiary — which marks a considerable reduction from the 235 operated prior to deregulation.

Cleveland has in recent years standardised on the Leyland Lynx and now runs 30. This gives the company a modern fleet, with its oldest buses being T-registered Fleetlines. Although not the last operator to buy a Fleetline (that was South Notts of Gotham) it was the last to place Fleetlines in service using eight chassis which were not bodied until 1983. They are the only Fleetlines with Y-suffix registrations. When Leyland ceased Fleetline production Cleveland switched its chassis business to Dennis and the only other double-deck buses in the fleet are Dominators. The newest of these entered service in 1986 and, like all of Cleveland's double-deck bus fleet, have Northern Counties bodies.

The company's livery is an attractive combination of green, white and yellow for buses, while coaches and dual-purpose vehicles are orange and yellow. Most of the single-deckers in both the Cleveland Transit and Cleveland Coaches fleets are Leyland Leopards with Plaxton Supreme bodies, some of which have been rebuilt with practical but ungainly destination boxes on their front domes. An unusual vehicle in the coach fleet is a Leyland Royal Tiger Doyen integral, purchased new in 1987 and one of the few of this comparatively rare type to have been operated by a local authority fleet. Most of the company's 25 minibuses are Renault S56s bodied by Northern Counties, some in bus fleet livery and some in orange and white.

Cleveland's fleet reduction over the last decade has been brought about partly by improvements in efficiency, including centralising operations in one depot in Stockton, and partly because of competition. The Teesside operation of Trimdon Motor Services, which put 60 Bristol LHs onto the streets served by Cleveland Transit, has already been mentioned. There were also some brief skirmishes with United. But there has been long-lasting competition from smaller fleets too.

Cleveland Transit was a staunch Fleetline user, placing its last examples in service in 1983. They have Northern Counties bodywork. D J Little

Cleveland Transit standardised on Leyland's Lynx from 1989 and now runs 30, a mix of Marks I and II. D J Little

For a number of years Cleveland Transit has operated a sizeable fleet of dual-purpose single-deckers, a type most often associated with NBC and SBG fleets. This 1980 Leopard has a Plaxton body which despite having tinted glazing has 55 bus seats. Malcolm King

From day one of deregulation Delta started running in Stockton with Bristol REs — two at first, but this figure quickly grew and Delta now operates 22 vehicles. Most of its buses are still REs, none newer than 1975. They are ECW-bodied and originated with a variety of NBC subsidiaries, generally reaching Delta as the third owner at least. Delta now also operates in Middlesbrough.

Robsons of Thornaby-on-Tees runs a small but varied fleet on services in both Stockton and Middlesbrough. Robson's brown and cream livery is worn by two Nationals, three ECW-bodied Bristol LHs, an ex-SBG Leopard and four minibuses.

A few miles north of Teesside lies Hartlepool, served by Tees & District and Hartlepool Transport which was local authority owned until June 1993 when it was bought by its employees. Hartlepool is one of those towns where time seems to have stood still — aided by Hartlepool Transport's fondness for Bristol REs, which it is still overhauling for further service. Roughly half of Hartlepool's 60-strong fleet is made up of Bristol REs delivered between 1970 and 1975. The company's main gesture to the new competitive market is the application of 'Your bus' logos to its fleet. When Leyland withdrew the Bristol RE from the British market, Hartlepool tried two batches of Nationals, and these still survive — seven National 1s and seven National 2s. Of more interest are its newest buses — Dennis Falcons delivered in 1983 with Wadham Stringer bodies and in 1985 with Northern Counties bodies.

The bus fleet is all single-deck, and most are of two-door layout. Since 1986 the only additions to the fleet have been six second-hand coaches — five Leopards and a 1984 Volvo B10M, all with Plaxton bodies — and four second-hand Nationals. Only two routes take Hartlepool's vehicles beyond the town boundary — one south to Middlesbrough and one north to the Gateshead Metrocentre.

Delta is adopting a new red and grey livery in place of its previous white with red and blue relief bands. A 1971 Bristol RE with ECW body in Stockton shows the current scheme. This bus was new to Eastern Counties and joined Delta from Cambus in 1987. D J Little

Robson of Thornaby-on-Tees runs three Bristol LHs like this one seen in Stockton. Mike Harris

Hartlepool has one batch of National 2s, new in 1980. Note the high-back seating fitted. It runs Mark 1 Nationals too. Malcolm King

Hartlepool Transport, privatised in 1993, runs a large fleet of Bristol RELLs with ECW bodies. All are Leyland-powered and the last – shown here – entered service in 1975.
Mike Harris

Hartlepool's newest buses are six Dennis Falcons with Northern Counties bodies. They were delivered in 1985.
Stewart J Brown

YORKSHIRE

A Leyland Olympian of East Yorkshire Motor Services at Hutton-le-Hole. Steve Warburton

Parts of North Yorkshire are served by operators covered in the North East of England section—Ripon by United, Whitby by Tees & District, for example. Both of these are Westcourt subsidiaries. The northernmost town of any substance to be served by a genuine Yorkshire operator is Scarborough where EYMS Group subsidiary Scarborough & District Motor Services holds sway. Scarborough was in fact served by United until 1986 when, shortly before deregulation, United's operations were transferred to EYMS. A year later EYMS took over Wallace Arnold's services out to Ebberston which had traded under the Hardwick's name, and ultimately the whole operation was reformed as Scarborough & District. Some ex-Wallace Arnold Leopards survive in the Scarborough & District fleet.

Most Scarborough town services are in the hands of Reeve Burgess bodied Mercedes-Benz minibuses which were introduced in the summer of 1989. Other services are operated either by elderly Leyland Leopards or, since 1992, by Leyland Nationals refurbished by East Lancs to Greenway specification. The minibuses carry a silver livery, while the Greenways are grey, and both types run under the Scarborough Skipper name. The Leopards carry a deep red and grey livery — the same as the parent East Yorkshire fleet — with Scarborough & District fleetnames. Two Leopards were rebodied by East Lancs in 1992.

The only regular year-round double-deck operation in Scarborough is by sister EYMS Group company Primrose Valley Coaches, based near Filey, seven miles to the south. Primrose Valley, in the same red and grey colours as Scarborough & District, runs VRTs, as well as a variety of coaches. Primrose Valley has been part of EYMS since 1990.

The main competitor for the EYMS Group in Scarborough is Applebys, whose headquarters are in Lincolnshire. Applebys use Scarborough as a base for both commercial and tendered services, generally using Leyland Leopard coaches. During the summer season Applebys also run open-top sea-front services, competing not only with EYMS but with an assortment of small operators who have come and gone with astonishing frequency.

Above: **Scarborough & District runs East Lancs National Greenways on local services. Introduced in 1992, they carry the Scarborough Skipper name which had previously been used only on Mercedes-Benz minibuses. A Greenway heads to Eastfield, location of Plaxton's body-building plant.** Michael Fowler

Left: **East Lancs has supplied Scarborough & District with EL2000 dual-purpose bodywork, fitted to an ex-Hardwicks Leopard which originally had a Plaxton body. Only the registration reveals the age of the chassis – and that has since been disguised by the purchase of a cherished number.** Malcolm King

The EYMS Group's headquarters are in Hull — which in the ancient aphorism ranked alongside Halifax and Hell as a place from which to seek divine deliverance. It isn't really that bad and although Hell may be warmer, Hull wins on bus interest.

East Yorkshire is currently locked in a battle for passengers with municipally-owned Kingston-upon-Hull City Transport. As in so many cities, in the days before deregulation the company operator, in this case East Yorkshire, ran the out-of-town services while the municipal transport department ran an essentially urban business.

That has gradually altered and while KHCT's management was in the throes of enforced change in 1992, EYMS took the opportunity to consolidate its position by taking over some of the smaller operators serving the city. The stars of the East Yorkshire fleet are without doubt its Routemasters. The company has approaching 20, all run in Hull, and they wear the traditional dark blue and primrose scheme which was abandoned by NBC 20 years ago when corporate image was all the rage. Which isn't to say that the rest of the fleet is uninteresting — far from it.

EYMS is the first operator north of Watford to run a Spectra, the all-new double-deck design unveiled by Optare in the autumn of 1991. The Spectra is DAF-powered and is the spiritual successor to the MCW Metrobus, although the two designs have very little in common. For routine fleet replacement EYMS has since 1990 standardised on Leyland Olympians with Northern Counties bodies. Older Olympians in the fleet are standard NBC types with ECW bodies, although there are also four of the extra-long-wheelbase one-time Green Line coaches. These run on longer-distance services from Hull.

Older 'deckers are VRTs (both Leyland and Gardner engined and both new and second-hand) with a smattering of second-hand Atlanteans. Most interesting among these are some former Cleveland Transit buses which have 1970 PDR1A/1 chassis and mid-1980s Northern Counties bodies. They joined the fleet in 1990 and were quickly re-registered with dateless Ulster marks to replace the original H-suffix registrations. Outside Scarborough minibuses play a small part in the EYMS Group's operations, although there are a number in the subsidiary East Yorkshire Travel and Cottingham Mini Coaches operations.

Expansion and acquisition has seen an amazing variety of buses join the East Yorkshire fleet. Among its older acquisitions is this 1969 Atlantean with Roe bodywork which was new to Kingston-upon-Hull. Paul Gainsbury

Old and new. The only Optare Spectra in the north is operated by East Yorkshire. It passes a Routemaster outside Hull station. Malcolm King

Hull & District livery is carried on a few Atlanteans used mainly for schools services. This 1976 ECW-bodied bus was acquired from Northern General in 1986. A window from a lowheight ECW body has been fitted where the exit door used to be. Malcolm King

The Hull municipal fleet is a varied one which has witnessed a succession of changes in vehicle policy. From the early 1960s Hull standardised on Leyland's Atlantean with Roe bodywork. The oldest examples of this combination still in use date back to 1972; the newest are 1982 X-registered buses. Hull tried MCW Metropolitans in the mid-1970s and all have gone, outlived by older Atlanteans. But the disastrous Metropolitan experience did not put Hull off either the bodybuilder, MCW, or the component supplier, Scania. A fleet of 30 Metrobuses purchased in 1980-81 still serves the city and after a Dennis interlude from 1984-89, Hull switched to Scania for its new buses. The newest buses in the fleet are double- and single-deck N112s delivered between 1988 and 1990 and bodied by East Lancs. East Lancs also bodied most of the fleet's Dominators, but to Alexander's R-type design. However the first, B-registered, batch of Dennises do in fact have genuine Alexander bodies just to confuse the situation.

Apart from six Scanias, most of Hull's single-deckers are coaches, although there is one Leyland National 2, purchased in 1984, which was one of the first buses in Britain to be fully accessible to passengers in wheelchairs. It has since been joined by an ex-Leicester Dennis Lancet with a wheelchair-accessible Duple Dominant bus body. A fleet of 15 Iveco Ford Daily minibuses with Robin Hood bodies runs in a dark red livery under the Royale brand name. Coaches, which include unusual Dennis Dorchesters, trade under the Kingstonian banner. Many of the coaches are named, although some of the people so honoured seem somewhat obscure to non-natives of Hull. Who was Wilf Spaven, whose name now decorates a Dorchester? He was KHCT's first general manager.

Post-deregulation independents in Hull have had mixed, but generally declining, fortunes. KHCT took over Citilink in 1989 and kept the name, for around 20 Atlanteans in a two-tone green livery,

Kingston-upon-Hull runs 51 Dennis Dominators, with bodies by Alexander and East Lancs This 1985 bus has East Lancs bodywork which differs from the Alexander original only in small details. Malcolm King

until 1992. Surviving green liveried buses have KHCT blue and white fronts. In the autumn of 1992 EYMS absorbed the bus operations of Rhodes of Wawne and Metro City Bus. This was followed in February 1993 by the old-established local services of Connor & Graham of Easington. Some blue and white Nationals used on the Metro City Bus route to Bransholme were acquired by EYMS, as were three of Connor & Graham's second-hand Atlantean 'deckers. This leaves Pride of the Road with ageing Nationals. At the start of 1993 Pride of the Road (which had previously run buses in West Yorkshire) took over the operations of Humber Stagecoach (not related to Stagecoach Holdings).

Since 1989 all of Hull's new buses have been East Lancs-bodied Scanias. Most are double-deckers but the first six were N112 saloons with 47 coach seats and tinted windows. They are the only single-deck buses in the fleet apart from two which are used on duties needing wheelchair accessibility. Stewart J Brown

North Yorkshire is a land of moors and mystery. Head south and it becomes a land of heavy industry and both West Yorkshire and South Yorkshire are predominantly industrial counties. Leeds and the surrounding towns have a rich Victorian heritage. Look at any West Yorkshire town hall and it's not too difficult to imagine bewhiskered civic dignitaries presiding over the inauguration of municipal tramways powered by electricity.

Now they have to make do with buses and, by and large, private sector buses at that. Yorkshire Rider of Leeds was the first of the former PTE bus companies to be privatised when it was sold to its management and employees in October 1988. Yorkshire Rider was previously the West Yorkshire PTE bus operation, created in 1974 to take over the municipal fleets in Bradford, Leeds, Halifax and Huddersfield and the Calderdale (previously Todmorden and Halifax) Joint Omnibus Committee. The Yorkshire Rider name was adopted in 1986 when the PTE was required by legislation to reform its bus operations as a free-standing company.

The heart of the Yorkshire Rider operation remains in Leeds, where there are four depots. There is one depot in each of Bradford, Halifax, Huddersfield and Todmorden. The fleet is predominantly double-decked although there are signs that this could change in the future as recent orders have specified single-deckers from Scania and Volvo.

The PTE standard bus was the Atlantean with Roe body. These were numbered from 6001 in 1974 and the series finished at 6361 in 1981. Smaller numbers of Fleetlines – 156 in all – were delivered at the same time, including some with lowheight Northern Counties bodies for operation in Halifax and Todmorden. Yorkshire Rider's buses do cross the Pennines into Lancashire and Greater Manchester, including a service from Halifax to Burnley.

In the early 1980s orders were split between Leyland (Roe-bodied Olympians) and MCW (Metrobuses, including some with Alexander bodies). When Yorkshire Rider was formed a number of these modern buses were sold by the PTE, with Metrobuses going to London and Stevensons of Uttoxeter and Olympians to a range of operators including A1 Services, Blackpool Transport, Cheltenham & Gloucester, Metrobus of Orpington and Wilts & Dorset. Only two Alexander-bodied Metrobuses remain out of a batch of 10 delivered in 1982. No sooner had these modern buses been sold than Yorkshire Rider started buying second-hand 'deckers from Manchester. There are some 50 former Greater Manchester Fleetlines in the Yorkshire Rider fleet, all operating in Halifax. There are also ex-Manchester Atlanteans in Leeds along with one-time London Country Atlanteans acquired from Sovereign Bus & Coach.

Single-deck buses have played a small part in Yorkshire Rider's traditional operating area. The PTE bought a batch of National 2s in 1980, most of which are still in operation. However in their early days they were particularly unreliable in service and the next batch of single-deck buses were Leyland

Tigers with Duple Dominant bus bodies fitted with high-backed coach seats. These were operated in the predominantly cream Gold Rider coach livery, but are now in standard green and cream bus colours.

Deregulation saw Yorkshire Rider under threat from United Transport, which had plans to launch a network of minibuses in Leeds to complement its Bee Line Buzz operation in Manchester. Yorkshire Rider took pre-emptive action, with a large fleet of Freight Rover Sherpas which run under the Micro Rider name. These were later joined by other types including MCW Metroriders and a few Optare StarRiders. Many of the early Sherpas have been sold.

Yorkshire Rider's fleet features a wide variety of types, many inherited from the West Yorkshire PTE. Most of its early MCW Metrobuses have gone, but there are still over 50 of the simplified Mark II model in use, all dating from the mid-1980s. This is a Leeds based bus. Stewart J Brown

There are 50 ex-GM Buses Fleetlines in the Yorkshire Rider fleet, all with Northern Counties bodies. This one is seen unloading in Halifax bus station. Malcolm King

The first examples of Alexander's Strider body were delivered to Yorkshire Rider in the spring of 1993 on Volvo's new rear-engined B10B chassis. A Huddersfield-based bus pulls out of the loading area in the town's modern bus station. *Malcolm King*

Below left: **Plans are in hand for a guided busway in Leeds. This Alexander-bodied Mercedes-Benz 0405 Cityranger was borrowed by Yorkshire Rider as part of a demonstration of the system.** *Malcolm King*

Above right: **The last of Yorkshire Rider's 1993 delivery of Alexander-bodied Scania N113s carries a distinctive Superbus livery as part of the promotion of the guided busway.** *Malcolm King*

Optare's first double-deck bodies were built to Leyland designs on Olympian chassis. Those in the Yorkshire Rider fleet included some with coach seating which carry the Gold Rider coach livery. They are now being down-graded to bus work. *Mike Harris*

The United Transport threat receded and the late 1980s and early 1990s saw Yorkshire Rider invest in substantial numbers of conventional full-size buses. The first, 15 Olympians, maintained the link with Roe's Crossgates factory in the east of Leeds, being bodied by Optare who had taken over the Roe premises after Leyland closed the business. These were followed by batches of Olympians with lowheight bodies by Northern Counties (to replace ageing Fleetlines in Halifax and Todmorden) and by Alexander. The Alexander-bodied buses were dealer stock vehicles. More recent double-deckers have been supplied by Scania, most with Alexander bodies although there are five Northern Counties-bodied examples.

At the start of 1993 full-size single-deck purchases since the formation of Yorkshire Rider were limited to five Optare Deltas and 10 Plaxton-bodied Volvo B10Ms. The Deltas run in Leeds; the Volvos in Halifax and Huddersfield. However a major change is on the way with the delivery of of 55 single-deckers to replace double-deckers. These are 35 Scania N113 and 20 of Volvo's new rear-engined B10B, all bodied by Alexander to a revamped PS-type design which has been christened the Strider. The body's name recognises Yorkshire Rider's involvement in the design — which seems to make it the St Rider — and the first, on Britain's first Volvo B10Bs, are at Huddersfield.

When Yorkshire Rider was privatised, the former NBC-owned West Yorkshire Road Car Co was part of the AJS group and ran 400 buses, many in what could be regarded as Yorkshire Rider territory. This situation was set to change dramatically. In August 1989 Yorkshire Rider took over West Yorkshire's operations in Bradford and Otley, along with 120 buses. In July 1990 Yorkshire Rider added AJS's

York operations, once part of West Yorkshire but by this time reformed as York City & District. With York City & District came the associated Target Travel minibus business. The deal added 80 buses to Yorkshire Rider's fleet and significantly expanded its territory which had not previously included York. At the same time Yorkshire Rider acquired the Reynard Pullman business.

These acquisitions added a large number of non-standard types to the fleet. The AJS companies were running standard NBC Nationals, VRTs and Olympians, and Iveco Ford minibuses. These now wear Yorkshire Rider colours. Reynard Pullman's fleet included Bedford buses and a batch of Leopards which had been newly rebodied as buses by Plaxton.

Competition for Yorkshire Rider has come – and some of it has also gone again. The most interesting of the newcomers is Black Prince, an established coach operator which has moved into bus operation since deregulation. The Black Prince name comes from Prince William, commemorated by a statue in central Leeds, and the livery is a distinctive red and yellow with, on most vehicles, elaborate lining out. The front-line fleet consists of Alexander-bodied Ailsas, new to West Midlands and Maidstone & District, and an ex-South Yorkshire Ailsa with stylish Van Hool-McArdle body, built in Ireland and the only survivor of a rare type still to be seen in regular revenue-earning service. Other front-engined double-deckers include a pair of Routemasters and a pair of PD3 Titans. Rear-engined 'deckers are Atlanteans. Black Prince also runs a Volvo Citybus which started life in London, but reached Leeds by way of A1 Service in Scotland. Single-deckers include Nationals and an Alexander-bodied Scania which started its life as an evaluation vehicle with London Buses. Services are centred on Morley.

Black Prince runs a smart fleet of second-hand double-deckers which includes 15 Ailsas. This one was new in 1976 to Maidstone & District. It has an Alexander body. Malcolm King

Above: **Originally delivered to London Transport for trials with a fuel-saving hydraulic accumulator, this Volvo Citybus has now been converted to standard and runs for Black Prince after a short spell with A1, Ardrossan.** Colin Lloyd

Smaller operators serving Leeds include Amberley Travel, running ex-West Midlands Fleetlines, a B20-specification London DMS and assorted Nationals to Pudsey. Rhodes Coaches of Yeadon, in a bright blue and white livery, operate a number of services between Leeds and Otley. The one new bus in the fleet, a G-registered Leyland Lynx, shares the services with a variety of older buses including a Volvo B58 with Duple Dominant bus body (new to A1 Service), two Tiger buses, an East Lancs-bodied Scania and the only Van Hool A600 bus in Britain.

Taylor's Coaches of Morley operate to central Leeds with an ex-South Yorkshire Atlantean, an ex-London/West Midlands Ailsa and three Bristol VRTs. The livery is red although some buses operate in their previous owners' colours. Also serving Morley is Miramare, with a National and a Leopard.

The most recent arrival in the city is Quickstep, which started in February 1992 running a fleet of eight Leyland Nationals on cross-city services, which it has since doubled to 16. In Huddersfield, K-Line Travel operates MCW Metroriders and Leyland Nationals on local services.

To the north of Yorkshire Rider's territory Blazefield Holdings, the successor to AJS, operates the majority of services around Keighley, best known in transport circles as the end of the line for the Keighley & Worth Valley Railway, and in the grand and genteel spa town of Harrogate. Both were, of course, previously served by West Yorkshire. In the distant past Keighley had a municipal transport fleet — in 1924 its was the first British municipal electric tramway to be abandoned.

Keighley & District Travel was formed in the summer of 1989 and runs 100 buses. Its services reach south to Bradford and north to the Bronte country, with a picturesque service which passes Haworth. The fleet livery is red and grey in a variety of styles which reflect the company's evolution. The initial livery was predominantly grey (or chinchilla, as the company preferred to describe it) but increasing amounts of red have been applied.

There is a high proportion of double-deckers in the fleet — all Leyland Olympians. The oldest are 1983 ex-West Yorkshire buses to standard NBC specification; the newest are 1991 buses with lowheight Northern Counties bodies which were bought new. There are also some former London Country examples, identifiable by their Park Royal style windscreens in place of the standard BET screen. These came from sister AJS companies County and Sovereign. Single-deckers are Nationals and Lynxes and there are also Iveco Ford minibuses in Keighley Hoppa colours. Coaches run under the Northern Rose name.

In Harrogate there are two Blazefield subsidiaries. Harrogate & District is the West Yorkshire successor running 45 buses in red and cream. The older vehicles in the fleet are former West Yorkshire Olympians and Iveco Ford minis. New additions since privatisation have been Leyland Lynxes and further Iveco Ford and Renault minibuses.

The Keighley & District fleet's new livery is white with grey and red relief. A Northern Counties-bodied Olympian purchased in 1991 loads in The Headrow, Leeds. Mike Harris

Coaches in the Keighley & District fleet carry a white and blue livery with Northern Rose fleetnames. This is a 1986 ECW-bodied Olympian in Keighley bus station. David Harman

The newest buses in the Harrogate & District fleet were delivered in 1990. These include six Renault S75s with Reeve Burgess Beaver bodywork. Colin Lloyd

Harrogate Independent Travel was formed at the start of 1987 by a group of redundant West Yorkshire drivers with six new Dodge S56s with Northern Counties bodies. These were soon joined by three Leyland Swifts, the first examples of Leyland's new lightweight to enter service in England. (The very first Swift was delivered to a Channel Islands operator.) In 1989 Harrogate Independent sold out to AJS. Its original vehicles are still running but have been joined by assorted second-hand big buses from other AJS companies including Leyland Leopards and the company's first double-deckers, Bristol VRTs transferred from York City & District. The Harrogate Independent fleet now totals 20 vehicles. Some carry the Challenger fleetname, coined in the company's early days when it was a more accurate description of the company's mission than it is now.

Blazefield has a fourth subsidiary, Yorkshire Coastliner, operating from Leeds to Scarborough, Hull and Bridlington. The blue and cream fleet comprises Plaxton-bodied Tigers and Leopards, and ECW and Northern Counties-bodied Olympians.

Skipton, on the edge of Keighley & District territory, is served by old-established independent Pennine Motor Services whose garage is in Gargrave, a few miles west of the town. For almost 70 years Pennine has been a loyal Leyland user and its current fleet of just under 20 vehicles is not only 100 per cent Leyland, but also 100 per cent PSU3 Leopard — not even a Tiger, the Leopard's successor, prowls in Pennine's attractive colours. All of the Leopards have Plaxton bodies and the last new one was bought in 1980. Pennine did buy a pair of Leyland Swifts in 1991 — but quickly decided they were not quite what they wanted and sold them again.

Yorkshire Coastliner operates lengthy inter-town services. An ECW-bodied Olympian passes through York on its way from Scarborough to Leeds.
Peter Rowlands

Typical of the newer vehicles in the all-Leopard/Plaxton fleet operated by Pennine of Gargrave is this 1978 example with Supreme IV body. It loads outside Pennine's depot on a journey to Skipton.
Stewart J Brown

The other significant operator in West Yorkshire is Caldaire Holdings, a management buy-out from NBC of West Riding and its associates in 1987. Based in Wakefield, Caldaire has maintained a policy of steady fleet replacement since privatisation with large numbers of Leyland Lynxes being taken into stock. With the end of Lynx production in 1992 Caldaire ordered five Volvo B10Bs and 30 Dennis Lances. The B10Bs, with Alexander bodies, entered service (in Selby) in March 1993; the first of the Lances followed in May. The Lynx fleet contains both Mark I and Mark II models and a small number

of second-hand specimens including former demonstrators and some Merthyr Tydfil buses. The remainder of the single-deck fleet is made up of Leyland Nationals, most of which are second-hand National 2s. With around 50 National 2s which originated with a range of operators – such as East Yorkshire, Eastern Scottish, Halton, Merseyside and Trent, to name but a few – Caldaire has the most varied collection of the type in the country.

The double-deck fleet is standardised on Olympians and VRTs, all with ECW bodies and Gardner engines, and all to standard NBC

Yorkshire Buses is the trading name of the Yorkshire Woollen District Transport Co. ECW-bodied Olympians are the most modern double-deck buses in the fleet. Colin Lloyd

One of a substantial number of second-hand National 2s in Caldaire's ownership, this 1985 bus came from Stevensons in 1989. One of the group's 130-odd Lynxes follows. Colin Lloyd

specifications. The newest Olympians date from 1985; no double-deckers have been purchased since privatisation. Minibuses play a small part in Caldaire's operations. There are 35 Optare MetroRiders (mainly in Wakefield) and a similar number of Alexander-bodied Renault S56s.

Caldaire actually trades through three subsidiaries – West Riding, Yorkshire Woollen and Selby & District. The standard livery layout is cream relieved by a band of colour which is swept up at the front: green for West Riding and Selby & District, and dark red for Yorkshire Woollen. Selby & District,

with just over 20 buses based in the town is far and away the smallest of Caldaire's subsidiaries. Yorkshire Woollen, which operates from Dewsbury and Heckmondwike, runs 125 buses, while West Riding, with depots in Castleford and Wakefield, runs 225. Caldaire had bus interests in north east England, based on United Automobile Services, but these were sold in 1992 to Westcourt, formed by a splitting of the Caldaire management. It also operated Compass Buses in Wakefield from 1989 to 1991, and for a short while after deregulation ran services in Sheffield with the Sheffield & District name.

Caldaire's standard minibus is the Optare MetroRider, with 35 in service or on order. This is a 1990 bus, a short 23-seater. Malcolm King

Selby & District is the smallest of the Caldaire group's subsidiaries with just under 30 buses. The newest are five Volvo B10Bs with Alexander Strider bodywork. Malcolm King

The first Dennis Darts in Yorkshire were operated by Jaronda Travel, who took two Carlyle-bodied buses in 1990. Jaronda now has a third Dart, this time with Plaxton bodywork. This is Selby bus station with a Selby & District Olympian behind Jaronda's first Dart. Malcolm King

Delivered new to London Buses' Harrow Buses unit, this Mark II Metrobus is one of 29 that came on the market in 1991 and found homes in various parts of the country. Longstaff's purchase is seen at Dewsbury on its regular duty. Mike Harris

Yorkshire Travel started operating in 1992. Its fleet includes three ex-Merseyside Nationals. Malcolm King

Among the more interesting small fleets in Caldaire country is Jaronda Travel which was one of the first small operators to buy a Dennis Dart. It now has three, two with Carlyle bodies and one bodied by Plaxton, which run from Selby to York. Jaronda also runs from Selby to Drax and Carlton, and the Darts are backed up by a trio of Bristol LH buses. All wear a white and two-tone blue livery. Among the Yorkshire Woollen buses in Dewsbury, Longstaff runs a service to Mirfield. The standard vehicle for this is a Mark II MCW Metrobus which was one of the fleet operated by London Buses on the Harrow Buses network. Longstaff's other bus is a 1979 Volvo B58 with 63-seat Duple Dominant bus body. Longstaff also runs Volvo coaches and every vehicle in the fleet apart from the Metrobus was purchased new.

Other operators in Dewsbury are Ron Lyles of Batley with a Leyland National and Yorkshire Travel with yellow and blue-liveried Nationals running to Wakefield.

Moving south, Sheffield is the hub of the South Yorkshire conurbation and has since deregulation been host to some long drawn out bus battles. These have ranged from bus wars in the city's streets, to the legal arguments in the refined atmosphere of the House of Lords between the region's major operator, South Yorkshire Transport, and the Monopolies & Mergers Commission.

SYT moved to defend its routes in the late 1980s by buying out much of its competition. In a supposedly free market this might seem a reasonable enough thing to do – except that the government's commitment to a free market for bus services fell foul of its desire to foster competition. The MMC ruled in 1990 that SYT's acquisitiveness was anti-competitive. Most recently, after a series of appeals, the House of Lords (a body which one imagines does not have vast experience of buses) has ruled that the MMC is right and that SYT should dispose of its SUT and Sheaf Line operations which were taken over in 1989.

SYT is in the throes of a change of identity. In the spring of 1989 it set up Sheffield Mainline as a high-quality service with a fleet of buses repainted bright yellow and red. The main fleet livery at this time was red, brown and cream – an average but unexciting sort of livery. Sheffield Mainline was a success and the concept was extended in 1990 to Rotherham, in yellow and blue, and to Doncaster in grey and red. In 1992 SYT decided to adopt the name Mainline for all its operations, with a livery based on the Sheffield yellow and red.

Whether or not this devalues the original quality concept of Mainline, only time will tell. Buses in the now somewhat dowdy-looking old red, brown and cream livery have been given Mainline fleetnames – which might in itself be evidence enough of devaluation of the concept.

The separate Mainline liveries used by SYT in Sheffield, Doncaster and Rotherham are being abandoned as the whole fleet adopts a unified Mainline identity. A Volvo B6R with Plaxton Pointer body – currently a unique combination – demonstrates the latest livery.
Malcolm King

The Mainline identity is being applied to all SYT buses, as illustrated by this 1985 Metrobus II in central Sheffield. The previous livery is seen on the Roe-bodied Atlantean behind. Stewart J. Brown

After a history of double-deck operation, SYT in 1990 switched to single-deckers in a big way with an order for 50 Volvo B10Ms with Alexander PS bodies. The twin aims of this move were improvements to service quality and a reduction in vandalism, a growing problem on the top deck of double-deckers. SYT now has 115 B10Ms with Alexander bodies, giving it the country's largest fleet of PS types.

At the end of 1992 it took its first midibuses into stock. A Plaxton Pointer-bodied Volvo B6 (the only example of this combination built so far) is running in Sheffield on comparative trials alongside a Northern Counties-bodied Dennis Dart.

The older vehicles in SYT's fleet are mainly double-deckers. There are still a number of Atlanteans in use, including some with Marshall bodywork, an uncommon choice. There are Metrobuses too, including coach-seated versions. But the bulk of the double-deck fleet is made up of Dennis Dominators. With almost 330 of the type, SYT is easily the UK's biggest Dominator user. Most have Alexander R-type bodies but there are ten bodied by Northern Counties and 15 by East Lancs. The last 20 Dominators, D-registered vehicles, have coach seats and long-wheelbase chassis. Their Alexander bodies have an additional short bay in mid-wheelbase.

SYT's biggest buses are its 13 Leyland DAB artics, built in Denmark and dating from 1985. Ten are 60 seat standee buses with a nominal carrying capacity of almost 150 people; the remaining three are 67-seat dual-purpose vehicles. They are powered by 245bhp Leyland TL11H engines (as used in many Tigers) and tend to be used on services to the vast Meadowhall shopping centre near the M1 motorway to the east of Sheffield. The only other articulated bus in Britain is a Mercedes running for Grampian Transport in Aberdeen.

From the biggest to the smallest: SYT's minibus fleet is based on the recently-discontinued Dodge/Renault S56. Most have Reeve Burgess bodies although there are 20 – part of the inaugural Eager Beaver fleet – which were bodied by Northern Counties. SYT also bought 19 minibuses from Lincoln City Transport when Lincoln's foray into Scunthorpe failed at the start of 1989 after only nine months. These were Reeve Burgess Beavers on Renault (15) and Iveco (four) chassis.

SYT's current standard bus is the Volvo B10M with Alexander PS type body. There are 115 in use. One of the 1991 delivery is seen at Meadowhall with the now obsolete Sheffield Mainline name. Roy Marshall

Most of SYT's artics run to the massive Meadowhall shopping complex near the M1 motorway. This one carries an appropriate livery. Tony Wilson

SYT minibuses run as Eager Beavers in a colourful livery. Most Eager Beavers are Renaults with, appropriately, Reeve Burgess Beaver bodywork. A 1990 bus loads at the busy Meadowhall Interchange. Later vehicles have full-size destination displays as on this bus while earlier examples have a much smaller destination box. Stewart J Brown

SYT is still owned by the PTE and since the MMC's interference in 1989 independents have become a touchy subject. Those which provoked the MMC's interest were SUT (purchased from National Express who had in turn taken it over from ATL Holdings), Sheaf Line (started by redundant PTE employees in 1986 and purchased when it seemed likely that Drawlane was about to buy it), Sheffield & District (acquired from Caldaire) and Groves Coaches.

These were merged into new SUT and Sheaf Line operations, run as a low-cost subsidiary of SYT. SUT's livery was off-white with maroon relief while Sheaf Line's was white with red and blue. The SUT livery has all but vanished with nearly all of the buses now being in Sheaf Line's patriotic red, white and blue. The company runs 100 buses, all but four of which are Leyland Nationals which come from an incredible variety of companies from Midland Scottish in the north to Plymouth City Transport in the south, although most have some NBC Yorkshire parentage. The two oddest buses in the fleet are Britain's only Neoplan SLIIs. These date from ATL Holdings' ownership of SUT. ATL also owned Carlton PSV, then as now the UK Neoplan importer, and had grand plans to import buses as well as coaches. The two running in Sheffield are monuments to a failed plan. Sheaf Line also runs two Atlanteans.

A separate SYT subsidiary is Don Valley Buses, running white and green minibuses from central Sheffield out to Meadowhall and beyond. The fleet is a mix of Mercs and Renaults and the business was acquired by SYT in 1991. It was originally owned by Skills of Nottingham. Meadowhall has one of Britain's better bus stations with well-designed shelters and a comprehensive passenger information system to cope with the high number of departures which it handles.

SYT's purchases back in 1989 have not inhibited competition in Sheffield, whatever the MMC might say. Andrews is a post-deregulation bus operator with 50 assorted Fleetlines, which means that the newest bus in the fleet is actually 15 years old. The Andrews standards are ex-West Midlands buses, but there are also former Greater Manchester and Cleveland Transit vehicles in the fleet. The livery is pale blue and yellow and most of the buses are named after a disparate selection of celebrities which ranges from Mandy to Captain Cook.

The standard Sheaf Line bus is the Mark I Leyland National, of which there are over 70 in the fleet. Mike Harris

Don Valley Buses is a subsidiary of SYT, acquired in 1991 from Skills of Nottingham. It runs a fleet of Mercedes-Benz minibuses. This one has an Alexander body. Stewart J Brown

Andrews of Sheffield has since late 1992 been owned by Yorkshire Traction. This has not yet had any outward effect on the company, whose operations are still entrusted in the main to ageing Fleetlines. This is one of three which were new in 1976 to Cleveland Transit and are unusual amongst Andrews buses in having Leyland engines. Northern Counties built the lowheight body. Malcolm King

Sheffield Omnibus started running in January 1991 with a fleet of seven former Preston Borough Transport Atlanteans. These retained Preston's blue and cream livery and were soon joined by further similar buses, and by other second-hand Atlanteans which were repainted blue and cream to match the Preston buses. More recent acquisitions have included further Atlanteans from a variety of sources and ex-Northampton Transport Alexander-bodied Bristol VRTs, pressed into service in Northampton red and cream but with blue and cream front ends. Some stretched Atlantean chassis have been rebodied with East Lancs EL2000 single-deck bodies. The first new buses for Sheffield Omnibus arrived in the autumn of 1992 and were Alexander-bodied Volvo B10M single-deckers, similar to those run by SYT, which were purchased from dealer stock.

Yorkshire Terrier has been snapping at SYT's heels with increasing success since 1988 when it was formed by redundant SYT employees. The company started with 12 Leyland Nationals and by 1991 had over 40 – all turned out in a neat green, yellow and white livery – as it expanded its network of services. One of the Nationals has been re-powered using a Volvo engine. There are examples from Eastern National and Western National, East Kent and Cumberland, Midland Red and Merseyside. Vehicle variety appeared in 1992 with the purchase of six East Lancs-bodied Scanias from British Airways. These had originally operated at London's Heathrow airport on inter-terminal passenger transfer duties and had large side baggage lockers, but were rebuilt to a conventional layout before hitting Sheffield's streets. Yorkshire Terrier's first new buses, Dennis Darts, arrived in 1993.

A new operator, South Riding, started up in Sheffield in the summer of 1992 with second-hand Nationals. SYT took exception to its red and beige livery and this was modified by the addition of a green band after the threat of legal action.

Most of Sheffield Omnibuses' omnibuses are double-deckers, but a few single-deckers appeared in 1992. These included this Atlantean, which was one of two lengthened and fitted with a new East Lancs EL2000 body. The blue livery was inspired by the company's first buses, ex-Preston Atlanteans. Malcolm King

Yorkshire Terrier standardised on Mark I Leyland Nationals until 1992 when it bought six Scania N112s from British Airways. They have East Lancs bodies. Michael Fowler

South Riding is Sheffield's newest operator, running almost 30 Leyland Nationals. Green was added to the red and cream livery after complaints by SYT that the original colours looked too much like SYT's. Michael Fowler

Above: **Northern Bus is a big Bristol user with both REs and VRTs in service. This RELH6L was new in 1972 to Bristol Omnibus. With 40 REs in the fleet, it is the country's biggest user of the type.** Malcolm King

Below: **Over 80 per cent of the Northern Bus fleet has ECW bodywork. This 1982 Leopard joined the fleet in 1992.** Mike Harris

The Northern Bus Company (note the initials, NBC, which were applied briefly to some vehicles) took over the business of Wigmore of Dinnington in 1987. The company is a great lover of the Bristol RE and runs 40, some of which are used on regular all-day service. There's a mixture of Gardner and Leyland engines and different styles of ECW bodies including both flat and curved windscreen varieties. Northern Bus was the first operator to buy an Optare Delta, although this was sold after two years to Walls of Manchester. There is a growing fleet of double-deckers, mainly Bristol VRTs but including one Olympian coach. Northern Bus, in a smart cream and dark blue livery, links Sheffield, Rotherham and Dinnington.

As well as being the country's biggest user of Bristol REs, Northern Bus has one of the few fleets of MCW Metroliner coaches for its private hire operation. It runs four of the rare single-deck model, all post-1985 models with the improved body styling of the final Metroliner. And all are smartly turned out, which is not something that can always be said of unpopular models which find themselves prematurely withdrawn by their original operators. Recent additions to the coach fleet have been former NBC (the real NBC) Leopards and Tigers with ECW's unloved B51 coach body.

South Yorkshire of Pontefract runs Fleetlines and Olympians, all bought new and all with Northern Counties bodies. A 1980 Fleetline pauses in Pontefract bus station.
Michael Fowler

Fleetlines dominate Leon's double-deck fleet. This Northern Counties-bodied FE30AGR came from GM Buses. Michael Fowler

In Doncaster SYT's services meet those of the original user of the South Yorkshire name, South Yorkshire Road Transport. This South Yorkshire, which is based in Pontefract, can trace its roots back to 1929. It is unusual for a small fleet in that all of its two dozen buses and coaches have been bought new, including 15 double-deckers. These are all Northern Counties-bodied. The older examples are Leyland-engined Fleetlines while newer deliveries are Olympians, with Leyland engines in the earlier examples and Cummins engines in the more recent deliveries.

South Yorkshire's two-tone blue and white livery was developed by a design consultant – back in the early 1970s when such things were unheard of in the bus industry. The company's trunk service runs from Doncaster to Leeds but there are also local services around Pontefract and a Pontefract to Barnsley route.

Doncaster was for many years a centre of independent bus operation. The creation of the South Yorkshire PTE almost brought this to an end as it quickly bought up as many of the small family-owned firms as it could, a job which was continued, albeit with less fervour, by South Yorkshire Transport after deregulation. Now only one of the original Doncaster independents survives, Leon Motor Services of Finningley. Leon runs from Doncaster to Finningley, Misson and Wroot – all long-established services – and since deregulation has won a number of contracted services which it runs on behalf of the PTE. Ten years ago Leon ran 20 buses and coaches, now it runs over 30.

Leon used to buy new double-deckers and there are two Fleetlines in operation which joined the fleet new in 1976 and 1980, bodied by Northern Counties and Alexander respectively. The latter is to SBG specification, complete with triangular destination display. Expansion has been catered for by second-hand purchases including Fleetlines from West Midlands, GM Buses, Western Scottish and AA Buses and three Atlanteans. Two Lynxes purchased from Southampton Citybus are used on a Humberside county tendered service from Doncaster to Scunthorpe. There are also three Leyland Cubs with Optare bodies, new in 1986 to the West Yorkshire PTE, but acquired by Leon when only a year old. Leon's livery is an unusual and attractive blue and grey.

Wifreda Beehive operate local services around Doncaster using Leyland Nationals, most of which came from Bristol Omnibus. Three dual-door Nationals have been fitted with wheelchair lifts for use on mobility services and one has been rebuilt to Greenway specification by East Lancs. The only service bus in the fleet not a National is a rare Leyland Cub with an even rarer HTI Maxeta body.

Barnsley is the headquarters of the Yorkshire Traction Company, privatised in a management buy-out from NBC in 1987. Yorkshire Traction – or Tracky as it is known locally – runs around 375 buses and coaches from depots in Barnsley, Doncaster, Huddersfield, Rawmarsh, Shafton and Wombwell. It also owns Strathtay Scottish Omnibuses, Lincolnshire Road Car, Lincoln City Transport, Barnsley & District and Andrews of Sheffield.

The most common type in the YTC fleet is the standard NBC ECW-bodied Olympian, of which there are over 70, all Gardner-engined, and including six with coach seats for Fastlink services which take YTC as far north as Bradford. The company also runs MCW Metrobuses, which are unique in having lowheight bodies with a few inches shaved off the standard MCW body shell to give them a rather squat appearance. There are also five former West Midlands Metrobuses in the fleet. The oldest double-deckers are P-registered Bristol VRTs.

Above right:
Wilfreda Beehive has built up a fleet of almost 20 MkI Leyland Nationals. Tees & District was the previous operator of this 1978 bus.
Mike Harris

Yorkshire Traction has bought only single-deckers since privatisation. These have been a mixture of Scanias and Dennis Darts. A Plaxton-bodied Dart shows the latest bright red and white livery with a blue relief band. It is operating in Barnsley.
Stewart J Brown

Yorkshire Traction's single-deck fleet at privatisation was made up of the inevitable Leyland Nationals. Since 1987 the company has bought no new double-deckers, but has instead gone for single-deckers. These have been a mixture of full-size Scanias and midi-sized Dennis Darts. There are also eight Leyland Lynxes which came into the fleet in 1991 when YTC took over Shearings' bus operations in the area. The first Scanias were Alexander-bodied N113s with transverse 11-litre engines. More recent examples have been K93s with in-line 9-litre engines and the first examples of Wright Endeavour bodywork, built in Ballymena using the Alusuisse system of aluminium extrusions.

The first Darts had Plaxton Pointer bodies but subsequent deliveries have been bodied by Wright. Smaller buses are in the main MCW Metroriders, but there are a number of Mercedes with a variety of bodies and one batch of Renault S75s. The minibuses generally wear Town Link names and are in a white livery with blue and orange relief bands. The big bus livery is in the throes of change. After privatisation the company abandoned NBC poppy red in favour of a traditional dark red with white relief. The amount of white relief has been gradually increased, until in 1992 an improved layout of dark red and white with a blue band was adopted as standard. A variant of this is replacing the white minibus livery too.

Another post-privatisation move was the reintroduction of old names and liveries for a small number of buses. Just over a dozen Huddersfield-based buses are in blue and cream with County Motors names. County Motors was a company which from 1927 to 1967 was owned jointly by Yorkshire Traction, Yorkshire Woollen and West Riding. It disappeared after the formation of NBC in 1969. Around 12 buses carry the Mexborough & Swinton name and a green and cream livery. Mexborough & Swinton was the last BET company to operate electric traction (trolleybuses, withdrawn in 1961) and like County it was absorbed by Yorkshire Traction in 1969. Most County-liveried buses are double-deckers; most Mexborough & Swinton-liveried buses are single-deckers. Both liveries are now being phased out.

Another name in the Barnsley area is Barnsley & District, set up as a YTC subsidiary in 1990 to take over the bus operations of Tom Jowitt. Barnsley & District, in blue, white and red (as opposed to YTC's red, white and blue) operates in the main Mark 1 Leyland Nationals. The Barnsley & District name is another revival, being YTC's predecessor in the area. The name was last used in 1928.

Yorkshire Traction has frequent services in and around all of the main towns in South Yorkshire and up into West Yorkshire.

Other operators in Yorkshire Traction territory include Aldham Coaches of Wombwell, running Leyland Leopard coaches in maroon and cream and Globe of Barnsley, with a mixed fleet of small buses in white with striking pink and dark red stripes – a livery which sits more comfortably on Globe's high-quality coach fleet.

Yorkshire Traction has been buying bodies by Wrights of Ballymena on Dennis Dart and Scania K93 chassis. There are two batches of Scanias, the second entering service in August 1993. Malcolm King

Below: **Around ten Yorkshire Traction buses operate under the County name, which is being phased out. These include Metrobuses and, as here, Olympians.** Stewart J Brown

Top right: **Mexborough & Swinton colours are carried by around a dozen Yorkshire Traction buses, most of which are National 2s.** Stewart J Brown

Right: **Barnsley & District was set up in 1990 and runs a fleet made up mainly of Leyland Nationals transferred from Yorkshire Traction. This one was new in 1978.** Malcolm King

Bottom right: **Globe of Barnsley run, among other buses, this Leyland Cub with Optare bodywork. It was new in 1986 to West Yorkshire PTE.** David Harman

THE MIDLANDS

A West Midlands Travel Scania in Birmingham City Centre. Malcolm Keeley

Birmingham and the Black Country dominate what is generally considered to be the English Midlands, although the area actually extends much further than this tight industrial belt. To the east the Midlands take in Nottingham, and for the purposes of this volume that eastern area extends across to the coast.

The heart of the Midlands lies in Birmingham, the city with more miles of canals than Venice — although few would dispute that those in Venice are perhaps a shade prettier which is proof, if proof were needed, that size isn't everything.

Size is one of the attributes of West Midlands Travel which with almost 1,800 buses is Britain's biggest single private sector bus company. WMT was owned by the West Midlands PTE until December 1991 when it was sold to its employees. This was the culmination of a long campaign to keep the company as a single entity when it was privatised. WMT's success in achieving this is in sharp contrast with the directed split up of Greater Manchester Buses, and is a tribute to the astuteness and pragmatism of politicians in the West Midlands.

WMT was set up in 1986 and took over the former West Midlands PTE direct bus operations. These dated back to 1969 when the PTE had in its turn taken over the municipal bus fleets of Birmingham, Walsall, West Bromwich and Wolverhampton. To this the PTE added a sizeable chunk of Midland Red in 1973, and the Coventry municipal fleet when local government was reorganised in 1974. The blue relief used on WMT's silver livery serves as a reminder of Birmingham City Transport's dark blue and cream colour scheme.

Recent additions to the WMT fleet are five Dennis Darts with Wright Handybus bodies which are running in Walsall and were the last buses purchased before WMT's privatisation. They entered service at the end of 1991. The most common single-deck type is the Leyland Lynx. WMT is the world's biggest Lynx operator, having ordered 250 for delivery in 1988-89 after a trial of six early examples of the breed in 1986. Before that single-deckers played a smaller part in the company's operations, with batches of Nationals being delivered in the 1970s and one batch of National 2s in 1980.

The world's biggest Leyland Lynx user is West Midlands Travel with 256, most of which were delivered in 1989 and have Cummins L10 engines. Malcolm King

WMT's newest buses are five Wright-bodied Darts which operate in Walsall. There are two styles – some have flat single-piece windscreens as on this vehicle; others have a two-piece screen with the section in front of the driver angled back. R Whitehead

The Fleetline plays an ever-reducing role in West Midlands Travel's operations. Of those that remain, a small number have East Lancs bodywork. Most WMPTE body orders went to MCW and Park Royal. Malcolm King

The newest double-deckers are 40 Scania N113s with Alexander bodies, an order which marked a distinct change of policy for WMT which had no Scanias in its fleet and no Alexander bodies other than the P-types on six trial Citybuses. The Scanias are all based at Birmingham Central garage.

The policy change was forced on WMT following the closure of MCW which had supplied all of the fleet's new double-deckers from 1980 to 1990. WMT operates 1,100 Metrobuses with a mix of Mark I and Mark II versions and they are operated throughout the region. This is the largest MCW fleet outside London.

The Metrobus became the standard West Midlands bus when Leyland made it clear that the fleet's previous standard, the Fleetline, was to be phased out of production. Birmingham City Transport was an early Fleetline user and this bus, with its chassis built locally in Coventry, was adopted as the PTE standard. Over 200 are still in use out of the 2,000 which the PTE has owned, mostly with S- and T- suffix registrations and bodywork by MCW or Park Royal. Both bodies are to a PTE design but with detail differences which help the eagle-eyed to differentiate. Most obvious is the front upper deck dome and window layout.

There are only two fleets with over 1,000 MCW Metrobuses – West Midlands Travel and London Buses. The Metrobus was built in the West Midlands and in buying them the West Midlands PTE, WMT's predecessor, was supporting local industry. To mark the employee buy-out of West Midlands Travel, one Metrobus at each depot was repainted in a promotional livery. This is a Mark II in Wolverhampton. Malcolm King

WMT operates a relatively small number of minibuses. Most are MCW Metroriders, but there is a batch of 20 Mercedes 709Ds with Carlyle bodies which were delivered in 1990 and operate in south Birmingham and Solihull. Carlyle, like MCW, was a locally-based manufacturer which closed down during the recession which followed the late 1980s economic boom.

Most WMT buses are in the current attractive blue, silver and red livery although a few still carry the previous silver with blue relief restricted to the skirt. The current livery layout is similar to the layout designed by Best Impressions for London operator Grey-Green. A few longer-distance limited stop services run under the Timesaver name. These are operated by coach-seated Metrobuses in overall blue with gold lettering and relief which is intended to add a touch of class to the operation, but in reality the overall effect is a bit dull. A number of Metrobuses are also running in a livery which publicises the employee buy-out.

WMT has garages in Coventry, Dudley, Hartshill, Walsall, West Bromwich and Wolverhampton, and no fewer than eight around Birmingham.

The company has not suffered from the intense competition which has characterised, say, Liverpool or Manchester. It has preserved much of its pre-deregulation network and suffered little from incursions by new or existing operators. The most visible in the Birmingham area is Your Bus, operated by Smiths of Tysoe. Your Bus competes head on with WMT's Scanias between Birmingham and Druids Heath, to the south of the city. It also runs services in the southern suburbs and in Solihull, and the fleet has grown quickly with a mixture of new and second-hand buses. Indeed, second-hand buses introduced the current livery — an adaptation of Greater Manchester Transport's brown, orange and white.

The bulk of the double-deck fleet is made up of former South Yorkshire Atlanteans with Alexander and Roe bodies, which to anyone familiar with Manchester's buses in the 1980s look just a bit strange in pseudo-GMT livery. There are also Fleetlines from SYT and a solitary ex-Cardiff Bristol VRT. The single-deck fleet is, by contrast, made up mainly of new buses. First were eight Tigers with Plaxton Derwent bodies in 1988. These were followed in 1990 by five DAF SB220s with Optare Delta bodies (including an ex-demonstrator) and 11 Volvo B10Ms with Plaxton Derwent bodies. Then came eight more SB220s, this time with Ikarus bodywork, and most recently six Dennis Darts with Plaxton Pointer bodywork. Your Bus now operates around 60 vehicles.

GMT's livery influenced another of WMT's competitors, Chase Bus Services. Chase's base is in Chasetown, Staffordshire, but it operates frequent services into Walsall as well as running to Birmingham, Cannock and Lichfield. There are over 40 Mark 1 Nationals in the fleet, including 25 ex-London vehicles, and around half a dozen Leopard buses, most of which came from Inter Valley Link when it was taken over by National Welsh in 1989.

Metrowest, with 20 Nationals in a dark green livery on services around Dudley and Wolverhampton, was taken over by West Midlands Travel in July 1993 and retained as a separate unit. Steve Warburton

Your Bus, run by Smiths of Tysoe, competes with West Midlands Travel to the south of Birmingham. Smiths run a sizeable fleet of modern single-deckers which include this DAF formerly used on Boro' Line park-and-ride services. T K Brookes

The most common type in the Chase Bus Services fleet is the Mk 1 Leyland National. The livery is a copy of that used by Greater Manchester in the early 1980s. Malcolm King

The Birmingham Coach Company of Smethwick is another confirmed National user, also running over 50 of the type on services to Birmingham and West Bromwich, among other places. They come from a wide variety of sources including Shearings, Western Scottish and Merseybus. Many are at the very least third-hand or, as car dealers coyly describe it, are pre-owned — but well-kept in red and cream livery.

A smaller fleet, equally well-kept, is Caves of Shirley with services into Birmingham and around Solihull. Caves' main claim to fame is operation of a unique Willowbrook-bodied ACE Cougar, bought in 1991, which makes the company's Carlyle-bodied Dart seem positively mundane. In the Longbridge area Pattersons run Mercedes minis on tendered services to Bearwood.

Merry Hill, one of Britain's biggest shopping centres, started running Merry Hill Minibus in 1988 with the aim of having 100 buses on services to the shopping complex. The recession put paid to that, but there are 46 silver-liveried Sherpas running to Merry Hill. The shopping centre is also served by a monorail with four stations. Further south, at Halesowen, Ludlows operates a growing number of local services. The company started on PTE tenders with Nationals. It now has 20 Nationals, but the most recent additions to its fleet have been two Carlyle-bodied Darts.

Flights, one of the region's most respected coach operators, runs PMT-bodied Mercs on a tendered service in Perry Barr. Dudley is served by Taj/Transol operating Nationals to Wolverhampton and Walsall. In Walsall, Midland Choice runs Nationals to Wolverhampton. And in Wolverhampton, Green Bus Service runs some amazing vintage machinery northwards into Midland Red North country — Stafford, Cannock and Rugeley.

Green Bus runs 24 vehicles, all but one of Leyland manufacture, and with an average age of around 20 years. Most are East Lancs-bodied Leopards acquired from Rossendale, but the star of the fleet is the surviving PD3 Titan, a 1965 bus which was new to Caerphilly. The oldest Leyland is an Olympian (a 1950s single-decker, that is); the newest, two S-registered Atlanteans. The livery is two-tone green and cream with yellow relief.

Two recent operators in the Tamworth area are Frontline, running Nationals and ex-West Midlands Fleetlines, and Serverse Travel with Nationals. Both operators run into Birmingham.

The Birmingham Coach Company is another National user. This bus came from Western Scottish. Ken Jubb

Only two operators run ACE Cougars, with one apiece. That operated by Caves of Shirley has a 40-seat Willowbrook Warrior body. The other Cougar is operated on the south coast by People's Provincial. Malcolm King

Pattersons of Selly Oak run Mercedes-Benz minibuses in south Birmingham. This is a 1991 709D with Reeve Burgess Beaver body. Stewart J Brown

The standard Merry Hill minibus is the Freight Rover Sherpa with Carlyle bodywork - Carlyle had a stake in the company when it was set up. There are 46 buses of this type in the fleet. Ken Jubb

Frontline Buses' ex-West Midlands Fleetlines include this East Lancs bodied bus. Malcolm King

Green Bus Service runs ageing Leopards, most of them ex-Rossendale 10m-long PSU4s with 46-seat East Lancs bodies. There are four 1971 examples which joined Green Bus in 1988. K R Crawley

East Midland Motor Services is based in Chesterfield and after being bought by its management from NBC, was sold to Stagecoach in 1989. Stagecoach's corporate white livery has now virtually eliminated the attractive two-tone green and cream previously used. Older buses in the fleet are standard NBC types: Mark 1 and 2 Nationals, Bristol VRTs and Leyland Olympians. For aficionados of the VRT there is a bit of hidden variety with engines. Most have the standard Gardner 6LXB, but there are eight with Leyland 501 turbocharged engines and five with Gardner's more powerful 6LXCT.

Alexander-bodied single-deckers feature in the fleet. Ten of the angular P-type bus bodies were purchased in 1985: nine on new Tigers and the tenth on a six-year old Leopard which had originally had a Willowbrook body. Four Alexander TE express coach bodies on Tigers were also purchased in 1985, and there is a solitary ex-SBG Y-type Leopard. At the same time as one Leopard was rebodied by Alexander, four were given new Duple Dominant bus bodies. These rebodied Leopards all have DWF-V registration marks.

Since the Stagecoach takeover new buses have been predominantly Alexander-bodied Olympians, with both long- and standard-wheelbase versions. Non-standard deliveries were eight Mercedes 811Ds and 15 Iveco Dailys, all bodied by Reeve Burgess; these were ordered by East Midland when it was management-owned but were delivered after the Stagecoach takeover.

Buses based in Mansfield carry Mansfield & District fleetnames. Mansfield & District was a tramway operator which changed its name to Mansfield District (no '&') in 1929 and was ultimately absorbed by East Midland under NBC control in 1975. The depot at Sutton Bank trades as Maun Buses—Maun was a company taken over in 1990— while coaches run under the Midland Travel name, built up on the Rainworth Travel business which was also acquired in 1990. All are, of course, in corporate Stagecoach livery.

East Midland's routes stretch north to Sheffield and Doncaster and the company also has depots in towns strung along the eastern side of the M1 motorway at Clowne (where the company was founded), Harworth, Shirebrook and Worksop.

Among the more unusual vehicles to carry corporate Stagecoach colours are ten East Midland buses with Alexander P-type bodies. Nine are on Leyland Tigers which were new to East Midland in 1985 and were an unusual choice for an NBC company. The tenth, shown here, was used to rebody a 1979 Leopard/Willowbrook. Michael Fowler

Chesterfield runs new and second-hand Nationals. Most of the latter came from Greater Manchester Buses or Midland Red West. This 1975 bus was purchased by Chesterfield in 1990. Malcolm King

Chesterfield's Spire Sprinter minibuses are mainly Alexander-bodied Mercedes. This is one of seven 811Ds delivered in 1992. Malcolm King

Chesterfield Transport was, in April 1990, the first English municipal bus operation to be privatised. It was purchased by its employees and in recognition of this change many buses quickly received the wording 'It's our business to get you there' under the fleetname. The company's livery is an attractive blue, yellow and white. Recent years have seen a swing away from double-deck operation. The last new double-deckers were actually purchased in 1978 — S-registered Roe-bodied Fleetlines — but these have been joined by a small number of second-hand examples — two ex-Greater Manchester Fleetlines and two Roe-bodied Olympians which came from South Yorkshire, where they were a non-standard type. All of the Fleetlines bought new by Chesterfield are of two-door layout.

Single-deckers form the bulk of the fleet. The newest are 11 Leyland Lynxes bought in the late 1980s; most of the rest are Nationals, both Marks 1 and 2, and both new and second-hand. One Leyland Panther, once a common sight in the town, has recently been refurbished for further service. Minibuses — Alexander-bodied Mercedes running as Spire Sprinters — appeared in 1988 and since privatisation more have been added, most recently in 1992. The Spire Sprinter fleetname is an allusion to Chesterfield's most famous landmark, the church with the crooked spire.

The only significant small operator running into Chesterfield is Hulley's of Baslow, operating between Chesterfield, Bakewell and Matlock and also running services to Castleton from Bakewell and Sheffield. The Hulley's blue and white liveried fleet is made up of assorted second-hand acquisitions which include Leopards from Barton Transport, an ex-Trent RE and former Maidstone Bedford YMTs with Wadham Stringer Vanguard bodywork.

In 1988 Chesterfield won tenders to operate services in the Retford area and the buses now used on those services are second-hand Leyland Leopards which carry Retford & District fleetnames. These have come from a variety of sources including Western Scottish (Alexander Y-types); Lancaster City Transport (Alexander T-types) and Midland Red West (Marshall BET-style bodies). The ex-Lancaster buses were new to East Midland, so are effectively back in home territory.

Chesterfield's gain in Retford was Kettlewell's loss. Kettlewell's of Retford had expanded into local bus operation after deregulation, even buying new buses — three East Lancs-bodied Scania K-series. Local services are still run and take Kettlewell's buses up to Gainsborough, and the company also operates a substantial number of schools contracts. The older buses in its fleet include an unusual MCW-bodied VRT which came from West Midlands.

Retford & District was set up by Chesterfield Transport in 1988 to operate tendered services which it won from local small operators. There are 16 buses at Retford – 15 Leopards and a Dodge S56. This Leopard is one of six with Alexander Y-type body which came from Western Scottish. It was new in 1977. Michael Fowler

Kettlewell's run a varied fleet of new and second-hand buses and coaches including three former London Buses Leyland Nationals. Mike Harris

The area to the west of the M1 is the preserve of Trent. Trent was an early NBC privatisaton, being bought by its management at the end of 1986. The company is in the process of a livery change which retains the base Ayres red, but uses cream and black relief in place of grey (and before that, silver).

The company has spent large sums of money maintaining a modern fleet and since 1988 has bought 23 Alexander-bodied Volvo Citybus double-deckers and 53 Optare Deltas. A number of the Deltas carry Barton fleetnames: Barton was taken over by Trent in 1989.

Despite the influx of new buses there are still significant numbers of Leyland Nationals in use. Trent has no National 2s, but has some of the last National 1s to be built; these have V-suffix registrations. Double-deckers from the NBC era are standard Olympians and VRTs, plus a few ECW-bodied Atlanteans including some late W-registered vehicles. The oddest 'decker in the fleet is a 1976 Atlantean which was rebodied by Willowbrook in 1977 after being damaged by fire. This unique bus is now allocated to Barton and is one of Barton's few double-deckers.

Barton took advantage of the government's new bus grant in the 1970s to standardise on Leyland Leopards with Plaxton coach bodies, all fitted with power doors for use on local bus services. The oldest survivors are M-registered, the newest are 1982 models with Y-suffixes. Leyland failed to convince Barton of the merits of its new Tiger and from 1983 Barton bought the mid-engined DAF MB series, still with Plaxton bodywork. There are 21 DAFs in the fleet. The engine in the MB has much in common with that used in the SB220 which forms the base for the Optare Delta.

Trent's older coaches are Leopards with bodies by Duple, Plaxton and Willowbrook.

Trent's territory stretches a long way from the river from which it takes its name. Its northernmost depot is at Matlock, its southernmost at Melton Mowbray. Its strongest centres of operation are around Nottingham and in its headquarters town of Derby.

Trent's double-deck fleet includes standard NBC-style ECW-bodied Olympians. This Gardner-powered bus dates from 1983. Steve Warburton

Trent has disposed of its National 2s, but retained National 1s. This is the latest livery, freshly applied to a 1979 11.3m National in Derby. Trent's original post-privatisation colours were red and silver. Peter Rowlands

Trent is one of the biggest users of Optare Deltas with 53 in operation, some of which carry Barton fleetnames. A 1991 Barton bus loads in Derby on the Nottingham service. Michael Fowler

Indeed, Derby is almost Optare City. Stand in the city centre and you can see Trent's new Deltas running alongside Derby City Transport's CityPacers. The combination gives a glimpse of just how attractive urban buses can be — even if in most places the reality isn't quite so bright. Derby City Transport runs 25 CityPacers, all bought second-hand. There are 15 which were originally operated in Loughborough, four from Southend Transport and six from Yorkshire Rider. The Loughborough buses had been operated by Leicester City Transport in competition with Midland Fox and made their way to Derby when Leicester admitted defeat and sold its Loughborough services to Midland Fox.

Most of the rest of Derby City Transport's operations use big buses. The oldest are Northern Counties-bodied Fleetlines. When the Fleetline was discontinued Derby switched first to Ailsas (it runs 15) and then to mid-engined Volvo Citybuses, of which there are 28. Most of the Ailsas and the newest Citybuses have Northern Counties bodies, but there are two Ailsas and 13 Citybuses with Marshall bodies, and five Citybuses bodied by East Lancs. Olympians were run for a short time but these have all been sold. The company's newest buses are seven Alexander-bodied Scania K-series single-deckers.

Derby City Transport still has the air of a municipal bus operation but it has since 1989 been owned by a consortium formed of the company's employees (75 per cent) and Luton & District (25 per cent). It briefly faced intense competition from Midland Red North minibuses which it countered by running double-deckers in Tamworth, a move which involved around 60 miles of dead running per bus each day. This farcical situation ceased when Derby bought out Midland Red North's operations in the city. The next purchase by Derby was of the services of Camms of Nottingham, and it is running them with some of its own elderly Fleetlines painted in Camms' orange and cream.

An old-established operator running into Derby is Felix Bus Services, which started in 1922. Felix runs between Ilkeston and Derby with a maroon and red Tiger with Plaxton Derwent bus body, bought new in 1988, and a Lynx.

There are 25 Optare CityPacers in the Derby fleet and 15 of these came from Loughborough Coach & Bus which had been set up by Leicester CityBus to compete with Midland Fox. A Northern Counties-bodied Volvo Citybus loads in the background. Michael Fowler

Camms were competing with Derby City Transport using an assortment of second-hand buses, but the operation was purchased by Derby in the spring of 1993. Camms' buses have been replaced by ex-Derby buses running in Camms' colours. This is a Northern Counties-bodied Fleetline. Michael Fowler

One of two service buses in the Felix fleet is a 1988 Tiger with 54-seat Plaxton Derwent body, seen arriving in Derby from Ilkeston. Michael Fowler

Nottingham City Transport is still in local authority ownership, although the harsh commercial realities of deregulation have seen major changes in its vehicle policy. In the good old days Nottingham's buying policy was individualistic at best or idiosyncratic at worst. It had East Lancs and Northern Counties building bodies to designs which no other operator wanted. First, there was a single-width entrance door, with a separate exit immediately behind the front wheel. There were some unusual seating layouts which included inward-facing seats at the front of the upper deck. This did have a practical pay-off with the exceptionally high seating capacity of 80 in a two-door 9m-long double-decker at a time when most operators settled for 74 in a single-door bus of the same length.

The bodies looked different too. Most had a BET windscreen on the lower deck, and a curved upper deck screen which was that used on the rear of 1960s BET single-deckers. Where all other operators had a solid metal panel beside the staircase at lower-deck window level, Nottingham specified glazing — which not only continued the window line unbroken, but shed extra light on the stairs. So it wasn't quite as odd as it seemed. The company also pioneered the use of bonded glazing on double-deckers, but quickly abandoned it. Massive bumpers are another practical Nottingham feature, designed to cut bodywork repair bills.

So the older buses in the fleet are distinctive. Most are Atlanteans, but there is one batch of S-registered Fleetlines. Orders in the 1970s were divided between the two models. When quick delivery was needed Nottingham took a batch of ten Roe-bodied Atlanteans in 1980 built to the standard NBC/Park Royal-Roe design — although even these had 80 seats squeezed into them, where the standard NBC body had 76.

Nottingham's quest for high capacity saw it switch to the mid-engined Volvo Citybus and Nottingham's interest in this chassis played a part in the development of the Leyland Lion, built in Denmark by Leyland-DAB. Nottingham has 13 Lions which are the only ones in England — although there are others in Scotland. Five have striking East Lancs coach bodies.

Nottingham's distinctive bodywork is seen on a 1979 East Lancs-bodied Atlantean which despite having two doors has 78 seats. The hefty front bumper was a Nottingham speciality. Richard Eversden

The only underfloor-engined Leyland Lions in England are 13 operated by Nottingham, who were influential in the model's development. The first three, new in 1986, have Northern Counties bodies. Stewart J Brown

The unusual green livery used on its double-deck coaches is also carried by a batch of eight Nottingham Scania N113s delivered in 1990. They have Alexander PS bodies. Ken Jubb

The Citybuses delivered up to 1988 have bodies to Nottingham specification; but the few which have joined the fleet since 1989 have standard Alexander R-type bodies and include two former demonstrators.

Nottingham showed interest in Scania products as long ago as 1981, when it took an ex-Scania double-deck demonstrator into stock. More former demonstrators have followed since, along with orders for 18 new N113 double-deckers and eight N113 single-deckers, all bodied by Alexander and delivered in 1989-90. Other second-hand Scanias include an Alexander-bodied 'decker from Harris of Grays and an East Lancs-bodied bus from A1 of Ardrossan; both are E-registered.

Nottingham's special requirements for double-deck bodywork were not echoed on its single-deckers. These are mainly National 2s (including some second-hand ones) and Lynxes. There are no Mark 1 Nationals in the fleet, and only one Lynx II, an ex-Volvo demonstrator. Minibuses are a mixture of Renault S56s and Mercedes 709Ds, most of which have Reeve Burgess Beaver bodies.

In 1991 Nottingham purchased the business of South Notts of Gotham — no doubt to the horror of Batman and Robin — and with it a fleet of Fleetlines. Most were bodied by Northern Counties but the last two had ECW bodies and were the last Fleetline chassis built, although not the last to enter service. Unusually, all of South Notts' Fleetlines were Leyland-engined; most smaller operators standardised on Gardner power. South Notts' two newest buses were long-wheelbase Olympians with Northern Counties bodies, and to these Nottingham added another pair with East Lancs bodies in 1992.

To replace South Notts' oldest Fleetlines which were 20-year-old veterans, Nottingham has transferred four National 2s from the main fleet, repainting them in South Notts blue and cream livery. It also had 11 new minibuses delivered in South Notts colours in 1991. As well as a depot at Gotham, Nottingham City Transport has another one outside the city at Ilkeston, which was taken over with Erewash Valley Services in 1988.

Nottingham runs coaches in a beige and brown livery. Most are Tigers, but there are also two Royal Tiger Doyen integrals.

Nottingham is among the operators to have purchased ex-London Buses Titans, three entering service in summer 1993 after conversion to single door layout. David Stewart

Six new Carlyle-bodied Mercedes 811Ds were added to the Nottingham fleet in 1991, marking a break from the Reeve Burgess/ Plaxton Beaver which had previously been the preferred choice. Roy Marshall

Since taking over South Notts, Nottingham has added new minibuses to the fleet and, more recently, a pair of long-wheelbase East Lancs-bodied Olympians. On the lengthened version of its copy of the Alexander R-type body East Lancs use equal-length windows where Alexander insert a short bay in mid-wheelbase. Michael Fowler

Apart from Camms, small operators did not have a major presence in Nottingham until the arrival of Kinch in 1990. Kinch's operations to Clifton are seen as having hastened the demise of South Notts as an independent company. These are run by a variety of acquired vehicles with a preponderance of Nationals and, more recently, Leyland Titans purchased from London Buses.

Dunn-Line of Nottingham operates mainly on tendered services which take the company's buses as far out as Hucknall and Mansfield. New buses in the fleet are three MCW Metroriders, but these are in sharp contrast with Dunn-Line's other buses, former SBG Leopards, PMT Nationals and three ex-Derby Fleetlines which are to be found on services such as Derby to Ashbourne and on peak evening journeys from Nottingham to Hucknall, Heanor and Mansfield.

Sheffield Omnibus has set up a Nottingham Omnibus operation initially with Alexander-bodied Bristol VRTs acquired from Northampton Transport. These run alongside ECW-bodied VRTs and all carry the Preston-inspired blue and cream livery.

Skills, best known as a coach operator, runs a few Mercedes minicoaches on tendered services which take them to Burton and Derby. The company also has two Ailsas, its only double-deckers, for contract work.

Pathfinder of Newark runs from Nottingham to Southwell and on to Newark. The company also runs north from Newark to Collingham. Pathfinder operates 17 minibuses, all delivered new since 1989. Most are Mercs, with bodies by Reeve Burgess and Dormobile, but there are half a dozen tri-axle Talbots, a rare choice for a small fleet — or, indeed, for any bus fleet, come to that.

Wright of Newark runs to Ollerton, Eagle via Collingham, and Carlton-le-Moorland. These routes are generally operated by coaches, which include a Plaxton-bodied Bristol LHS, although Wright has one small bus purchased for tendered services, a Reeve Burgess-bodied Mercedes-Benz.

Kinch operate services in Nottingham with a fleet which includes smartly presented ex-London Buses Leyland Titans. Michael Fowler

Dunn-Line operate three of these ex-Derby Fleetlines, often seen on the Derby to Ashbourne service. T K Brookes

Nottingham Omnibus, an offshoot of Sheffield Omnibus, uses the same Preston-inspired livery but runs Bristol VRTs rather than the Atlanteans favoured for Sheffield. David Stewart

Interpreting the East Midlands loosely to include anything south of the Humber which isn't claimed by Yorkshire, if you keep heading north-east from Nottingham you come to Lincoln. Bus operation here is in the throes of change. Lincoln City Transport expanded dramatically, doubling its fleet between 1986 and 1988. But it contracted equally rapidly and by 1991 was back to its original size and in private sector ownership. It was sold to its employees during 1991, with Derby City Transport taking a 40 per cent share. The cut-backs saw Lincoln give up its Lincoln Limo operation, run by a fleet of FX4 taxis, and pull out of ill-fated adventures in Scunthorpe and Gainsborough.

At the start of 1993 control of the company passed to Yorkshire Traction, who already owned Lincolnshire Road Car, more of which shortly. So, from a peak of almost 100 vehicles, the slimmed-down Lincoln City Transport fleet now consists of under 30 buses, the oldest of which are eight of its once-larger fleet of VRTs dating from 1977-80. Between 1982 and 1985 Lincoln bought East Lancs-bodied long-wheelbase Olympians. Its last new buses were four East Lancs-bodied Citybuses with coach seats. These were transferred to the parent Yorkshire Traction company in the spring of 1993. Recent additions to the fleet have included 11 Dodge S56 minibuses from South Yorkshire Transport, new in 1987 and purchased by Lincoln in 1992. These replaced VRTs which were sold to Luton & District who were linked to Lincoln because L&D owned 25 per cent of Derby City Transport which owned 40 per cent of Lincoln. The route network in Lincoln was rationalised in 1993 so that City Transport and Road Car no longer conflict.

One small operator serving Lincoln is Enterprise & Silver Dawn, a new company which has resurrected an old name. It is based in Waddington, and runs from there to the city. Insofar as the fleet has a livery, it is brown and cream, which are the colours worn by two ex-Grimsby-Cleethorpes buses acquired in 1990 and not yet repainted. These are one-time London DMS Fleetlines. There is also an ex-South Yorkshire Atlantean, still in SYT colours.

PC Coaches runs from Lincoln to Saxilby, usually with a Reeve Burgess-bodied Mercedes 811D, appropriately registered J1PCC. Older vehicles are operated on contracts and a former Eastern Counties Leyland National is the standard performer on a circular service in Lincoln.

The new livery now being applied to Lincoln City Transport's small fleet is seen on this Leyland National acquired from Cumberland in 1993. G B Wise

The livery treatment currently being applied to Lincoln City double deckers is seen on 1836 (which still carries its LCT number also), an East Lancs bodied VRT of 1980. Malcolm King

Enterprise & Silver Dawn operate services from Lincoln. A one-time London DMS-type Fleetline pulls out of the bus station on its way to Waddington. Malcolm King

Lincolnshire Road Car buses used to have Lincolnshire as a fleetname; now they have Road Car — or, on minibuses, Road Runner. Yorkshire Traction purchased the company from NBC in 1988. Road Car has a large but sparsely-populated operating area with services running across the Humber Bridge to Hull in the north, and stretching from the coast inland to Gainsborough, Grantham and Newark. It has a depot in each of these towns and in Scunthorpe, Louth and the coastal towns of Grimsby and Skegness, the last-named made famous by the LNER poster which, in the absence of any other attraction, proclaimed of the resort: 'It's so bracing!'

In NBC days Lincolnshire, as it was then, received steady deliveries of Bristol VRTs and many of these are still around. They have been joined by over 50 transferred from the parent Yorkshire Traction fleet, of which 43 were in stock in summer 1993. Minority double-deck types in the fleet are the Leyland Olympian of which there are three coach-seated ECW-bodied examples allocated to the Scunthorpe to Hull Humberlink service and the Leyland Atlantean, represented by but 10 vehicles, most of which came from Greater Manchester and run in Skegness. In the summer Skegness hosts open-top VRTs.

Genuine single-deck buses (as distinct from Leopard dual-purpose coaches) are few in number. There are around two dozen Nationals, most of which are refugees from Yorkshire Traction, and a handful of survivors of a once large fleet of Bristol LHs. Former SBG Alexander Y-type Leopards make up the rest of the single-deck bus fleet.

The nature of Road Car's territory, with longish inter-town services, means that there is plenty of work for that compromise, the dual-purpose bus. Road Car has Leopards with a wide variety of d-p bodywork: Duple Dominant, ECW B51, Plaxton Supreme and Willowbrook 003. There are also three Tigers rebuilt with East Lancs dual purpose bodywork in 1992.

In 1989 Road Car took over Gash of Newark and there are still a number of ex-Gash buses in the fleet, mostly operating around their home town. These include a V-registered Roe-bodied Atlantean bought new, a Marshall-bodied LH and assorted Leopards including a pair with Plaxton Derwent bodies and a pair of former Western Scottish buses.

Wright bodywork is to be found in a number of Yorkshire Traction group fleets and Road Car is no exception with this 1992 Dennis Dart. It is one of three long-wheelbase 40-seaters operating in Gainsborough. Malcolm King

Blue is substituted for green to good effect on this Road Car open-top VRT which operates in Skegness in the summer. New in 1973, it came from Yorkshire Traction in 1989. Michael Fowler

Small buses in the Road Car fleet carry Road Runner names and an unusual grey livery. Two ECW-bodied Bristol LHS6Ls were acquired from Yorkshire Traction in 1988. They were new in 1974 to London Country. This one is in Lincoln. K R Crawley

The major operator in Grimsby is not Road Car, but Grimsby-Cleethorpes Transport which is still municipally-owned. Minibuses were introduced to the fleet at deregulation but have since been reduced in number, with only ten MCW Metroriders remaining. Grimsby-Cleethorpes' recent purchases have been Dennises, with 15 Dominators entering service between 1989 and 1992. These have Alexander R-type bodies (on F- and G-registered buses) and East Lancs R-type look-alikes on the H- and J-registered vehicles.

Older double-deckers are one batch of A-registered Olympians with ECW bodies, and an assortment of Fleetlines which were either purchased new with dual-door Roe bodies (an unusual layout for a small town fleet) or bought second-hand from London in the great Fleetline bonanza of the early 1980s.

Dennis Lance single-deckers with East Lancs bodies entered service in the spring of 1993. They joined four 1983 Falcons with Wadham Stringer bodies and four 1988 Leyland Tigers with Alexander P-type bodies. The Tigers are unusual in having Gardner engines, an option specified by few operators outside the Scottish Bus Group.

Grimsby-Cleethorpes owns Peter Sheffield Coaches running R-series Fords, Leyland Leopards and Tigers, and a Dennis Javelin.

One of the biggest family-owned businesses in Lincolnshire is Applebys of Louth, with depots in Grimsby, Horncastle, Lincoln and North Somercotes. The company operates a large number of predominantly rural services in the area, generally using Bedford Y-series coaches which have been downgraded from private hire and excursion work. Most have Plaxton bodies. There is a small fleet of double-deckers, mainly Fleetlines from Chester, South Yorkshire, Southend and Thamesdown and these are used on contracts.

As mentioned in the Yorkshire chapter, Applebys also operate services in Scarborough.

Grimsby-Cleethorpes' last Fleetlines entered service in 1980 and have dual-door Roe bodywork. Since then most new buses have been of single-door layout. Malcolm King

The newest buses in the Grimsby-Cleethorpes fleet are four East Lancs-bodied Dennis Lances, delivered in the spring of 1993. Malcolm King

With almost 90 vehicles, Applebys is Lincolnshire's biggest family-run coach business. Bedfords and Leyland Leopards are generally used on the company's predominantly rural routes. Stuart Jones

In Gainsborough, Road Car faces competition from Eagre which runs locally in the town and also up to Scunthorpe and down to Lincoln. The front-line bus fleet comprises three former Alder Valley South Nationals which have been curiously re-registered with AFE-A marks in place of their original M- and N-suffix registrations. Eagre also runs a mixture of double-deckers with two former NBC VRTs, two Atlanteans from GM Buses and the unique low-height Ailsa which started life with Derby as RTO1R but is now TRR814R. Eagre is not some rustic pronunciation of the name of the owning family — Eaglen — but the name of a little-known tidal bore on the Trent, which flows alongside the depot at Morton.

Ashby, just outside Scunthorpe, is the base of Hornsby Travel Services, which runs a service connecting the two. There are also services from Scunthorpe to Brigg and surrounding villages. The bus fleet is small but interesting. There are ex-London DMSs which have now spent as long with Hornsby as they did in the capital. There is a 1977 Roe-bodied Atlantean, bought new. There are three Carlyle-bodied Mercedes 811Ds bought in 1990-91. But pride of place has to go to the fleet's Renault which is not one of the usual S56 minibuses, but one of only two full-size PR100s on local bus operation. New in 1989, this was bodied by Northern Counties to Renault designs and used as a demonstrator. It failed to drum up much business — one PR100 for London Buses and three for Luton Airport was the sum of its successes — and it was bought from Northern Counties in 1991. When new it was registered F100AKB; it is now WUK155.

In south Lincolnshire, operations around Boston have largely been given up by Road Car and the town and surrounding areas are now served by small firms. Brylaine Travel is based in Boston and runs 36 buses and coaches. Until 1990 Brylaine was much smaller: in that year it took over Hogg of Boston and and two-thirds of the current fleet are ex-Hogg vehicles. Brylaine's routes reach out to Spalding, Skegness and Coningsby and the fleet consists mainly of elderly light-weight coaches — Bedfords and Fords built between 1973 and 1983.

Eagre's Nationals, purchased from Alder Valley South, now have 30-year old registrations to disguise the fact that the buses are 20 years old. As this picture shows, the vehicles are very well turned out. Alan Simpkins

The Renault PR100 failed to make any impact on British bus operators. This former demonstrator is now with Hornsby of Ashby. Alan Simpkins

Most Brylaine vehicles are Ford and Bedford coaches but there are four double-deck buses in the shape of former Burnley & Pendle VRTs with East Lancs bodies. Alan Simpkins

Skegness is also served by Hunt's of Alford, running in from Chapel St Leonards, a few miles up the coast. Hunt's also serves Louth and Boston. Double-deckers in Skegness — two one-time London Fleetlines and two ex-NBC VRTs — carry Skegness & District Services fleetnames. The single-deck fleet is noteworthy in having one of the last Leyland Panthers in regular use, a Pennine-bodied bus which started life in Preston and reached the east coast by way of the Isle of Man and Citibus of Manchester.

Sleaford lies inland from Boston and the two towns are connected by Kime's of Folkingham running Fleetlines in green and cream. These have come from a variety of sources, often third-hand, but originated with Cleveland, London, Merseyside and Southend. The company runs one of the few MCW Metropolitans still in service, a former London example which spent six years in the capital and has now spent 11 in Lincolnshire.

Between Boston and Spalding lies Gosberton, home of Elseys, which has grown since deregulation at Road Car's expense. Elseys runs between Boston and Spalding and provides a Boston town service. The fleet includes four buses — two Nationals, a Duple-bodied Javelin bought new in 1989, and a 1976 Leopard with a 1989 Willowbrook Warrior body. Some of the company's older coaches are also used on service.

Spalding is served by Fowler's of Holbeach, running to King's Lynn and to Wisbech. Fowler's, like Elseys, has benefited from retrenchment at Road Car. Unusually for such a small operator it runs a new double-decker, a 1989 Scania N113 with Alexander body. With it came three K93s with Plaxton Derwent bodies. The new buses were bought for the busy hourly route from Spalding to King's Lynn via Holbeach, formerly one of Road Car's last Bristol Lodekka services. Older double-deckers, used mainly on school services, are ECW-bodied VRTs. The company also runs an assorted coach fleet.

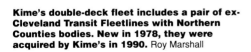

Kime's double-deck fleet includes a pair of ex-Cleveland Transit Fleetlines with Northern Counties bodies. New in 1978, they were acquired by Kime's in 1990. Roy Marshall

Elseys of Gosberton, near Spalding, run this Willowbrook Warrior rebody of a Leyland Leopard. An Ulster registration effectively disguises both its age and its origins. Alan Simpkins

The only new double-decker operated by Fowler's of Holbeach is an Alexander-bodied Scania N113, seen in King's Lynn. M Fowler

Delaine of Bourne operates from Bourne to Peterborough, Sleaford, Deeping St James and Stamford. It is a fleet renowned for its well-kept vehicles, currently 22-strong. Newest is a 1988 Tiger with Duple 300-series bus body. Oldest is a 1956 Willowbrook-bodied PD2. The company also still owns its now unique Yeates-bodied PD3 Titan, one of only two double-deckers ever produced by the Loughborough-based builder — both of which were owned by Delaine. The fleet is made up mainly of Duple-bodied Tigers with Dominant buses, ex-Green Line Dominant IV expresses, and a Laser. Apart from the venerable Titans and an RM, double-deckers operated are five Northern Counties-bodied Atlanteans, one of which was bought new. The others came from Greater Manchester (three) and Whippet of Fenstanton.

Bourne is one of the many destinations reached by Reliance of Great Gonerby, whose services stretch as far west as Nottingham, usually served by a Dennis Javelin coach. The heart of Reliance's operation is Grantham, where it competes with Road Car. Older buses in the Reliance fleet are Duple-bodied Leopards bought new in the mid-1970s. They have been joined by second-hand Leopards. Both MCW and Optare MetroRiders are in the fleet, and Reliance has the only Lynx in Lincolnshire, bought new in 1989.

The Delaine fleet has a reputation for high standards of maintenance. The youngest bus in the Delaine fleet is a 1988 Leyland Tiger with a rare Duple 300-series bus body. Mike Harris

Delaine's Titans still see passenger service; the Yeates bodied PD3 is seen on a special service in connection with a vintage running day at the end of August 1993. G A Rixon

Reliance of Great Gonerby serve Grantham with both big and small buses. This Leyland Lynx was purchased new by the company in 1989. Ken Jubb

Moving west and back towards the heartland of the Midlands, Leicester is the next major centre, served by Leicester CityBus and Midland Fox, with Kinch now adding extra competition.

Leicester CityBus has recently undergone a livery change which turns the clock back 30 years. The bright red, grey and white adopted as the city council's corporate colours in the early 1980s are being replaced by a dull maroon and cream.

If the livery is old and dark, the bus fleet is certainly neither. The standard bus is the Dennis Dominator, of which there are over 120. Three have Marshall bodies and the rest are bodied by East Lancs, in a variety of styles. The oldest are S-registered and include the first production Dominator, recently restored to its original 1978 livery; the newest are F-registered. The most unusual double-deckers are four MCW Metrobuses with lowheight Alexander R-type bodies, a combination for which the only other buyer was the Scottish Bus Group. These originally operated with Gibson of Barlestone fleetnames — Gibson being an independent taken over in 1979. Leicester CityBus still stations vehicles at Barlestone.

The only other 'deckers are around 20 MCW Metropolitans, the biggest surviving fleet of that ill-fated type. Most other operators gave up an unequal battle against body corrosion, but Leicester has managed to keep in operation some of what was the first substantial fleet of the model.

The newest big buses are Dennis Falcons. Six with East Lancs bodies were delivered in 1991 and were followed by four more at the start of 1993. Two Falcons with Northern Counties Paladin bodies were also delivered in 1993. The only Leylands are six Tiger coaches, of which four were bought new and two came from Ribble.

Minibuses are mainly Carlyle-bodied Ivecos, although more recent deliveries have been Northern Counties-bodied Renaults including what may well prove to be Britain's last Renault buses, delivered in 1992.

CityBus and Midland Fox provide the bulk of Leicester's bus services, but that expansionist operator, Kinch, started running competitive commercial services in 1993 with ex-London Buses DMSs. Before this, Kinch's main interest in Leicester had been the provision of a tendered outer circle service using Reeve Burgess-bodied Mercedes minis.

Leicester CityBus has recently returned its first Dennis Dominator to its original 1978 livery. It has an East Lancs body. The MCW Metropolitan behind carries the current fleet colours. K R Crawley

Single-deck buses were re-introduced to the Leicester CityBus fleet in 1991 with the arrival of six Dennis Falcons. More have since followed. The first buses had East Lancs EL2000 bodies and the latest have Northern Counties Paladin bodywork with revised livery treatment. K R Crawley/Brian Gilliam

After the West Midlands PTE acquired the heart of Midland Red's operations back in 1973, NBC eventually (in 1981) split what was left into four companies — imaginatively christened Midland Red East, Midland Red West, Midland Red North and Midland Red South. Midland Red East was the first to break the mould, becoming Midland Fox in 1984. Midland Fox was sold to its management in 1987, with Stevensons of Uttoxeter having a minority stake. In 1989 ownership of the company passed to Drawlane. This firm already owned Midland Red North, which it bought from NBC in 1988. Both companies continue as separate subsidiaries under British Bus, as Drawlane is now known.

Midland Red South was sold to Western Travel in 1987, which has gradually dropped the word South from the fleetname. Midland Red West was sold to its management at the end of 1986, but passed to the Badgerline group in 1988.

Leicester-based Midland Fox uses a striking red and yellow livery with a stylised fox motif. Minibuses are branded as Fox Cubs. Second-hand vehicles play a major role in the fleet. Around 105 of the company's 125 double-deckers have come from other fleets. The only ones bought new are 14 A-registered ECW-bodied Olympians which date back to NBC days, and five Alexander-bodied Olympians purchased in 1989 during the short period between NBC and Drawlane ownership.

This means, of course, an interesting and varied fleet. There are large numbers of Fleetlines purchased from South Yorkshire Transport and from London, including B20 models which joined the fleet in 1992. There are also smaller numbers of former West Midland Fleetlines, one-time South Yorkshire Metrobuses, and a few former SBG Alexander-bodied Metrobuses which came from North Western Road Car in 1992. Most of these types can be seen in Leicester, the centre of Midland Fox's operations.

The company's full-size single-deck buses are all Leyland Nationals, although Leopard coaches are used regularly on longer-distance services. Some Nationals running into Leicester carry cream and red Wreake Valley Travel livery, while a number in Loughborough are in the green and cream Loughborough Coach & Bus colours.

Midland Fox was an early convert to minibuses and its oldest Transits date from 1985. They have proved remarkably long-lived, confounding the expectations of NBC's engineers that they would last for a maximum of five years on arduous local bus operation. There are almost 100 Transits still in use, but since 1988 the company has standardised on the bigger Iveco DailyBus with bodywork by Carlyle. There are second-hand Ivecos in the fleet from London Buses and Bee Line Buzz, among others.

The company has a fairly simplistic attitude to fleet numbering, generally adding a digit to the registration number — Fleetlines and Metrobuses are 2, Nationals are 3, Olympians are 4 — thus ex-SYT Fleetline SHE538S has fleet number 2538. There are, however, exceptions to this general rule.

Moving round to Midland Red North, the adjacent British Bus subsidiary, the picture is quite different, with considerable expenditure on new and rebodied buses since privatisation. Midland Red North is based in Cannock but its territory now extends up to Crewe, where it has taken over the former Crosville depot and operations, and west to Oswestry which was previously part of Crosville Wales. It retains its traditional Staffordshire and West Midlands operations too, with its southernmost depot being at Tamworth.

The company's use of the Midland Red name is generally linked with a locality name, often inherited from the days of NBC. Thus around Cannock and Stafford buses carry the name Chaserider Midland Red, in Telford and Wellington it is Tellus Midland Red, around Tamworth it is Mercian Midland Red and in Shrewsbury the name is Hotspur Midland Red. The former Crosville operations in Crewe trade as Midland Redline; the Oswestry buses run as Cambrian Midland Red. Midland Red North took control of C-Line, another British Bus subsidiary, early in 1993 and some vehicles transferred to that operation carry C-Line Midland Red names — and reach as far north as Manchester.

The nearest thing to a current standard Midland Red North bus is the Leyland Tiger rebodied by East Lancs. The first were treated in 1989, when 11 redundant Tigers with ECW's plain B51 coach body were purchased from sister Drawlane subsidiary London Country South West. The ECW bodies were scrapped and new East Lancs bodies fitted. More have since followed, including some which originally had high-floor Berkhof coach bodies. New single-deckers have been two Dennis Darts which run in Crewe and were the first Darts to be bodied by East Lancs. Some new East Lancs-bodied Dennis Falcons arrived in 1993 to join six similar buses transferred from London Country South West in 1991 when they were just a year old. The other modern single-deckers in the fleet are a trio of 1990 Plaxton-bodied Scania K93s which came with the local bus services of Happy Days of Woodseaves in 1991.

Double-deckers play a small part in the fleet and are a mix of types. Oldest are VRTs acquired with the Crosville Oswestry operations in 1991. Then there are standard NBC-style Olympians. Under Drawlane ownership Midland Red North has bought four new Olympians and six new Dominators with East Lancs bodies and three X-registered Alexander-bodied Metrobuses from Kelvin Scottish.

Minibuses are varied too, with Transits, Sherpas, Ivecos, Renaults and Mercedes spread throughout the fleet, including examples acquired from sister Drawlane companies.

Midland Red North has revived an old-style all-over red livery as used by Midland Red in times gone by. Buses so far repainted include this 1989 East Lancs-bodied Olympian. Ken Jubb

Few operators were buying Dennis Falcons in 1993, most having opted for the lighter and simpler Lance for full-size single-deck operation. Midland Red North is an exception, and has added nine Falcons with East Lancs bodies to its fleet. Malcolm King

PMT last bought full-size buses in 1990 with a mixture of Leyland Lynxes and Optare Deltas. There are nine Deltas, based on DAF SB220 underframes. Malcolm King

Below: **In 1989 PMT bought 10 Olympians with Leyland bodywork. Seven were finished as dual-purpose 72-seaters in a special livery for the Hanley to Crewe service. This one illustrates the spread of the Crosville-style vehicle classification to the main PMT fleet.** Alan Simpkins

PMT stands for Potteries Motor Traction, the name by which the company used to be known. PMT was part of NBC until the end of 1986 when it was bought by its management. The Potteries area is still the company's heartland, but since privatisation it has expanded its territory quite considerably. At first it grew by winning local authority tenders. This established it on the Wirral peninsula, where it traded as Red Rider. Then in 1990 it acquired a substantial part of the Crosville business with depots in Chester, Crewe, Ellesmere Port and Birkenhead. This added 164 buses to the fleet. The former Crosville operations now wear the same bright red and yellow livery as the rest of the PMT fleet, but with Crosville fleetnames.

Rapid growth has brought with it a mixture of vehicles. The buses which remain from PMT's NBC days are a few Leyland Nationals, some 50 Bristol VRTs and 15 Leyland Olympians. A few of the VRTs have ECW bodies built to a non-standard height of 13ft 5in (the standard VRT was 13ft 8in high). These can be identified by the beading above the windscreen which is lower than on a standard VRT. There are also around 50 minibuses which date from the NBC era. Most are Mercedes L608D vans with bus conversions carried out in PMT's own workshops, an activity which led to a short-lived body-building operation.

After privatisation more minibuses were purchased, with Mercedes still predominating although there was one batch of Freight Rover Sherpas. The Sherpas had coachbuilt PMT Bursley bodies, with an unusual sloping waist line which adds a bit of style to a basically unglamorous bus. The smaller Mercs had PMT Hanbridge conversions of van shells, while the bigger Mercs had coachbuilt PMT Ami bodies which looked vaguely (but only vaguely) like Optare StarRiders with their sloping fronts designed to make them look just a bit more appealing than bodies built on the standard snub-nosed Mercedes chassis cowl. Imitation is the sincerest form of flattery. Bodies were also bought from outside builders — Alexander in 1987 (on Dodges) and Reeve Burgess in 1990 (on Mercs).

The only new double-deckers since privatisation have been 10 Leyland-bodied Olympians, seven of which have coach seats and a striking silver-based livery for the Hanley to Crewe service. Instead the privatised PMT has invested in single-deckers. In 1990 it bought nine Optare Deltas and 11 Leyland Lynxes to compare the two types on one of the main routes connecting the Potteries towns. Since then it has turned to the Dennis Dart and now runs 18 of the type with Plaxton Pointer bodies. The Darts weren't PMT's first midis. That honour goes to 10 Leyland Swifts with PMT Knype bodies. The body looks almost as strange as the name. Blame for the body's name can apparently be laid at the door of the local writer Arnold Bennett. No one has as yet admitted responsibility for its looks.

Several services in the Potteries have been route-branded, leading to minor livery variations.

In 1988 PMT took over the business of Turner of Brown Edge. Two ex-West Yorkshire Olympians acquired from Turner still run between Brown Edge and Hanley in Turner's brown livery and have been joined by a PMT National 2 which has been re-painted brown. Another old-established name in the Potteries, Procters of Hanley, survives as an independent business. The company has been running for 70 years and currently uses second-hand Leopard coaches on its service from Hanley to Leek: in the 1960s and 1970s it ran new double-deckers.

Knotty Bus run a number of AECs including an ex-London Country Reliance and this ex-Merseyside Swift. It has a Marshall body and was ordered by St Helens Transport. Ken Jubb

PMT's fleet includes 10 Leyland Swifts with unusually-styled PMT Knype bodies. Malcolm King

PMT retains the Turner name from a company taken over in 1988. Buses in Turner livery include this Olympian. Ken Jubb

Stevensons of Uttoxeter is the other major operator in the North Midlands. Its growth has been phenomenal. In 1982 it had 52 vehicles – 27 double-deckers, 24 single-deckers and a minibus. Ten years later it had 222 – 44 double-deckers, 76 single-deckers, 19 midis and 83 minis. Only two of the 1982 fleet, a pair of Leopard coaches, were still in use in 1992. Here is an operator who has seized the opportunities of deregulation with enthusiasm. The first signs of an expansionist tendency were actually displayed back in 1985, before deregulation, when the company took over the operations of East Staffordshire District Council – perhaps better known by its pre-1974 title of Burton-on-Trent Corporation Transport.

The company runs Metrobuses from a range of sources—South Yorkshire, West Midlands, Greater Manchester, West Yorkshire (with Alexander bodies), and even the solitary example once owned by Tayside. Newest is an F-registered ex-MCW demonstrator; the oldest is one of MCW's original S-registered demonstrators.

There are only six Olympians, but these are interesting too. Two are B-registered examples which started life as coaches with Eastbourne. One is a former Ipswich bus. Two have Alexander lowheight bodies and were bought new in 1988. And the sixth is the first prototype, B45-01, which was built as a test rig by Leyland and has the unique combination of an ECW Olympian-style body with a

standard VRT windscreen and grille. It was sold as a shell by Leyland and trimmed and prepared for service by Stevensons. It carries a Q-prefix registration.

The single-deck fleet is quite a mixture, with new midis and predominantly second-hand full-size buses. The midis are Leyland Swifts and Stevensons runs 11 of this short-lived model, the biggest fleet in public bus service (as distinct from welfare or social services operations). Oddest of the Swifts are four with Wright bodies which look like tall Handybuses.

The big single-deckers include a few ex-SBG Seddon Pennine 7s with Alexander bodies and three contrasting Scanias bought new; two K93s and one N113. All three have Alexander PS bodies. There are two Lynxes bought new, but of more interest are those bought second-hand. Stevensons runs the only Lynx ever owned by SBG — it came from Kelvin Scottish in 1991 — and there are seven Lynxes with Alexander bodies which were purchased from Belfast Citybus in 1992. They are the only Alexander-bodied Lynxes around and were non-standard in the Citybus fleet.

Stevensons' heartland remains around Uttoxeter, but its routes now encompass Derby, Burton, Lichfield and parts of Birmingham. It did have operations in Stockport for a time, but these were taken over by PMT in 1992. In exchange Stevensons took over PMT operations around Wolverhampton. No vehicles changed hands in this deal.

Midland Red West is the smallest of the Midland Red companies. It is based in Worcester, a city which was among the first to undergo the wholesale replacement of big buses by minibuses in 1986. There are depots in Birmingham, Evesham, Hereford, Kidderminster and Redditch — and numerous outstations as well. There are almost 175 minibuses in the 350-strong fleet, and no double-deckers at all. The newest big buses are 50 Leyland Lynxes which entered service in 1990 and most of which are based in Birmingham. The rest of the big-bus fleet is made up of Mark 1 Nationals (there are no Mark 2s in the fleet) and Leopard and Tiger coaches, many of which run in all-over red with Midland Red Coaches fleetnames. The bus livery is red and cream.

The minibus fleet is remarkably standardised, with most being Mercedes 608D and 609D van conversions. There are a few Iveco Dailys and one batch of seven Peugeot-Talbot Pullman triaxles which operate on contract to Centro (as the West Midlands PTE now likes to be known) in Centro's yellow and green Quickstep livery.

Small operators in Midland Red West territory include Blue Line, running minibuses on tendered services around Hereford, and Go-Whittle of Kidderminster running rural services in parts of Shropshire and Worcestershire. Most Go-Whittle services are operated by Bedford coaches, but two Northern Counties-bodied Dennis Darts were purchased in 1992. One is used on the Ludlow town service, the other runs from Kidderminster. Local services in Kidderminster are run by Hollands, with second-hand minibuses. In Redditch Midland Red West competes with Kingfisher, running town services with white-liveried ex-West Midlands Fleetlines.

In Shrewsbury there are local services provided by Williamsons, who also run to Telford and to Birmingham. Coaches are used on out-of-town services and the newest vehicles in the fleet, two J-registered Darts with Carlyle bodies, are to be found on a Shrewsbury park-and-ride service.

The largest old-established private sector operator in Hereford is Yeomans Canyon Travel. Yeomans runs just under 40 vehicles with a preponderance of Bedfords, most of which have Duple or Plaxton coach bodies. The most recent fleet additions have been Dennis Darts—one bodied by Carlyle and the other, unusually for a small operator, by Alexander.

Midland Red West, owned by Badgerline, runs 50 Leyland Lynxes. They were new in 1990. Stewart J Brown

Older vehicles in the Midland Red West fleet are mainly Mark 1 Leyland Nationals. There are 80, including this example in Redditch which came from Western National. K R Crawley

Midland Red West's minibus fleet is made up mainly of Mercedes. Non-standard types include seven Peugeot-Talbot Pullman three-axle 22-seaters used on West Midlands PTE tenders. Stewart J Brown

Go-Whittle runs two Dennis Darts with Northern Counties CountyBus bodies. One is used on the Ludlow town service. Stewart J Brown

Williamsons operate Dennis Darts on the Shrewsbury park-and-ride service. The newest has Marshall bodywork to the same design as earlier Carlyle-bodied deliveries. Malcolm King

Yeomans run two Dennis Darts, one with Carlyle Dartline body and the other with Alexander Dash body. The Alexander-bodied bus was new in 1991 and is a short 30-seat 8.5m model. Malcolm King

Completing the circle of Midland Red companies is Midland Red South of Rugby, which still uses NBC poppy red for its livery, but with attractive white and grey relief. No new full-sized buses have been purchased since the company was privatised in 1987. Instead the investment has been in small buses, mainly Wright-bodied Mercedes-Benz 811Ds, and these have been replacing time-expired Leyland Nationals. There are still Nationals in the fleet, both new and second-hand. Some have been fitted with DAF engines.

Double-deckers are in a minority. There are 17 Olympians dating back to NBC days while post-privatisation double-deck additions have been four London DMS Fleetlines (from Stevensons of Uttoxeter) and four Greater Manchester Fleetlines. Buses in Stratford-on-Avon, including five double-deckers, are painted blue and white and carry Stratford Blue fleetnames, reviving an identity lost under NBC ownership over 20 years ago when the Stratford Blue fleet was absorbed by Midland Red. Stratford is the birthplace and headquarters of the Guide Friday organisation which runs open-top tours in more than a dozen towns and cities in Britain. The green and cream liveried fleet includes two 1946 Beadle bodied AEC Regals ex-Hastings.

Midland Red South has depots at Banbury, Leamington, Nuneaton and Stratford as well as at its Rugby headquarters. The Banbury fleet includes half a dozen coaches acquired from Tanners International in 1989 when Tanners gave up competing with Midland Red South in the town. These are recognisable by their 1xxx series fleet numbers. The company is also unusual in running a coach with a Q-prefix registration, issued by the DVLA to vehicles whose date of construction cannot be accurately identified, and rare on a bus or coach. The coach in question is a 1976 Leopard which suffered fire damage and was rebodied by Plaxton in 1984.

The Leamington garage is shared with another Western Travel subsidiary, G&G Travel. G&G (a Mr Green and a Mr Griffen) started its business in 1954 and was taken over by Western Travel at the end of 1989. The company established new services after deregulation and still runs between Leamington and Coventry. It has two buses bought new, F-registered Lynxes. The rest of its fleet is an assortment of second-hand units including West Midlands Fleetlines, Inter Valley Link Leopards and Merseybus Atlanteans. Sherpa minibuses run a park-and-ride service in Coventry. The fleet livery is two shades of blue.

Another Western Travel subsidiary running into Coventry is Vanguard of Bedworth. Vanguard was bought by Western in 1989, since when the entire 34-vehicle fleet has changed, rapidly. All are second-hand and most are Leylands with a mixture of Nationals, Leopards and Tigers. Some have come from other Western Travel companies, but the majority are from outside the group. Vanguard runs from Coventry to Nuneaton, where it also provides local services.

Left: **There are 17 standard NBC-style ECW-bodied Olympians in the Midland Red South fleet. This bus, seen in Coventry on the Leamington service, dates from 1983.** K R Crawley

Centre left: **Midland Red South runs over 50 Leyland Nationals, most of which are Mark Is new in the late 1970s.** Alan Simpkins

Bottom left: **Midland Red South trades as Stratford Blue in Stratford-upon-Avon. Double-deckers are very much in the minority – four Olympians like this one and a DMS type Fleetline.** Ken Jubb

Midland Red South runs a growing fleet of Mercedes minis. Most have been bought new and have Wright bodywork. This is a 1991 811D in Stratford. Ken Jubb

G&G Travel of Leamington is a sister company of Midland Red South in the Western Travel group. It operates second-hand Fleetlines. This one came from West Midlands Travel in 1990 and has MCW bodywork. K R Crawley

The Vanguard fleet, also part of Western Travel, is made up primarily of second-hand Nationals, Tigers and, as here, Leopards. This 1980 PSU3 with Willowbrook 003 bodywork was transferred from Midland Red South in 1989. Colin Lloyd

The much-reduced United Counties company, bereft of its Luton and Milton Keynes operations since the 1986 split, serves the South Midlands with its main operations in Bedford, Northampton, Kettering and Corby. United Counties was bought by Stagecoach in 1987 and with the departure of the last of its Routemasters in September 1993, the great bulk of the fleet is in the Stagecoach group's corporate colours.

Stagecoach inherited a fleet of Nationals, VRTs and Olympians, along with Iveco minibuses and Leopard and Tiger coaches. It introduced the Routemasters in 1988 and then upgraded the fleet with almost 30 Series 3 VRTs purchased from Devon General in 1989. A smaller number were also transferred from sister company Hampshire Bus. New additions to the fleet have been 35 Alexander-bodied Olympians and 15 with Northern Counties bodies. Express services have retained the Coachlinks name used by United Counties before the takeover and this appears on such disparate vehicles as ECW-bodied Olympians with coach seats and Plaxton-bodied Volvo B10Ms.

United Counties also runs one of the trio of three-axle Olympian Megadekkas owned by Stagecoach. The other two are with Cumberland Motor Services.

There is one municipal fleet in the United Counties area, Northampton Transport, which demonstrates its arm's length relationship with its owners by rather unnecessarily displaying 'Ltd' in large letters after its fleetname in a triumph of politics over marketing. Northampton has escaped the worst excesses of competition and the 70-strong Northampton Transport fleet has maintained a steady policy of fleet renewal. Its oldest buses are Alexander-bodied Bristol VRTs, an unusual municipal choice in 1977, although these are gradually being replaced by new Volvo Citybuses with Alexander and East Lancs bodies. There are also half a dozen East Lancs-bodied VRTs and the same number of East Lancs-bodied Olympians. Single-deckers are four Volvo B10Ms with Duple 300 series bus bodies. Minibuses were introduced in 1987 but have since been phased out. Since deregulation most new buses have been given names with local connections.

Yorks of Northampton runs between Northampton and Milton Keynes, generally with a 1977 Leopard which was rebodied as a bus by Plaxton in 1987. Yorks is primarily a coach operator and older Fords are available as back-up for service. The entire fleet is named after battleships: the Leopard bus is, perhaps appropriately, HMS Tireless.

In Milton Keynes the main operator is Milton Keynes City Bus. MKCB took over United Counties' operation in the new town in 1986, and promptly converted the whole network to Mercedes minibuses in an uninspiring grey and cream livery. The operation is still minibus-based, although larger coachbuilt buses have replaced some of the original van conversions and a few have even been rebodied to increase carrying capacity – an event so far unique in the annals of minibus work in Britain.

MKCB was bought by its management in 1987 and expanded by taking over Johnson of Hanslope, running full-sized vehicles on services to Milton Keynes in an all-over blue livery. Johnson remains a separate operation. Another distinct operation set up by MKCB is the Buckinghamshire Road Car Co in a green and yellow livery, and running 20 Mercedes minibuses on services in Buckinghamshire and Bedfordshire. Big buses never disappeared entirely, with a few Nationals and VRTs surviving. These have more recently been joined by Bristol REs for both the Johnson fleet and a maroon-liveried County Line operation. MKCB and its associates were taken over by Cambus Holdings in 1992, but continue to operate separately. An improved livery of cream and red started to replace MKCB's grey in summer 1993.

Competition in Milton Keynes comes from London-based R&I Tours, running Leyland Nationals, a Plaxton-bodied Dart and four short Bedford YMQ-S models with utilitarian-looking Lex Maxeta bodies on local services. Buffalo of Flitwick, to the east of Milton Keynes, not only serves the new town but also runs to Dunstable, Bedford and Hitchin as well as having services in the St Albans, Watford and Hemel Hempstead areas. The vehicles are mostly second-hand and include four Northern Counties-bodied Dennis Dominators which were new to Greater Manchester, some ex-London DMS Fleetlines and four new (in 1988) Volvo B10Ms with Plaxton Derwent bus bodies. Buffalo's newest buses are two Plaxton-bodied Darts, purchased in 1993 for a service in the Watford area. The livery is white with yellow and red stripes. Cedar of Bedford has a mixed fleet of acquired double-deckers and the single-deck fleet includes an unusual Wadham Stringer-bodied Dennis Lancet and an ex-Western Scottish Seddon Pennine VII. Services are operated from Bedford to St Neots and Bolnhurst.

Top left: **The Leyland Olympian, with three different makes of body, forms a strong part of the United Counties double-deck fleet. An ECW bus is seen in Northampton.** Stewart Brown

Centre left: **Interest in Volvo's mid-engined Citybus has declined in the 1990s and the most recent deliveries have been six for Northampton Transport.** Ken Jubb

Left: **Milton Keynes City Bus runs a fleet made up mainly of Mercedes-Benz minibuses. A 1986 L608D is seen here.** Roger Whitehead

Top right: **County Line is a trading name for Milton Keynes City Bus. An ECW-bodied RE waits for passengers in Central Milton Keynes.** David Harman

Centre right: **R&I of London started competing with Milton Keynes City Bus in 1992, trading as Inter MK. Most services are operated by Mark I Nationals.** David Harman

Right: **Few double-deck Dennis Falcons were built and few survive in service. Cedar Coaches run this former Nottingham bus with 94-seat East Lancs body.** G R Mills

EAST ANGLIA

A Plaxton bodied Dennis Javelin in the picturesque village of Kersey. G R Mills

Eastern Counties has the distinction of having Britain's most easterly bus depot, in Lowestoft, Suffolk. The company is not quite as big as it once was: its western operations were split off by NBC in 1984 to form the Cambridge-based Cambus company. At the same time its coaching activities passed to Ambassador Travel. What was left, with its headquarters in Norwich, was privatised in a management buy-out in February 1987.

Eastern Counties has a large operating area with depots scattered throughout the flatlands of East Anglia from the north Norfolk coast down to the Suffolk/Essex border in the south. There are depots at Norwich, Lowestoft, Great Yarmouth, Bury St Edmunds, King's Lynn and Ipswich. As with most former NBC operators, the older buses in the fleet are fairly standardised: VRTs and Leyland Nationals. The VRTs include some of the last to be built, with X registrations, and four with highbridge bodies which came from Hastings & District in 1985. The highbridge VRTs operate in Norwich and have an attractive non-standard livery layout with a cream roof instead of the normal red. The takeover of Dack's Rosemary Coaches in July 1993 brought some elderly vehicles with it.

Eastern Counties provides all the city services in Norwich and these are largely operated by Ford Transits and Mercedes-Benz 608Ds which carry City Line fleetnames. The newest buses running in Norwich are four green-liveried Dennis Darts with Plaxton Pointer bodies. These are used on park-and-ride services which were introduced at the start of 1993 to help reduce the city's chronic traffic congestion.

Since privatisation Eastern Counties has bought an interesting mixture of new double- and single-deck buses. The 'deckers have been Leyland Olympians and the first five, with Northern Counties bodies, entered service in 1989. They were the company's first Olympians, and its first new double-deckers since 1981. Two were delivered in a predominantly cream livery with coach seats for use on the Eastline service from Norwich to Peterborough via King's Lynn. A further five similar buses were ordered for delivery in 1991, but the body order was switched to Leyland when Northern Counties called in the administrative receivers. The irony of this was, of course, that Northern Counties survived but Leyland's Workington plant did not.

The four highbridge Bristol VRTs in the Eastern Counties fleet are immediately identifiable by their cream roofs. Lowheight double-deckers have red roofs. These buses were bought from Hastings & District in 1985. K R Crawley

New single-deckers have all been supplied by Dennis. Since 1989 the company has received 15 Javelin buses, five bodied by Duple and 10 by Plaxton. At the start of 1993 it received five Dennis Lances, with Northern Counties' attractive Paladin body, one of which is seen at Southwold. T K Brookes

Great Yarmouth Transport's fleet includes Dennis Darts with Carlyle and East Lancs bodies. They replaced AEC Swifts. Malcolm King

The most recent double-deck additions to Great Yarmouth's fleet are ex-London Buses MCW Metrobus IIs. Malc McDonald

Flying Banana runs minibuses in Great Yarmouth in competition with Great Yarmouth Transport. A Transit pulls out of the bus station. G R Mills

There are two municipally-owned bus companies in Eastern Counties' area. The smaller of the two is Great Yarmouth Transport. Before deregulation its fleet was made up entirely of big buses; since deregulation most of the additions to its fleet have been small vehicles.

Three types of double-decker are operated, Bristol VRTs, MCW Metrobuses and Volvo Citybuses. The VRTs have standard lowheight ECW bodies which look particularly attractive in Great Yarmouth's blue and cream colours. The Citybuses have East Lancs coach bodies on the first pair, delivered in 1987, and more conventional Alexander R-type bus bodies on the second pair, delivered in 1989. The MCWs are second-hand Metrobus IIs which were originally used by London Buses on its Harrow network.

The remaining full-size single-deckers are 1973 ECW-bodied AEC Swifts, rare survivors indeed, although since deregulation these have been thinned out as smaller buses have replaced them. Initially Great Yarmouth went for the MCW Metrorider, of which it has eight, and then the Mercedes 811D with Reeve Burgess Beaver body of which there are four. The most recent deliveries have been Dennis Darts with East Lancs bodies. Competition in the town comes from a minibus operator, trading as the Flying Banana. Flying Banana runs ten minibuses on four services in Great Yarmouth and also provides Sunday services in Lowestoft.

While Great Yarmouth has been content to stay broadly within its established territory, municipally-owned Ipswich Buses has branched out into rural Suffolk, taking over a number of independent operators' services in the process. The fleet is an interesting one. Mainstay of the town's double-deck services is a fleet of dual-door Atlanteans with Roe bodies.

It is in the single-deck fleet that the variety is to be found. In the 1980s Ipswich standardised on the Dennis Falcon and it now has 28 of the type, giving it Britain's biggest Falcon fleet. Seven have Northern Counties bodies while the remainder have East Lancs bodies, most of which could best be described as rugged rather than attractive. (Well, how often have you seen a body builder adopt an off-centre front grille because the radiator is off-centre?) The newest Dennis in the fleet is a solitary East Lancs-

bodied Lance, which entered service in 1992 and was the first Lance outside London.

Ipswich Buses also runs rare Leyland B21s, a low-frame rear-engined export chassis which Leyland was hoping it could sell to Ulsterbus as a successor to the Bristol RE. It did sell six before abandoning the idea, and these now run in Ipswich. They joined four bought new by Ipswich in 1985 when Leyland was desperately seeking a buyer for some unsold stock chassis. All of the Ipswich B21s — which are the only B21s in Britain — have bodywork by Alexander (Belfast). Although sold as Leylands, the chassis were built by Bristol.

Since deregulation the company has bought a small number of small buses. The older examples are Dodge S56s, the newer ones are Optare MetroRiders. All of Ipswich Buses' vehicles are named. There is thus a Leyland called Albion.

Ipswich Buses is Britain's biggest user of Dennis Falcons, with 28. These include seven with Northern Counties bodies. The use of two-door buses is unusual in a relatively small town. Peter Rowlands

The B21 was a chassis developed by Leyland which used parts of the National driveline. Ipswich has four bought new and has added to them six which were built for operation in Northern Ireland. All have Alexander (Belfast) bodywork. Note the Suffolk Bus logo used for post-deregulation expansion outside the home town. Malcolm King

Throughout Norfolk and Suffolk there are many small operators, often running infrequent services with elderly coaches although some run modern buses, including new double-deckers.

Wisbech has been served since the 1930s by Towler. Bristol VRTs run market day services while a former Derby LHS is used on lighter workings. Cromer, on the north-east Norfolk coast, is served by Sanders of Holt, one of the county's largest operators with a fleet which includes over 50 Bedfords. Sanders operate weekday services with additional market day duties, particularly on Wednesdays and Thursdays — a pattern of operation which applies to many Norfolk bus companies.

Small firms running into Norwich include Neave of Catfield, Spratts of Wreningham and Anglian from Loddon. Semmence of Wymondham operates a large fleet of Bedfords. Most have coach bodies but there are two with angular Wright of Ballymena bodywork; these came from Maidstone Boro'line. Simonds of Botesdale also serves Norwich, running in from Diss. Other Simonds services run from Diss to Bury St Edmunds and to surrounding villages. The fleet is made up mainly of Bedfords and Fords, most of which have coach bodies and most of which are second-hand. The few buses in the fleet have 60-plus capacity thanks to the use of three-and-two seating. Oddest of these is a 69-seat Plaxton Paramount-bodied Bedford Venturer, built new with bus seats and normally allocated to the Bury St Edmunds service. Coach Services (Thetford) provides services with Ford and Bedford coaches in cream and red with the latest additions in a new maroon livery.

Partridge Coaches of Hadleigh serves Ipswich and also runs north to Bury St Edmunds and Stowmarket. The company's double-deckers are predominantly Daimler Fleetlines, including examples which originally ran for London Transport. These cover schools contracts as well as some service work.

Rules of Boxford reach both Bury St Edmunds and Colchester once a week but serve Sudbury every weekday. They run an elderly fleet of buses and coaches. These include that fast-disappearing type, the AEC Reliance, the oldest of which was new over 20 years ago. Rules is one of the few operators in Sudbury not to serve the large Great Cornard housing estate which is catered for by Eastern Counties, Beeston of Hadleigh, Chambers of Bures and Hedingham Omnibuses.

Bury St Edmunds is also served by Felix of Long Melford with black-and-white Mercedes minibuses, Galloways of Mendlesham and Mulleys of Ixworth (part of Beeston of Hadleigh).

Right: **The rural areas of North Norfolk are served by Sanders of Holt's large fleet which includes over fifty Bedford coaches many of which are dedicated to bus services. This one was originally one of batch of eighteen new to Eastern National fitted with bus grant specification doors ideally suited for rural bus workings. The Duple Dominant II bodied YMT is seen in Heath Drive, Holt bound for the Market Place terminus.** G R Mills

Far left: **Before coming to prominence with its Handybus bodies on Dennis Darts, the products of Wright of Ballymena were rarely seen in Britain. This Wright-bodied Bedford was new to Maidstone Borough Transport and now runs for Semmence.** G R Mills

Left: **Partridges are active in dealing in and the rebuilding of buses as well as having a long-established operation. This East Lancs bodied Atlantean was purchased seatless for spares but was considered worthy of re-entry to bus use.** G R Mills

Opposite centre: **The Simonds fleet is made up largely of Bedfords and Fords, all but one of which have Plaxton bodies.** Alan Simpkins

Above: **Beestons of Hadleigh have amassed a fleet of Leyland Nationals for local bus operation. This one is seen on the Great Cornard housing estate served by four operators.** G R Mills

Left: **Midland Red ran a large fleet of Fords in the early 1970s. Most have been scrapped, but this one survives with Rules of Boxford. New in 1970 it is an R192 with 45-seat Plaxton body.** G R Mills

Cambus was formed in 1984, taking over the western part of what had been Eastern Counties territory, and was privatised by a management buyout in 1986. In 1989 the Cambus company was divided, with its northern operations becoming the new Viscount Bus and Coach Co. Viscount and Cambus are both subsidiaries of what is now known as Cambus Holdings.

The first sign of an independent identity at Cambus was the adoption of a new — and, it has to be said, insipid — powder blue livery. This soon gave way to a much more attractive two-tone blue and cream or, more recently, white. Wavy lines in the fleetname are a subtle reference to the River Cam. The bulk of the company's operations are based in the university town of Cambridge, with a depot at Newmarket. The older buses in the fleet are standard NBC-specification VRTs and Nationals. The VRTs acquired from Eastern Counties have been joined by second-hand examples from a variety of sources including York City & District, Keighley & District and North Devon. There are no standard NBC-type Olympians in the fleet, instead Cambus has since privatisation bought new Olympians with bodywork by Optare (to Roe designs) and by Northern Counties. There is also a trio of Olympians purchased from the West Yorkshire PTE in 1987 when they were but five years old. The most recent Olympian additions have been the two long-wheelbase vehicles with striking Alexander RDC coach bodies, built for Eastern Scottish. These are used on limited-stop services. The only other Alexander bodies of this style are on a pair of Volvo Citybuses operated by Western Scottish.

Optare went on to become a supplier of small buses to Cambus — first of all with MAN-VW-based CityPacers and more recently with integral MetroRiders. The CityPacers include ex-Taff Ely examples and some are in a red, white and blue scheme for the link between Cambridge city centre and the railway station, which is some distance away.

In 1992, Cambus acquired the business of Millers Coaches of Cambridge and has retained the Millerbus name on some of the buses acquired with that operation. The Lynxes and Nationals of Millerbus identity are in a cream and red colour scheme.

The first Volvo B6s with Marshall bodies are running for Cambus, which is taking 14. The Marshall body is based on that originally developed by Duple for the Dennis Dart. The Cambus vehicles are 32 seaters. Malcolm King

After trying the Optare CityPacer, Cambus has switched to the bigger MetroRider integral. It now has 17 in service. This is a 1992 model. Mike Harris

Following the Miller takeover, Millerbus livery was applied to this 1981 National 2 allocated to park-and-ride operation in Cambridge. It was part of the fleet which Cambus acquired from Eastern Counties in 1984. Mike Harris

After Cambus, the biggest local operator running into Cambridge is Whippet Coaches of Fenstanton which runs to St Ives and to Huntingdon, where it also runs local services. The company trades as Go Whippet (a style of name coined by Whittle of Kidderminster in the early 1980s) and this, with a leaping dog logo appears on the side of a variety of double-deckers. For front-line service there are three Volvo Citybuses bought new, one bodied by Alexander and two by Northern Counties. The first of these arrived in 1988, eight years after Whippet's last new 'decker, a V-registered Northern Counties-bodied Atlantean which is still in use. There is also one second-hand Citybus. The company has amassed a collection of Scania-powered MCW Metropolitans. Most originated with London Transport but there are others from Hull, Reading and the Tyne & Wear PTE. These are used mainly on school work and constitute the biggest fleet of the type with a second owner. Even more unusual is a solitary Baghdad-specification Atlantean with Willowbrook body which was damaged before shipment to Iraq in 1980 and was bought by Whippet, converted to right-hand-drive, and put into service in 1987 with a D-prefix registration. At first it ran with Middle East style full depth sliding windows, but these were replaced by ones more suitable for the English climate during accident damage repair.

Whippet has a sizeable coach fleet, but until recently the only single-deck buses were three Volvo B10Ms with Duple Dominant bodies, two of which were bought new in 1980-81. These have been joined by four similarly-bodied Bedford YMQs which were new to South Wales Transport and are unusual for Bedfords in having automatic gearboxes.

One of the strangest Atlanteans running in Britain is Whippet's Baghdad-specification AN68 with Willowbrook body which was converted from left-hand drive. It has a nearside staircase (on what would have been the offside in Iraq) and the original centre exit door has been retained as an emergency exit. G R Mills

Whippet runs both Bedfords and Volvos with Duple Dominant bus bodies. This Volvo B58 came from Skills but was new in 1980 to Hutchison of Overtown. Mike Harris

An unusual conversion of a Metropolitan to open-top is to be found in the Whippet fleet. This bus was new to Hull in 1977 and is one of almost 20 of the MCW-Scania integrals run by Whippet. Geoff Mills

The older double-deckers in the Viscount fleet are Bristol VRTs, all with ECW bodywork. *Mike Harris*

Viscount supported local bodybuilder Marshall of Cambridge in 1992 with an order for seven 25-seat bodies on Iveco Ford 59.12 chassis. Marshall is building bodies to Carlyle designs following Carlyle's closure. *Mike Harris*

Peterborough Bus Co is a new name to appear in 1993, being applied to eight Viscount buses running in the city. This is a former London Buses Iveco Ford 49.10 with Robin Hood bodywork. *Mike Harris*

Viscount has distanced itself from Cambus with a new yellow and white livery and as well as having a base in Peterborough, also has depots at March, Market Deeping and Oundle. Viscount, with 80 vehicles, is smaller than Cambus (which has over 100) but its fleet is, not surprisingly, similar — VRTs, Optare CityPacers and Northern Counties-bodied Olympians. It did have Nationals but these have all gone, replaced largely by second-hand VRTs. Viscount also has Optare StarRiders and has more recently patronised local industry by buying Marshall-bodied Ivecos when Marshall of Cambridge re-entered bus body building in 1992 using designs purchased from Carlyle.

Few Bristol VRTs were bodied by Northern Counties. Reading Transport favoured the combination and took long-wheelbase VRT/LL models which were known as Jumbos. One survives with Morley of Whittlesey. It was new in 1976. **Mike Harris**

Morley runs three ex-Scottish Bus Group Seddon Pennine VIIs. All came from Western Scottish and were new in 1976-77. **Mike Harris**

Enterprise of Chatteris runs ex-London Fleetlines and Nationals into Peterborough. A National leaves for Ramsey. **Alan Simpkins**

Smaller operators running in Viscount's catchment area include Delaine of Bourne, whose services reach Peterborough, and Emblings of Guyhirn who run between March and Wisbech, using either a coach or a second-hand VRT. Morley's of Whittlesey run from Coates to Peterborough, usually with an ex-Western Scottish Alexander-bodied Seddon Pennine 7, a comparatively unusual choice for a small fleet, and a former London DMS Fleetline. Enterprise of Chatteris run a DMS from Ramsey to Huntingdon and a service to Peterborough using a National. Double-deck work is sometimes covered by an ex-Lothian Atlantean. The livery used by Enterprise is green and grey in a layout almost identical to that used by Luton & District. Enterprise operate tendered evening and Sunday services between March and Wisbech, operated commercially at other times by Emblings.

Moving south into Essex, Eastern National is another former NBC company privatised in a management buy-out. This took place at the end of 1986, but in April 1990 another change saw ownership pass to the Badgerline group. Badgerline quickly split the company in two, retaining the Eastern National name for operations east and north of Chelmsford, and setting up a new Thamesway company in July 1990. Thamesway is based in Basildon and runs services in south Essex and in London, where Eastern National had won a substantial number of LRT contracts all of which passed to Thamesway.

Eastern National's livery is a distinctive yellow and green and this is worn by some 230 buses which are based as far east as Clacton. During its spell in management ownership, Eastern National bought 30 new Leyland Lynxes and batches of Mercedes minibuses. These joined standard NBC-issue VRTs, Nationals and Olympians and some more unusual Leyland Tigers with Alexander TE express coach bodies, delivered in 1983 and initially used on longer-distance services. Eastern National took a number of ECW-bodied Olympian coaches, both the original extra-long-wheelbase type with somewhat bizarre styling, and a later and much neater variant with an attractive front end style using windscreens similar to those on Mancunian bodies of the late 1960s.

A new look was announced for Eastern National in the summer of 1993, with a brighter shade of green and a revised fleetname and colour division. Mike Harris

There are 13 ECW-bodied Olympians to standard NBC outline in Eastern National's fleet, although they differ from most buses of this type by the fitment of dual-purpose seats. A 1986 Gardner-powered bus shows the latest livery. Mike Harris

A Mark 1 National in the Eastern National fleet picks up outside Chelmsford station. A Mercedes-Benz minibus follows. The livery carried in both cases is the previous standard using a darker green. Stewart J Brown

Colchester Borough Transport, whose depot premises incorporate the former Corporation tram sheds, runs just over 50 vehicles and these stay primarily within the immediate area of the town and its environs. The company has maintained a consistent fleet replacement policy, adding new Lynxes and Olympians to its fleet in small numbers at a time. It has both Mark I and Mark II Lynxes, including a K-registered example, which is not a common sight. Its first Olympians, delivered in 1985, have ECW bodies. When ECW closed, body orders were placed with Leyland at Workington.

Before the arrival of the Olympian, the standard Colchester double-decker in the late 1970s was the ECW-bodied Atlantean and 22 of these remain in the fleet. The company runs a small coach fleet under the CBT Coachways name in a white and blue livery. The bus fleet colours are cream and deep crimson. Since October 1986, Eastern National have worked all of Colchester's town services on Sundays, on a contract from Essex County Council.

The traditional independents have made Colchester a mecca for transport enthusiasts over the years. The biggest to run into the town is Hedingham Omnibuses in a smart cream and red livery. Hedingham reaches Colchester from Halstead and Walton-on-the-Naze. The company has depots in Sible Hedingham, Little Tey, Kelvedon, Clacton, Nayland and Walton and its services cover much of north Essex and reach into parts of Suffolk.

The fleet is a mixture of new and second-hand vehicles. These are mainly single-deckers but there are 18 one-time NBC Bristol VRTs (mainly used for schools), five East Lancs-bodied Atlanteans acquired with the business of Norfolks of Nayland in 1991 and an Alexander-bodied Olympian bought new in 1990, which was the company's first new 'decker. Bedfords still figure in the fleet and these are bodied by Duple, Marshall, Plaxton, and Willowbrook. There are three Leyland Lynxes and the first Dennis Dart in Essex, an Alexander-bodied bus delivered in 1992 and used on the Maldon to Witham service. A few minibuses are used on tendered rural routes. The L-series fleet numbers carried on Hedingham buses are a throwback to the founder of what became Hedingham & District, A E Letch.

Colchester's late 1970s standard was the ECW-bodied Atlantean, a relatively rare combination outside NBC subsidiaries. There are 22 in the fleet. Dave Cole

Colchester is one of the few fleets running a K-registered Lynx, a type on which the operator standardised for its single-deck intake from introduction in 1986. This was its last. G R Mills

Hedingham Omnibuses has built up a fleet of Bristol VRTs, one of which is seen in the attractive village of Sible Hedingham when freshly repainted and about to work a school contract. G R Mills

The next major operator is Osborne's of Tollesbury, who have been running buses for over 75 years. Osborne's run from Tollesbury to Colchester and to Maldon and Witham. The double-deckers all date from the 1970s and include second-hand Fleetlines, with examples from London and Tayside, and an ex-Tayside Alexander-bodied VRT. The livery is red, cream and maroon. The single-deck fleet comprises a mixture of new and second-hand coaches on a wide variety of chassis. Some of the Leopard coaches appear on bus work; these are white with blue and red bands.

Chambers of Bures operate a service from Bury St Edmunds to Colchester, with a choice of three Alexander-bodied Leyland Olympians bought new in 1989 — after almost 20 years of running only single-deckers. Chambers run a Lynx on their Sudbury to Great Cornard service, and a few high-capacity Duple-bodied Bedford YMT buses, plus two Talbot Pullmans on a high frequency service to Long Melford. Chambers face competition from Beestons of Hadleigh running a variety of second-hand Nationals.

Cedrics of Wivenhoe, to the east of Colchester, operate from Brightlingsea to Colchester. The company has six Bristol VRTs available for this work including a pair of ex-Badgerline coach-seated examples.

South Essex is the scene of continuing bus wars, with Southend Transport and Badgerline's Thamesway subsidiary as the key protagonists. Since being split from Eastern National, Thamesway has purchased a large fleet of Mercedes-Benz minibuses with Reeve Burgess bodies many of which have been used to compete with Southend Transport services.

In the summer of 1992 Thamesway stepped up the pressure on Southend Transport by launching new commuter coach services to London, in competition with Southend's long-established operations to the capital. Southend Transport has lodged complaints about Thamesway's tactics with the Office of Fair Trading.

Thamesway, based in Basildon, operate throughout south Essex and in London as well. The fleet livery is an unusual and perhaps uncomfortable combination of a traditional dark maroon and a vibrant yellow. Apart from some of the minibuses, the Thamesway fleet in Essex is an Eastern National inheritance.

Osborne's of Tollesbury run five 33ft-long Alexander-bodied Fleetlines which were new to Tayside Transport in 1975. They have Alexander bodies. David Harman

The long established Colchester to Bury St Edmunds via Sudbury service provided by Chambers of Bures was the regular domain of Guy Arab double-deckers from the immediate post-war years until the early seventies. After nearly twenty years of bus bodied Bedfords plying the route, double deckers returned to woo the public when three new Leyland Olympians with Alexander coachwork were added to the fleet strength. G R Mills

Cedric's double-deckers are all Bristol VRTs with ECW bodies. This example came from Badgerline in 1992. G R Mills

Grahams of Kelvedon run locally using this Bedford YMQ-S with Wadham Stringer body. It was new to Eastern National in 1981, but came to Grahams from Hedingham Omnibuses. G R Mills

Minibuses have been used by Thamesway to compete in the Southend area. This Mercedes-Benz has a Reeve Burgess Beaver body, a combination which – with the body now built by Plaxton – is effectively the Badgerline group's standard. Colin Lloyd

Southend Transport operates an interesting selection of vehicles. The company was put up for sale by the borough council at the start of 1993, with British Bus taking over in the summer. This could impinge on both its vehicle policy and on its operational strategy in the face of Thamesway's competition.

The oldest buses in the fleet in mid-1993 were Routemasters, which were introduced in 1988 when they were on average 25 years old. The aim was to provide faster loading than on competitors' one-person-operated buses. The first 12 came direct from London Buses. These have since been joined by examples from Southampton and from Clydeside Scottish. Many are named after local places.

There are still a number of 33ft-long Fleetlines in use, all bodied by Northern Counties — and including five 1972 examples which were rebodied by Northern Counties in 1984/85. The newest Fleetlines date from 1981. More recent double-deckers have been Leyland Olympians. An Alexander-bodied bus bought from dealer stock in 1989 (and since sold to East Yorkshire) was quickly followed by four Leyland-bodied buses ordered from the factory. The most recent double-deckers have been a variety of ECW-bodied VRTs including highbridge examples from Ribble and standard-height buses from Crosville, Go-Ahead Northern, PMT and National Welsh. Other full-size buses include Leyland Nationals, introduced to the fleet in 1989 and acquired from a variety of sources. All are 10.3m-long single-door buses.

Southend Transport built up a sizeable coach fleet in the early 1980s and still runs Duple-bodied Leopards and Tigers. The Leopards are all second-hand while all but one of the Tigers were bought new. They generally operate on express services. Southend Transport has 10 coaches due in central London before 9am and runs an hourly service off-peak.

The coaches in Southend's fleet are blue and yellow; buses are blue and off-white. Both liveries incorporate red relief.

In Basildon, Thamesway is on the receiving end of some small-scale competition. District Bus, a child of deregulation, started running four Freight Rover Sherpas on a cross-town service and now has a nine-strong fleet. Jacksons of Bicknacre run to Basildon Hospital from South Woodham with a Sherpa. Nelson Independent Bus Services — NIBS — operates an ageing fleet of yellow-liveried ex-Western National Bristol REs on various services into Basildon. There are also several DMSs in the fleet

Tendering of Sunday services in East Anglia produces some unusual operations which include Ambassador Travel running locally in Norwich; all Colchester services being run by Eastern National; Carters of Colchester running to Chelmsford and Stephensons of Rochford operating between Southend and Chelmsford. Stephensons also run weekday services in Southend with Bristol VRTs and an LH, and a summer open top VRT service on Southend sea front.

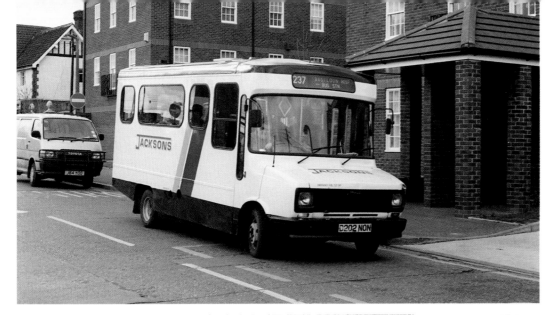

Facing page top: **A batch of 1972 Fleetlines in the Southend fleet were rebodied by Northern Counties in 1984-85 and re-registered with Q-prefix numbers in place of their original L-suffix marks. There are five of these CRL6-33s with 80-seat two-door bodies.** Geoff Mills

Facing page centre: **Southend's single-deckers are Leyland Nationals, of which it has 28, all second-hand and bought after the model ceased production. This one dates from 1977 and was one of the first to enter the Southend fleet in 1989.** Alan Simpkins

Facing page bottom: **District Bus operates from Basildon using Freight Rover minibuses. This one is seen in Romford.** Malcolm King

This page top: **The smallest bus in regular use by Jacksons of Bicknacre is this Freight Rover Sherpa with Carlyle body. It came from Ribble but was new to United.** Peter Rowlands

This page centre: **Bristol REs form the backbone of the Nelson fleet running into Basildon and are the oldest buses to be seen in the town nowadays.** G R Mills

This page bottom: **A Carter's VRT takes its layover in Colchester bus station. It was new to West Riding in 1977 but came to Carter's from Circle Line of Gloucester, in whose green livery it remains.** David Harman

SOUTH EAST ENGLAND

Kentish Bus in Piccadilly on LT contract route 19. Mike Harris

London may so far have escaped deregulation – a treat which the politicians assure us is still to come – but that does not mean it has escaped competition. The process of route tendering started by London Regional Transport in 1985 introduced a number of independent operators to London's bus services. The remainder of the network was put on to contracts during 1993 as a prelude to deregulation.

London Buses Ltd (LBL), with around 5,000 vehicles, remains Britain's biggest bus company – but not for much longer, since the Government is about to undo 60 years of co-ordination by privatising London Buses before unleashing deregulation in the capital. Privatisation will in itself raise interesting questions, such as the future of the world-famous red livery which for many visitors to the capital is synonymous with London's buses.

London Buses operates through 10 subsidiaries which during the currency of this book are due to be sold:

CentreWest London Buses
East London Bus & Coach Co
Leaside Bus Co
London Central Bus Co
London General Transport Services
London Northern Bus Co
London United Busways
Metroline Travel
South East London & Kent Bus Co (Selkent)
South London Transport

Stanwell Buses (Westlink) was entering the private sector as we went to press.

Although London no longer places large orders for many hundreds of standardised buses as was done in the past, LBL has maintained a fleet renewal programme which has benefited a number of manufacturers whose presence in the capital would have been unimaginable just a few years ago: Dennis, Scania, Northern Counties, Plaxton, Wright – none were significant suppliers of buses to London in the mid-1980s but all are now.

There are of course reminders of the times when London pursued the holy grail of standardis-ation and manufacturers bent over backwards to cater for London's needs. The AEC-Park Royal Routemaster integral, that classic of British bus design, soldiers on in the 1990s, long past its sell-by date but still doing sterling service. Routemaster operation is now concentrated in central London, but is restricted to weekdays only. On Sundays all services are one-person-operated, although Routemasters still appear on London Coaches sightseeing work.

Around 700 Routemasters remain in service and many of the 30ft long RMLs are being extensively refurbished with major work on subframes and bodywork, including the fitment of fluorescent lighting and new interior trim. Most Routemasters now have Cummins or Iveco engines. Odd non-standard types can be seen on the 15 in central London, on which East London run RMCs and – just to confuse passengers who want to hop on the open rear platform at traffic lights – a pair of forward-entrance RMAs.

Two generations of buses which followed the Routemaster, the Swifts and the Fleetlines, have disappeared from regular service, leaving Leyland Titans and MCW Metrobuses as some of the oldest vehicles in the fleet after the Routemasters. The newest Routemaster is 25 years old; the oldest Titan is 15.

Titans are outnumbered by Metrobuses. There are around 950 Titans against over 1,400 Metro-buses, the two types together accounting for almost half the fleet. Titans are being withdrawn more quickly and a number have already been sold. Titans tend to operate mainly in east and south London, while Metrobuses are much more widely spread, although there are none in east or south-east London. The Titans and Metrobuses are highly standardised but there are two Metrobus IIs bought new which run for South London, and also second-hand Metrobuses from Greater Manchester, Yorkshire Rider and Busways Travel Services, all working from London Northern's Potters Bar garage.

Most of London's Routemasters have been refurbished in a programme that should enable them to last into the 21st Century. RML 2551 is seen in Oxford Street. Capital Transport

The acquired Metrobuses and Titans are all single-doorway buses; those bought new by London were of two-door layout, although a few have been converted to single door. Two of the ex-Yorkshire Rider Metrobuses are unusual in having Alexander bodywork, a combination rarely found outside Scotland.

London Transport was the only operator buying the Leyland Titan in the early 1980s and Leyland was anxious to convert London to Olympians. Three trial vehicles were delivered in 1984, and led to what was to be London's last big order for double-deckers: 260 Olympians with ECW bodies delivered in 1986-87. The last of these was also the last bus to be bodied by ECW. These Olympians are all based south of the Thames.

The only single-deckers from the good old days of standardisation (if that's what they were) are Leyland Nationals and the bulk of these are National 2s concentrated on the central London Red Arrow network operated by London General. The apparent success of the RML refurbishment programme has seen London Buses commission a small number of East Lancs Greenway rebuilds of Nationals. The first two entered service at the end of 1992 and 41 more commenced delivery in summer 1993.

There are 16 Nationals retained by LRT for use by operators who win contracts to run suburban mobility bus services. These are all accessible to travellers in wheelchairs. All of the Nationals bought new by London were short 10.3m or 10.6m models, but two second-hand 11.3m Nationals are included in the mobility fleet.

Full-size single-deckers have never really been popular in the capital since the ill-fated attempt to introduce suburban standee services in the late 1960s. They are still few in number. There are 11 Leyland Lynxes, including three acquired from Merthyr Tydfil Transport and re-registered with numbers transferred from Routemasters. The only regular Lynx operation is on London United's 190 and CentreWest's 607.

Optare's DAF-based Delta has had more success. Nine are running for Stanwell Buses and 26 for East London. Selkent has 16 Dennis Lances with Alexander bodywork which entered service in 1992. A further 31 Lances arrived with Metroline in 1993. Also new in 1993 are the first of a new generation of 68 low-floor buses, designed to be accessible to wheelchairs and baby carriages. The chassis are being built by Dennis (38) and Scania (30), and both types will be bodied by Wright of Ballymena. The Dennises are planned to run for Metroline, London United and CentreWest; the Scanias for East London and Leaside.

Northern Counties' first major success in the capital (unless you count wartime Guys) came with an order for 27 two-door bodies on Volvo Citybus chassis for London General for an LRT service which started at the beginning of 1990. Further orders have since increased the number to 39, although it has to be said that the high-frame layout of the Citybus is not ideally suited to dual-door buses.

Left: **London is Britain's biggest user of both Leyland's Olympian and Titan. A London Central ECW-bodied Olympian passes a Workington-built London Northern Titan at Victoria.** Peter Rowlands

Right: **Links from central London to Heathrow Airport are provided by London United's Airbus operation run by Metrobuses with 50 coach seats. These buses have large luggage pens – there are only nine seats in the lower saloon – and are accessible to travellers in wheelchairs.** Stephen Madden

Left: **London Buses' first East Lancs National Greenway was this 1992 rebuild of a 1981 National 2 for operation on Red Arrow services. More Greenways are being delivered.** Stephen Madden

Right: **The most striking single-deckers in use with London Buses are Optare Deltas running for East London in a silver and red livery. The Delta is built on a DAF SB220 chassis.** Mike Harris

Left: **Deliveries of Dennis's full-size Lance started in 1992 with 16 Alexander-bodied buses for Selkent painted in an attractive variation of the standard red theme.** Malcolm King

Right: **The first Volvo single-deck buses for London arrived in 1993. These were 13 B10Bs with Northern Counties Paladin bodies. They introduced the Clapham Omnibus marketing name to London General service 88.** Colin Lloyd

More Olympians have been ordered too. London United has 23 with Leyland bodies allocated to its Riverside Bus tendered operation. These were delivered in 1989. In 1992 a fleet of 40 Alexander-bodied Olympians entered service with Leaside. These were followed by 25 eye-catching Optare Spectras of which 24 were for London Central and were put on to service 3, running to Oxford Circus, at the start of 1993. The remaining Spectra, initially allocated to Metroline, joined the others at Camberwell later in 1993 and then started touring other LBL companies for them to evaluate the design.

Nine Alexander-bodied double-deck Scanias arrived with London Northern in 1989 for tendered work and another 20 similar buses were delivered to the East London company in 1991. These were followed by 42 Northern Counties bodied Scanias.

A noteworthy feature of most new deliveries is that they have been registered by bodybuilders rather than by London Buses. Thus there are new vehicles carrying registrations issued by Ballymena (Wright), Birmingham (Carlyle), Edinburgh (Alexander), Leeds (Optare), Sheffield (Reeve Burgess) and Hull (Plaxton). Wright-bodied buses with London registrations are a particular rarity.

Since the start of LRT tendering London's bus purchasing policy has been turned head over heels, with large numbers of minibuses and midibuses being purchased to oust conventional big buses. First came Optare CityPacers in 1986 and MCW Metroriders in 1987. The CityPacers have gone, as have a few of the early Metroriders. The Metroriders were followed by 285 Mercedes-Benz 811Ds of which there are 134 with Alexander bodies, 123 with Optare StarRider bodies and smaller numbers bodied by Carlyle, Reeve Burgess and Wright.

There are also 124 Renaults, bodied by Wright and Reeve Burgess. Despite the French name, these S50-series chassis come from nowhere more exotic than Dunstable. Since the demise of MCW and the re-emergence of the MetroRider as an Optare product, over 100 Optare-built MetroRiders have joined London Buses. There have also been orders for small numbers of other types, most notably Ivecos and CVE Omnis – the latter going to the Westlink unit. London's minibuses are scattered around the metropolis although there are concentrations of Wright-bodied Renaults and Alexander-bodied Mercs at CentreWest, while the Reeve Burgess-bodied Renaults are with East London.

There are 42 Northern Counties-bodied Scania N113s running for East London. They entered service in 1992. Colin Lloyd

At the same time as Scanias were being added to East London, 40 Olympians with Alexander bodies were being added to the Leaside fleet. Stephen Madden

Optare's stylish Spectra is still an uncommon sight. London Buses, with 25, is the biggest user of this DAF-based bus. They perform regularly on route 3. Tony Wilson

Few minibus services reach the central area. Frank E Thorpe of Kensington runs two Alexander-bodied Mercedes 709Ds in red livery on the LRT Stationlink service. This circular route, previously known as Carelink, can carry wheelchairs and is designed to assist disabled travellers who have to make cross-London connections. Three LRT-owned CityPacers are in reserve, having been rendered spare when London General lost the Carelink contract to Thorpe.

Minibuses based on light truck chassis have their limitations, and the success story in London in the 1990s has to be the Dennis Dart, a purpose-built midibus chassis. There are nearly 700 in service or on order – to make up 14 per cent of the fleet. The first buses had bodywork by Duple, or by Carlyle to Duple designs. Both of these builders have closed down and the two major suppliers of Dart bodies in the early 1990s have been Wright with the Handybus and Reeve Burgess/Plaxton with the Pointer. All of London Buses' subsidiaries have Darts.

A substantial fleet of open-top Routemasters still runs in central London. These are operated by London Coaches which was until 1992 a part of the London Buses organisation. It is now owned by its managers and its double-deck fleet also includes two Dennis Dominators with Northern Counties bodies which were purchased for evaluation by London Buses in 1984. They joined London Coaches in 1991. London Coaches runs 45 DAF coaches and in 1992 added 10 DAF SB220 buses to its fleet to operate the LRT tendered 726 from Heathrow to Dartford, a one-time Green Line route. The SB220s have Ikarus bodies.

The London sightseeing business is highly competitive. London Coaches have already been mentioned and still run Routemasters. Other operators using Routemasters on tours are Blue Triangle and Big Bus Co. Both these companies also run ex-London DMSs, for many years virtually a standard for sightseeing (even though London Transport couldn't get them to work on regular services) and other DMS operators include London Sightseeing Tours and Cityrama. The latter also runs an open-top Optare-bodied Olympian which was a cancelled closed-top bus originally intended for Maidstone Boro'line.

London Buses is the biggest user of the Dennis Dart chassis, on which is mounted a variety of bodywork. A Carlyle-bodied bus crosses Hammersmith Bridge. Stephen Madden

London Coaches was the first part of London Buses Ltd to be privatised. Among the vehicles involved in the sale were the Sightseeing Tour Routemasters, some of which have been converted to convertible open-toppers. Geoff Rixon

London Coaches have 10 DAF SB220s wth Hungarian-built Ikarus bodies which are allocated to the Heathrow-Dartford Expresslink service, a remnant of the disappearing Green Line network. Malcolm King

LRT tendering has brought colour to the capital's streets – Grey-Green, Kentish Bus and London & Country all penetrate the heart of the West End. Move to the suburbs and a host of large and small operators are providing services on LRT's behalf.

Grey-Green operates the prestigious 24 from Pimlico through Parliament Square and Trafalgar Square to Hampstead, using F-registered Alexander-bodied Citybuses in a striking livery designed by Best Impressions. The company also runs a number of services in north, north-east and east London with an assortment of vehicles which include ex-South Yorkshire and Newport Metrobuses and ex-County Bus & Coach Olympians with Northern Counties bodies. Single-deckers bought new include Leyland Lynxes, Ikarus-bodied DAF SB220s and Volvo Citybuses with 41-seat East Lancs bodies. The last-named have a short rear overhang and are used on the 210 from Finsbury Park to Brent Cross.

As the emphasis of Grey-Green's operation has switched from coaches to buses, the company has cut the costs of expanding its bus fleet by having B-registered Volvo coaches rebodied as buses by East Lancs – both as single-deckers and as oddly-proportioned double-deckers which have retained the long 6.1m wheelbase of the 12m B10M coach, but with a noticeably reduced rear overhang. These are used on the 141 from Moorgate to Wood Green. Potters Bar, served by Ikarus-bodied DAFs, is the northernmost reach of Grey Green's operations which have grown in just seven years to 125 buses.

Kentish Bus reaches Oxford Circus (on the 55 from Clapton) and has a significant presence in inner east London. These routes are entrusted to a batch of 43 Northern Counties-bodied Olympians delivered in 1990. In 1993 Kentish Bus became the first private sector operator to take over a contract for a Routemaster-operated LRT route, for which it uses buses supplied by LRT but operated in Kentish Bus livery.

Not surprisingly, Kentish Bus is strongest on LRT routes in the south-east which border on its own operating territory in north-west Kent. Its position in the Bexley and Woolwich areas was strengthened at the start of 1992 when it took over the contracts previously operated by Maidstone Boro'line, shortly before the latter's collapse. This brought an odd mixture of buses into the fleet – Alexander-bodied Volvo Citybuses and Scanias, Olympians with bodies by Optare and Northern Counties, and Leyland Lynxes. Most have been repainted from Boro'line's attractive blue, yellow and grey into Kentish Bus cream and maroon.

Grey-Green has covered its growing number of London tendered services by having Volvo B10M coaches rebodied by East Lancs. The EL2000 single-deck body sits comfortably on the B10M coach chassis while the double-deck rebodies look a shade ungainly.
Malcolm King/Roy Waterhouse

Kentish Bus has added East Lancs National Greenways to its fleet. They carry a modified livery with a green band at wheelarch level.
Tony Wilson

Kentish Bus, owned by Proudmutual since privatisation in 1988, was formed in 1987 and had previously been London Country South East, an NBC subsidiary. Proudmutual also owns Northumbria Motor Services and is based in Newcastle-on-Tyne, which is why most new Kentish Bus vehicles have Newcastle registrations. There is some interchange of buses between fleets, with Northumbria Olympians having been transferred south to cover LRT contracts won by Kentish Bus. In August 1993, Kentish Bus were awarded nine more routes in south-east London for operation during the following winter. About 40 minibuses and ten double deckers will be needed, making Kentish Bus the largest LT contractor after London Buses, with almost 200 buses allocated to LT routes.

In Kent the company operates vehicles inherited from London Country – mainly B-series Nationals and Roe-bodied Atlanteans. Some East Lancs National Greenway rebuilds were introduced in 1992. Interesting small buses operate around Gravesend in the shape of 16 tri-axle Peugeot-Talbot Pullmans – the biggest fleet of the type in the South East.

Another Pullman operator in the area is Transcity of Sidcup, which uses them on LRT service B15 around Bexleyheath. Transcity, primarily a minibus operator, took a move towards the big league in 1992 with eight Plaxton-bodied Darts for the 286 which runs from Greenwich to Eltham. The company's dark green livery does nothing for the neat lines of the Pointer – or for any other buses in its fleet. Transcity also operates services in Kent.

Metrobus of Orpington, an established bus operator albeit on a small scale, has grown since 1986 with a mixture of LRT tendered work and new commercial services. Its presence is strongest around Bromley but it runs as far west as Croydon (on three different services). There are 15 Leyland-bodied Olympians bought new between 1988 and 1992 as well as 10 Roe-bodied ones which came from the West Yorkshire PTE in 1987. There is one long-wheelbase ECW-bodied Olympian coach, bought from Thamesway in 1991. Older double-deckers are ex-London Fleetlines. The single-deck fleet comprises new Dennis Darts with Plaxton Pointer bodies and an assortment of Leyland Lynxes – one bought new, two from Miller of Cambridge and three from Merthyr Tydfil.

A small number of former Maidstone Boro'line buses are still running in Boro'line colours but with Kentish Bus fleetnames. An Alexander-bodied Volvo Citybus drives through Woolwich. Stewart J Brown

The newest vehicles running for Metrobus of Orpington are Plaxton-bodied Darts. They are 8.5m long models with a short bay in mid-wheelbase. Malcolm King

Transcity have eight Dennis Darts with Plaxton bodies. They operate between Greenwich and Eltham. Malcolm King

North of the Thames, what was London Country North East has undergone significant changes. LCNE was privatised in 1988, being sold to the AJS Group. AJS split the company in two in 1989, with County Bus & Coach based at Harlow and Sovereign Bus & Coach at Stevenage. Sovereign is now part of Blazefield Holdings, successors to AJS, while AJS sold County to the Lynton Travel Group in 1990.

County Bus & Coach does not appear as a fleetname. The buses based in Grays trade as ThameSide, those in Harlow as TownLink and those at Ware as LeaValley. A minority of the buses in the fleet – Atlanteans, Olympians and Nationals – are of obvious London Country descent, as are ECW-bodied Tigers once considered fit for Green Line service but now demoted to bus work. Expansion, primarily on LT tenders in east and north-east London, has seen the acquisition of Dennis Darts, bodied by Plaxton and by Wright, Leyland Lynxes, and of batches of Mercedes minibuses. The Mercedes are used mainly in the Walthamstow area; the Lynxes run on the 66 between Romford and Leytonstone.

County competes in Harlow with the Buzz Co-operative, set up in 1988 by former LCNE employees with nine new Reeve Burgess-bodied Mercedes. These are still operated, along with a pair of ex-demonstration Optare StarRiders.

A small operator to have gained routes through tendering by Essex county council is West's of Woodford Green, running in Loughton, Ongar and Chingford. The second-hand Nationals which were used to introduce bus services in 1986 have gone, and West's now run nine MCW Metroriders, a Leyland Swift, two Optare Deltas and four Dennis Darts with Wright bodies. The Darts have J- and K-prefixed BUS registrations.

Services operated by Harris Bus of Grays meet those of County Bus & Coach. Harris's services run mainly in the Grays and Tilbury areas and out to the Lakeside shopping centre at West Thurrock (also served by County and Capital Citybus). The Harris fleet includes Volvo B9Ms with 38-seat Plaxton bus bodies, MCW Metroriders, Leyland Swifts and a pair of Scania N113s with Alexander R-type bodies. Ex-Northampton Alexander-bodied VRTs run services to the huge Lakeside shopping centre. Harris Bus uses a blue and cream livery inspired by a pair of former London Transport DMSs acquired from West Midlands PTE in 1986.

Double-deckers play an increasingly small part in the County Bus & Coach business, modernisation of the fleet largely being undertaken with single deckers and minibuses. A Dennis Dart is seen at Waltham Cross. Colin Lloyd

West's of Woodford Green is the only small operator in the south-east to run Dennis Darts with Wright Handybus bodies. The company has two, both 40-seat 9.8m-long models. Malcolm King

The Harris fleet in Grays includes some ex-Northampton VRTs with Alexander bodies. Malcolm King

Some local services in the Romford area are provided by Blue Triangle using Leyland Nationals. The Blue Triangle name is a reference to the badge used by AEC, and there are AECs in the fleet in the shape of two RTs and an RF, used on summer Sunday services sponsored by Essex county council, and an RCL and an RMA, used on sightseeing.

The north-east of London is also served by Basildon-based Thamesway, part of the Badgerline group. Some of Thamesway's LRT contracts were initially won by its predecessor, Eastern National. Thamesway contracts are generally operated by new buses bought specifically for tendered operation. Reeve Burgess-bodied Mercedes (the standard Badgerline group mini) are used on minibus routes and 17 Dennis Darts were purchased in 1992 for the 214 running from Parliament Hill Fields to Liverpool Street, a service which brought Thamesway into central London for the first time.

The Darts have Plaxton Pointer bodies with a large badger logo on the side. Four H-registered Leyland-bodied Olympians are allocated to the 307 which runs through Enfield from Barnet to Brimsdown, where they operate alongside older ECW-bodied Olympians.

The other major operator in east and north-east London is Capital Citybus, the successor to the operating arm of the long-established Ensign Bus dealership. Ensign started running on LRT contracted services in 1986 and expanded in 1989 with the acquisition from Stagecoach Holdings of East Midland Motor Services' Frontrunner South East operations. The business was taken over by CNT of Hong Kong, owners of Hong Kong Citybus, at the end of 1990. Since then the livery has been changed from blue and silver to yellow with red relief – although a number of buses still carry the old colours.

Capital Citybus now runs around 200 vehicles, of which around 150 are needed for LT contract services, making it one of the biggest of LT's private sector contractors. These comprise a mixture of new and modern second-hand buses. The company is strongest in the Romford and Walthamstow areas. The closest it gets to central London is Smithfield, on the 153 from Finsbury Park.

The fleet is one of the most varied serving London. There are Metrobuses, both new (in 1988) and secondhand. There are Dennis Dominators and Leyland Olympians, again both new and secondhand. The new Olympians have bodies by Alexander (1989), Leyland (1991) and Northern Counties (1991/2). The second-hand Olympians came from Highland Scottish in 1992 following that company's retrenchment after a bitter battle with Stagecoach in Inverness.

Since 1992 Capital Citybus has also run minibuses on tendered services with 20 Plaxton-bodied Mercedes 811Ds, 10 Optare MetroRiders and three Alexander-bodied Mercs. Conventional single-deckers in the fleet are seven Leyland Nationals and two K-series Scania high-capacity buses purchased from Kettlewells of Retford in 1992 to replace lowheight Fleetlines. The single-deckers (and a few VRTs) are needed to negotiate a low bridge at Cranham.

Capital Citybus's newest Olympians have an unusual line in personalised registrations. All start K888 (888 being a lucky number to the Chinese) and the registration letters are the initials of various company directors.

Docklands Transit re-appeared in March 1993 when it won tenders for LT minibus contracts in east London. These are run by Carlyle-bodied Mercedes transferred from Transit Holdings' Portsmouth operations. In its previous incarnation Docklands Transit had tried unsuccessfully to run commercial services in east London, pulling out in November 1990 after operating for 18 months.

Although no longer involved in bus operation, Ensign Bus still has a presence on the capital's streets with its London Pride sightseeing tours.

Full-sized single-deckers play a small part in the Capital Citybus fleet. Three Scanias were purchased from Kettlewell of Retford in 1992 to replace lowheight double-deckers and two remain. This is a 1987 K92 with East Lancs body. Tony Wilson

Northern Counties unveiled its new Palatine II body in 1993 with the first example being built for Capital Citybus on a Leyland Olympian chassis. It has distinctive deep windscreens and no rear lower deck window. Note the exterior lights above the entrance which are used to illuminate the kerb for passengers boarding or alighting after dark. Malcolm King

Docklands Transit re-appeared in 1993 running on London Transport tendered services in the Barking area. It uses Carlyle-bodied Mercedes transferred from associated Transit Holdings' operations in Portsmouth. Colin Lloyd

Moving back to outer London, Sovereign Bus & Coach operates mainly around Stevenage and St Albans with subsidiary Sovereign Buses (Harrow) running almost 30 Mercedes-Benz minibuses on LRT contracts in the Harrow area. Sovereign, part of Blazefield Holdings, has a big bus fleet which is a pale shadow of what London Country once was. There is a collection of largely second-hand Mark 1 Nationals, a trio of VRTs for school services and four ex-London Country Olympians. The only really modern big buses are 14 Leyland Lynxes.

The minibus fleet is a little more modern with 14 MCW Metroriders acquired from Jubilee of Stevenage in 1989 and a number of Mercedes, mostly with Reeve Burgess Beaver bodies. The Welwyn-Hatfield Line fleetname is carried by around a dozen minibuses and two Nationals. Welwyn-Hatfield was acquired in 1990.

Sovereign cut back its operations in Stevenage in 1990 when it sold 42 buses to Luton & District.

Indeed, moving anti-clockwise round London, Luton & District is the next major operator encountered. The company was formed in 1986 as NBC was splitting some of its bigger subsidiaries. Luton & District took over the southern part of what had been United Counties. It was sold to a management-led employee buy-out in 1987 and a few months later, at the start of 1988, it consolidated its position in Aylesbury with the purchase of Red Rover. However its biggest single expansion came in 1990 when it took over London Country North West from its management, which had in turn bought the company from NBC in 1987.

To the outsider there are in effect two Luton & District companies. The former LCNW operations retain that company's attractive green and grey livery and London-inspired fleet numbering system with a range of local names – Chiltern Bus, Hemel Bus and Watford Bus (the latter name having previously been used by Luckett, who now trade only as Lucky Bus). There was also a Slough Bus, but that part of the old LCNW business was sold to Q-Drive in early 1993. The original L&D fleet runs in cream and red – and the layout of the colours is being changed to copy that used by LCNW – with Aylesbury Bus, Dunstable Bus, Hitchin Bus, Luton Bus, Red Rover and Stevenage Bus fleetnames, and uses a straightforward sequential numbering system. Confused? You might well be. On top of all this, minibuses in what might be called L&D's red bus territory carry Hoppanstopper fleetnames on a white-based livery.

Looking firstly at the green buses there are a number of one-time London Country vehicles still around, most noticeably B-series Leyland Nationals and a few Roe-bodied Atlanteans and ECW-bodied Olympians. New Olympians with Leyland bodies were added to the fleet before L&D took over, along with four 12-month-old Northern Counties-bodied Olympians purchased from Ensign Bus. Other pre-L&D purchases included 30 MCW Metroriders in 1988 and eight Carlyle-bodied Dennis Darts. The Olympians and Darts were purchased for LT tendered work.

Left and below: **Most of Sovereign's single-deckers are Leyland Nationals. In the St Albans area, some trade under the name Blazefield Buses.**
Stewart Brown/Malcolm King

Bottom: **Luton & District has retained London Country North West's green and grey livery for buses running in what was LCNW territory. Buses from its Watford garage originally carried the fleetname Watford-wide but this is being changed to Watford Bus. This is one of 30 MetroRiders in the fleet.**
Keith Wood

Since L&D has taken over, the green bus fleet has received a varied selection of Bristol VRTs from Cambus (now withdrawn) and from Lincoln City Transport — in which L&D had, through its shareholding in Derby City Transport, a very indirect interest until early 1993. Most of the VRTs have, inevitably, ECW bodies but there are a few bodied by East Lancs and by Alexander. The Alexander-bodied buses are comparatively unusual long-wheelbase VRT/LL models and were new to Tayside.

The red L&D fleet includes standard NBC Nationals, VRTs and Olympians — either inherited from United Counties or bought secondhand. There are a few ex-Sovereign buses: Olympians and Lynxes standing out. New purchases since privatisation have been 25 Alexander-bodied Olympians in 1988-90, four Wadham Stringer-bodied Leyland Swifts and nine Leyland Lynxes, three of which carry Luton Flyer livery for a service linking Luton station and Luton airport. The minibus fleet is made up largely of Ivecos, but in 1992 nine Peugeot-Talbot Pullmans were acquired from East Midland and are still running in Stagecoach livery. These had been new to Zippy, United Transport's short-lived Preston adventure.

Small operators in the Luton area include Seamarks running Optare Deltas on contracted services, primarily for Hertfordshire county council. Reg's Coaches link Hertford and Hatfield. Five buses are owned — three G-registered Dennis Darts and two J-registered Mercedes 709Ds.

What were formerly private services for students at Hatfield Polytechnic have since early 1993 been transformed into commercial routes in the Hatfield, St Albans and Watford areas trading as Universitybus and running two Carlyle-bodied Darts and four ex-London Buses Nationals in an all-white livery.

In the Luton, Dunstable, St Albans and Borehamwood areas Luton & District faces competition from Challenger Transport running a fleet of two dozen Sherpa minibuses.

The original Luton & District fleet uses a red and cream livery which is now being modified and applied in the same style as the green and grey used on former LCNW operations. An ECW-bodied VRT is seen in Luton. R Whitehead

Buffalo of Flitwick have obtained some Hertfordshire county council contract work around Watford and have added two of these Darts to the fleet. Mike Harris

Seen at the same location, Watford Junction station, is a Dormobile Routemaker bodied Mercedes in the fleet of Red Rose of Aylesbury. Tony Wilson

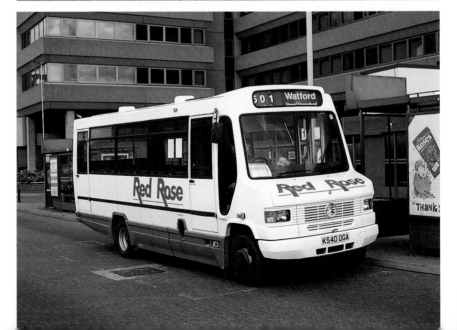

Seamarks was an early customer for Optare Deltas, and was also the first company in southern England to add the smaller MAN-based Vecta to its fleet. The Vecta is Optare's original demonstrator, built in 1991 and bought by Seamarks in 1992. Malcolm King

Stuart Palmer Travel of Dunstable has expanded gradually and in 1993 started running to Luton. The fleet is composed mainly of ex-London Fleetlines, of which it has 13. Colin Lloyd

Reg's Coaches of Hertford run in the Hertford, Stevenage and Welwyn Garden City areas, with Dennis Darts as their front-line buses. Carlyle completed the body on this example. Malcolm King

There are a number of smaller operators running LT contracted routes in outer north-west London. Harrow, served by London Buses, Luton & District and Sovereign, is also reached by BTS with Northern Counties-bodied Olympians on the 114 which connects Ruislip and Mill Hill. BTS also operate between Borehamwood and Colindale (the 292) using Alexander-bodied Scania N113s and in 1993 were awarded the contract for operation of RML route 13 into central London. The initials stand for Borehamwood Travel Services. Atlas Bus runs two routes, the 112 from Ealing Broadway to Wood Green, operated since 1988 with Leyland Lynxes, and the 107 from Edgware to New Barnet Station, run since 1989 with Northern Counties-bodied Olympians.

R&I is another coach operator to have taken advantage of LRT tendering. It runs from Golders Green to Finchley Road Station (the 268) and Hampstead (the H2), and the C11 and C12 which run from Archway to Brent Cross and from Finchley Road Station to King's Cross. The C11 and C12 are operated with 14 Carlyle-bodied Dennis Darts named after castles from Inverness in the north to Dover in the south. Iveco minis cover the H2 and new Plaxton-bodied Darts are used on the 268.

Scorpio runs between Ruislip Station and Northolt, using a second-hand Peugeot-Talbot Pullman and an ex-Lothian Leyland Cub.

London Buslines was started in 1985 by Len Wright, previously well-known for running high-specification sleeper coaches for top pop groups. The first route to be won under LRT's tendering procedure was the 81 from Hounslow to Slough, which was started with ex-London DMS-type Fleetlines, but is now operated by six Leyland Lynxes bought new in 1986. London Buslines operates 50 buses on routes which reach north to Edgware and south to Richmond. There are two batches of Olympians with bodywork by Alexander and Northern Counties and 10 Mercedes minis with Reeve Burgess/Plaxton Beaver bodies.

The London Buslines operation runs as far out as Slough. Q-Drive, the holding company for London Buslines, took over the Slough Bus operation of Luton & District in February 1993. This was amalgamated with the Berks Bucks Bus Co which was renamed Q-Drive Buses, but retained The Bee Line as a trading name. Slough's main claim to fame is the dingiest bus station in Britain – a dark, cavernous hole which is best avoided.

Armchair Passenger Transport runs two LT services in west London – the 65 from Ealing to Kingston, and the 260 between Shepherds Bush and North Finchley. These are operated by Leyland Olympians – G-registered Alexander-bodied buses on the 260, and H-registered Leyland-bodied examples on the 65. Half a dozen Atlanteans are held as spares. Armchair also runs Mercedes minibuses on routes in the Sunbury and Walton areas. A smaller coach operator, AML Coaches, has two ex-London Buses Titans and an SM-class AEC Swift in use on routes around Molesey and Ashford.

The BTS fleet includes new Scania and Leyland double-deckers. The latter are Olympians with Northern Counties bodies. All are used on tendered services. Stewart J Brown

Below: A London Buslines Lynx on route 81, one of the first routes to be put out to tender by LRT. In the background is the dingy Slough bus station. Gerald Mead

Bottom: Six one-time South Yorkshire Atlanteans provide back-up on Armchair contracts for routes 65 and 260. The buses date from 1978/9. G A Rixon

Above: **Westlink was set up as a low-cost unit of London Buses in response to the loss of routes to other operators under LRT tendering. In early 1993 its stock of Titans was replaced by newer ones in advance of privatisation.** G A Rixon

Below: **AML Coaches has recently started running tendered services in south west Middlesex and Surrey using ex-London Buses' Titans. Still carrying its LBL fleet number, T60 is seen at West Molesey.** G A Rixon

The main operator in outer south-west London and Surrey is London & Country, based in Reigate. This is the former London Country South West operation, purchased from NBC by Drawlane in 1988. The London & Country trading name was adopted in 1989 and this is another fleet to have benefited from a Best Impressions livery. The west Surrey operations of Alder Valley were acquired at the end of 1990 and are now run by Guildford & West Surrey Buses. To further complicate things, London & Country runs the Gem Fairtax operation in Crawley and the Tellings Golden Miller LT tendered bus operation, TGM Buses.

London & Country has had considerable successes in securing LT tenders and some of these are run from a modern garage at Beddington, near Croydon. There are two fleet numbering systems in use, which conveniently differentiate buses from the NBC era from those bought new by the company since its takeover by Drawlane. However, lest this appear too straightforward, some second-hand purchases have old-style LCSW fleet numbers with prefix letters such as LNB (Long National Bus). The ghost of London Transport's Country Area lives on.

The older vehicles in this fleet, as in the other ex-London Country companies, are Atlanteans, Olympians and Nationals. The Alder Valley takeover added more Nationals and assorted minibuses to the fleet. But the impressive fact about London & Country has been its vast intake of new buses, largely for operation in London. Since 1989 the company has acquired 74 Volvo Citybuses, nine Dennis Dominators, ten Dennis Falcons, six Leyland Lynxes and nine Renault S56s. It also received the first East Lancs National Greenway, and took 12 more in late 1992 for LT work.

TGM Buses, originally a Midland Fox company but now more logically associated with London & Country (both are British Bus subsidiaries), runs six ageing Nationals and six National Greenway conversions in a blue and white livery on LT services 116 and 117 from Brentford to Bedfont Green and Staines. The Gem Fairtax fleet in Crawley includes four Nationals taken over from short-lived Panther Buses in 1991.

Epsom Buses, part of the old-established Epsom Coaches company, has routes into Kingston, Croydon and Leatherhead. Its fleet includes four Darts, four Plaxton bodied Bedfords and nine assorted Mercedes minibuses.

London & Country invested heavily in new buses in the late 1980s. These included 21 Northern Counties-bodied Volvo Citybuses. Stephen Madden

Epsom Buses runs a number of services based on its home town. Two Dennis Darts in its smart fleet are seen in Leatherhead. Malcolm King

Gem Fairtax is part of London & Country, running Leyland Nationals in Crawley. This is an ex-London bus. Malcolm King

Guildford has a long history of private sector bus operation and there are three significant small businesses serving the cathedral city, all established in the 1920s. Blue Saloon is the smallest and its main operation is a local Hoppa-Shoppa service using ECW-bodied Bristol LHs. Safeguard has a varied fleet including Duple bodied Leopards and Tigers, Lynxes and Dennis Darts.

Tillingbourne Bus Co, based in Cranleigh, has the most widespread operations, running not only in Guildford but in a number of nearby towns including Aldershot and Farnborough, and with separate operations as far south as Redhill and Horsham. There are 20 minibuses in the fleet – Mercedes and Ivecos with a variety of bodies – but the real interest is in the big buses. These include such delights as Dennis Dorchesters with Wadham Stringer bodies, bought new in 1983, Bedford YMTs with Plaxton bus bodies, second-hand Bedford YMP-S models with rare Lex Maxeta bodywork and an E-registered Volvo B10M rebodied in 1992 by Northern Counties with its new Paladin body.

Alder Valley's history is complex. Go back 20 years and it was created by NBC as a fusion of Aldershot & District (a former BET company) and Thames Valley (an ex-Tilling company). The name is a combination of the two constituent companies' names – and not a reference to some mythical river valley. Those were the days when big was beautiful. When big ceased to be beautiful and privatisation was looming, the company was split in two at the start of 1986 with the remarkably original names of Alder Valley South and Alder Valley North and operating territories not dissimilar to those of 15 years earlier. Alder Valley South was sold by NBC in 1987 to the short-lived Frontsource organisation. Alder Valley North was renamed the Berks Bucks Bus Co in 1987 and thankfully eschewed this title in favour of The Bee Line as its trading name. It was bought by Q-Drive in 1987. Q-Drive then bought Alder Valley South in 1988 – giving it ownership of both the former Alder Valley operations – and dropped South from the title in 1989.

There then followed a period of retrenchment, which saw part of Alder Valley being sold to London & Country. That is now Guildford & West Surrey Buses. In October 1992 the rest of the company was sold to Stagecoach South, trading as Stagecoach Hants & Surrey.

Guildford & West Surrey's mixed fleet has adopted a new livery and shortened fleetname in 1993, seen on one of the company's Nationals. G A Rixon

The newer vehicles in Safeguard's fleet include Leyland Lynxes and – the newest – Pointer-bodied Darts. Malcolm King

A rare type in the Tillingbourne fleet is the Bedford YMP-S with Lex Maxeta body. Alder Valley bought two in 1985 and both are now with Tillingbourne.

Reading Transport expanded its fleet and its operating territory by taking over the Reading and Newbury operations of Bee Line in 1992. Operations in Reading operate as Reading Buses while those in Newbury trade as Newbury Buses – both in a mainly cream and maroon livery with a turquoise relief band for the former and a green relief band for the latter. The most impressive buses in the Reading-based fleet are a trio of Optare Spectras. Reading was the first operator to receive a Spectra and its first was the star of the 1991 Bus & Coach Show. The Spectra is built on a DAF DB250 chassis which is an extensive reworking of the MCW Metrobus underframe.

Reading runs Metrobuses too, with over 50 bought new plus fifteen 1987 models bought from London Buses in 1991 after London lost the contract from LRT to run the Harrow Buses network. Leyland buses have never played a major part in Reading's fleet but it does have 12 integral Titans, the only ones supplied to a municipal fleet, and 15 Olympians with bodywork by ECW and Optare. The takeover of Bee Line has added ECW-bodied VRTs to this variety. Single-deckers bought new are 10 Optare Deltas and eight MAN/Vectas. These have been joined in Reading by a few ex-Bee Line Nationals.

Services in Newbury are provided mainly by Nationals and minibuses, including Optare StarRiders. Most of the big buses are still in Bee Line yellow with the addition of Newbury Buses fleetnames, but all the minibuses have been repainted. Reading Transport runs express services to London with a mixture of double- and single-deck coaches. The former are Olympians, the latter are a mix of Scanias, DAFs and the occasional Duple 425 Integral. Coaches have been given an unusual shaded blue livery.

Chiltern Queens, based in Oxfordshire, operates into Reading and also runs a local service in Henley. There are four AEC Reliances with bus bodies still in use, including one acquired from the Ministry of Defence. The company also runs Leopards – both buses and coaches – and has recently added two Mercedes minis to its fleet. Tappin of Wallingford operates a tendered service in Reading using a Plaxton-bodied Dennis Dart in the distinctive orange and black colours used on the company's coaches.

Reading was the first operator to buy Optare Spectras and now runs three. The new-style Spectra makes a sharp contrast with the ex-Berks Bucks Bus Company Bristol VRT just visible in the background. Malcolm King

After buying Deltas and Spectras, Reading ordered Optare Vectas. This one is in the Newbury Buses fleet. Malcolm King

AEC Reliance buses are becoming increasingly rare. Chiltern Queens runs four, including this Plaxton-bodied example which was bought new in 1972, although a Mercedes minibus is often used on the company's Reading route. Malcolm King

North of Reading services are provided by City of Oxford Motor Services which trades as the Oxford Bus Company and the Wycombe Bus Company. Both reach Reading. The history of the Oxford operation can be traced back to tramway days. More recently it was privatised in a management buy-out from NBC in 1987. Services in Oxford are provided mainly by VRTs, Titans and Olympians, alongside green MCW and Optare MetroRiders. The Optares were bought in 1990 to introduce services in Exeter, retaliating against Exeter-based Transit Holdings' competition in Oxford, but now look unlikely ever to head south west.

The older Olympians are standard NBC buses, but unusual in being of dual-door layout. To these the privatised Oxford Bus Company has added four ex-Atomic Energy Authority buses, and 11 new Olympians with Alexander lowheight bodies which again are unusual in being of two-door layout. These have double-curvature BET screens, offered by Alexander in the interests of parts commonality with ECW-bodied buses. The most interesting Olympian is a far-travelled demonstrator which was built in 1980 and shipped to Singapore. It joined the Oxford fleet in 1987 and has an Alexander body.

Unusually for a major operator, Oxford has extended the lives of ageing Leyland Leopard coaches by having them rebodied as buses by Willowbrook. Six are in use.

Much of the High Wycombe fleet, taken over from the Bee Line in 1990, has now been repainted in Oxford's red and white livery. The takeover introduced Leyland Nationals to the one NBC fleet which had pointedly avoided the type for the duration of its production life. The Bee Line takeover also introduced Leyland Lynxes to the fleet. VRTs dominate the High Wycombe operation and include two bought from Mayne of Manchester. At High Wycombe it is possible to see buses still in The Bee Line's yellow colours belonging to two different operators – City of Oxford and Reading Buses.

Motts of Aylesbury, trading as Yellow Bus, serve High Wycombe, Aylesbury and Oxford. The fleet includes six ex-South Yorkshire Metrobuses, five ex-London DMS Fleetlines and several Leopard dual-purpose vehicles.

Competition in Oxford comes from Thames Transit, part of Transit Holdings. Thames Transit introduced a fleet of 16-seat Mellor-bodied Ford Transits to Oxford in 1987, sparking off a major bus war. These are still running, and have been joined by bigger Mercedes-Benz 709Ds which operate on longer-distance services, reaching out to Witney, Chipping Norton, Abingdon, Wantage and Didcot. A fleet of dual-door Iveco minibuses has entered service in Oxford. They have Mellor bodies and are Britain's first small buses to feature two doors. The company also operates coaches from Oxford to London under the Oxford Tube name. The newest are Ikarus-bodied Volvo B10Ms. This competes with City of Oxford's Citylink 190, which uses a mixture of DAFs and Dennis Javelins with automatic gearboxes and Plaxton Premiere bodies.

Above left: City of Oxford Motor Services now trades under the more manageable Oxford Bus Company title. Most of its double-deckers are of dual-door layout and these include 11 Alexander-bodied Leyland Olympians bought since privatisation. Like most City of Oxford double-deckers they have Gardner engines. K R Crawley

Above right: **City of Oxford trades as the Wycombe Bus Company in High Wycombe. This VRT was one of the 51 buses taken over from the Berks Bucks Bus Company in 1990 when City of Oxford purchased its Wycombe operations.** Graham Jones

Below: **Yellow Bus operates a mixture of vehicles in the Aylesbury, Oxford, Reading and High Wycombe areas. These include ex-South Yorkshire MCW Metrobuses.** K R Crawley

With parts of The Bee Line having been sold to Reading and Oxford, the remaining operations are from one depot, at Bracknell. Its bus fleet, which reaches as far north-east as Slough and Windsor, is made up mainly of Leyland Nationals, Bristol VRTs and Mercedes-Benz minibuses. The only new buses added since privatisation have been five Northern Counties-bodied Olympians which are still in the fleet and 10 Optare StarRiders which passed to Reading Transport. Seven Berkhof-bodied Scania K113 coaches, new in 1991, are used on the Reading to Heathrow Railair Link.

Windsor, where London & Country and The Bee Line meet, is still served by White Bus Services with ageing Bedford buses in an operation which looks as though it has been untouched by the changes which have taken place around it.

Stagecoach South, with just over 400 buses, is the biggest operator south of London with an operating area embracing parts of Hampshire, Surrey, East Sussex and West Sussex. It has depots strung across these counties, from Winchester in the west to Rye in the east. Its headquarters are at Lewes.

Stagecoach South was born of Hampshire Bus and Southdown Motor Services. Hampshire Bus, still a trading name in the Andover, Basingstoke and Winchester areas, was Stagecoach's first venture south of the Scottish border and was purchased from NBC in April 1987. Southdown was privatised in October of that year, being bought by its management who then sold it to Stagecoach in 1989. To this Stagecoach added Portsmouth Citybus, which attracted the wrath of the Department of Trade & Industry who effectively forced a demerger, and Hastings & District, another former NBC management buy-out company.

Standard Stagecoach long-wheelbase 85-seat Olympians – 40 in all – were delivered between 1989 and 1992 and run for Hampshire Bus and the two new divisions created out of what was Southdown – South Coast Buses and Sussex Coastline Buses. The biggest influx of new buses for the south of England since deregulation came with no fewer than 80 Alexander-bodied Dennis Darts delivered to Stagecoach South in 1992. These are spread across the company's operations.

Operations by The Bee Line are now concentrated on Bracknell, Maidenhead and Slough. The only double-deckers bought new since privatisation in 1987 have been five Northern Counties-bodied Olympians. Two stand in Bracknell bus station. Peter Rowlands

Most of The Bee Line's single-deck buses are Mark I Leyland Nationals. This one was inherited from Alder Valley when The Bee Line was set up in 1986. Mike Harris

The last new buses bought by Southdown before the Stagecoach takeover were 12 Volvo Citybuses with Northern Counties bodies. Three are now with Fife Scottish, but the remaining nine are still with Stagecoach South. Stewart J Brown

The rest of the Stagecoach South fleet is made up mainly of buses acquired from its constituents. These are primarily Nationals and VRTs which originated with Hampshire Bus and Southdown, although there are some odd buses of greater interest such as Volvo Citybuses with Northern Counties bodies, which were Southdown's last new buses before the Stagecoach takeover, and National 2s from Portsmouth Citybus (most of which are in Hastings). There are a couple of former Eastbourne Atlanteans – the only ones in the fleet – which have survived from the absorption of Hastings Top Line, a short-lived joint operation set up by Southdown and Eastbourne Buses in 1987. The Atlanteans have remained in Hastings, which also hosts two Bristol REs.

The Hastings & District company was previously part of Maidstone & District and many of the VRTs now running with South Coast Buses betray their M&D ancestry by their Kent registrations. One odd VRT which came from M&D is an East Lancs-bodied bus new to the South Yorkshire PTE. There are few opportunities to play jokes with fleet numbers – but one of South Coast Buses' Tiger coaches is numbered 1066, one of the few dates in English history which all schoolboys know. A number of MCW Metrorider minibuses and Leyland coaches carry reversed DCD registrations from withdrawn Southdown PD3 Titans. Two of these distinctive buses with fully-fronted Northern Counties open-top bodywork survive, still in Southdown green. There is also an ex-East Kent Regent V, carrying Hastings & District names on a blue and yellow livery.

Alder Valley's contribution was made up mainly of Nationals, VRTs and Renault and Iveco minibuses which operate from garages in Aldershot and Hindhead. Buses formerly run by Alder Valley at Alton carry Hampshire Bus names. Only weeks before the Alder Valley company was sold to Stagecoach it received its first new big buses for over 10 years: two K-registered Lynx IIs. These ran briefly for Stagecoach South but are now back with Q-Drive, repainted yellow and running for The Bee Line. Hants & Surrey has since received an influx of Darts and Mercedes minibuses which have contributed to the quick disappearance of Alder Valley's green and yellow livery.

Within the Stagecoach South area there are two local authority bus fleets at Brighton and Eastbourne. A third, Southampton, lies on the south-west corner. There are also two significant major private sector operators, the Brighton & Hove Bus and Coach Co and Transit Holdings.

Southampton Citybus has expanded beyond its traditional urban operating area with services which now take its red-liveried buses out into rural Hampshire. For many years the standard Southampton bus was the East Lancs-bodied Atlantean. There are still almost 100 in use, delivered between 1972 and 1982. But standardisation has been forgotten. The last double-deckers were Dennis Dominators bought in 1988, which have since been sold to Capital Citybus. Since then the company has switched to single-deckers. First came Lynxes,

before a decision was made to try midibuses. One of these is a Wadham Stringer-bodied Dennis Lancet, new in 1982 to Portsmouth City Transport and purchased in 1989. It has been followed by eight Dennis Darts with three different bodies – Duple, Reeve Burgess (the first Pointer built) and Wadham Stringer.

A further change of policy saw the company start recycling Atlanteans, having their old East Lancs double-deck bodies replaced by new East Lancs single-deck bodies. The result is a good-looking 35-seater but with a considerable weight penalty; a single-deck Atlantean weighs almost twice as much as a Dennis Dart.

Coaches are operated under the Red Ensign name and include two second-hand Setra double-deckers and four East Lancs-bodied long-wheelbase Olympians, two of which were new to London Coaches.

One of the biggest fleets of Darts outside London is with Stagecoach South, which runs 80. All have Alexander Dash bodies.
Malcolm King

Southampton Citybus was the first customer for the Reeve Burgess Pointer body, taking this, the original prototype. It also runs Darts with bodywork by Duple and Wadham Stringer, but has more recently been having Atlanteans rebodied as single-deckers to fulfil its need for midi-sized buses.
Malcolm King

The other major player in Southampton is Solent Blue Line, a post-deregulation operation started in the spring of 1987 with backing from Southern Vectis. It grew later that year by buying part of the Hampshire Bus company, which had been recently purchased from NBC by Stagecoach. Solent Blue Line runs in an attractive two-tone blue and yellow livery with a mixture of Bristol VRTs, Leyland Olympians, Leyland Nationals and Iveco Dailys. The VRTs include comparatively unusual highbridge ECW-bodied buses which were new to Ribble. The Olympians include ex-Hampshire Bus and ex-Southern Vectis buses and 14 supplied new with Leyland bodywork. The newest minis, five Ivecos with Car Chair bodies, have an unusual seating layout with conventional foward-facing pairs of seats on the offside and a long inward-facing bench seat on the nearside. This is designed to create more space.

The Solent Blue Line livery is also carried on buses operated by Marchwood Motorways who run services under a franchise arrangement, a unique set-up in the UK. Marchwood have two Optare Deltas, two Dennis Darts and a few ex-Solent Blue Line Nationals running in blue and yellow.

Southern Vectis operates on the scenic Isle of Wight, where it is the major operator. Its bus fleet is similar to that run by Solent Blue Line on the mainland, with VRTs, Olympians, Nationals and a small number of minibuses. The company is one which sees tourist potential in its vehicle heritage with a prewar open-top Bristol K5G, three closed-top and one open-top Lodekka and a J-registered flat-fronted Series 1 VRT. These carry period liveries. The most unusual open-topper is a Bristol RE based at Shanklin, which runs as Shanklin's Pony.

With British Rail privatisation now on the political agenda, Southern Vectis is part of a locally-based consortium which has expressed an interest in taking over BR's Isle of Wight line, currently operated by ex-London Transport tube trains in full Network South East livery. Interestingly, the Southern Vectis name dates back to the days when railway companies were buying into the bus business . Before 1929 and involvement by the Southern Railway the company was simply Vectis, the Roman name for the island. It also explains why there's no Northern Vectis, or Eastern or Western Vectis.

The other major city on the mainland facing the Isle of Wight is Portsmouth. Portsmouth City Transport was one of the first significant casualties of deregulation. It was sold in 1988 by the city council to a consortium headed by Southampton Citybus after a deal with Southern Vectis fell through. In 1989 the business passed to Stagecoach, who merged it with Southdown in a new Southdown Portsmouth operation. In 1990 there was an MMC investigation of Stagecoach's alleged monopoly in Portsmouth which led to an instruction that the former Portsmouth City Transport operations be sold. This happened at the start of 1991, when Transit Holdings took over and quickly got rid of the decrepit collection of buses which it inherited, converting the services to high-frequency minibus operations. These run in and around the city as Blue

Admiral (mainly Ford Transits displaced from the failed Docklands Transit services in London) and out of town as Red Admiral (mainly bigger Mercedes), reaching as far inland as Petersfield.

A novel feature of Transit Holdings' operations in Portsmouth is the use of colour-coded destination screens which identify the main corridors served by each group of routes in a complex network. Transit Holdings claim that the conversion to small buses has created a substantial growth in bus use.

As well as Stagecoach South, People's Provincial of Fareham runs services in Gosport, Fareham, Portsmouth and Southsea. People's Provincial is unique among ex-NBC companies in being owned by its employees. It runs a standardised fleet with almost 60 second-hand Nationals acquired from eight different sources, as well as around 30 bought new, including two National 2s. Since privatisation in 1987 new Iveco minibuses have been bought, along with a rare ACE Cougar bodied by Wadham Stringer. Two open-top ex-Bournemouth Fleetlines appear in Southsea in the summer. The only closed-top double-deckers are 11 second-hand VRTs. People's Provincial also has a limited presence in Southampton.

Hants & Sussex of Emsworth serves Havant and Chichester. Its services are operated by what is now a very rare type – former London Transport AEC Merlins. These are now 24 years old which is quite a remarkable age for a breed of bus consigned to the scrap heap by London Transport after barely five years in service. Sussex Bus also runs services around Chichester, mainly with Willowbrook Warrior-rebodied Leopards although there is also a rare Marshall-bodied single-deck Dennis Dominator which came from Thamesdown. Most are in a red and white livery which advertises the Evening Argus newspaper.

Top left: **Solent Blue Line is in effect a mainland extension of Isle of Wight-based Southern Vectis. Its latest livery is seen on one of its VRs.** Malcolm King

Centre left: **Leyland-bodied Olympians are also operated by Southern Vectis on the Isle of Wight, but with a more conventional livery than their mainland counterparts.** Ken Jubb

Bottom left: **The two Transit Holdings fleets in Portsmouth are Blue Admiral and Red Admiral, with appropriately-coloured minibuses. Blue Admiral run primarily in the city area while Red Admiral's routes reach further out.** Stewart J Brown

Top right: **The People's Provincial fleet is made up largely of Mark 1 Leyland Nationals. This one came from National Welsh.** Stewart J Brown

Centre right: **Hants & Sussex is one of the few operators still running ex-London Merlins. This bus was new in 1969.** Stewart J Brown

Right: **Sussex Bus is one of a number of fleets in the south to have been attracted by the Willowbrook Warrior body as a means of extending the lives of trusty Leyland Leopard chassis. It runs three.** Malcolm King

Along the coast in Brighton there is little evidence of Stagecoach South. It operates out-of-town services, but the local network is covered by Brighton Borough Transport and Brighton & Hove. Brighton Borough Transport – trading as Brighton Buses – operates mainly, but not exclusively, within the town. It has a depot at Lewes, set up after the purchase of Lewes Coaches in 1988. The Lewes Coaches name has been retained (but with Brighton's blue livery) and is carried on buses which operate tendered services running as far inland as Crawley.

The newest buses in the Brighton fleet are 1992 Dennis Darts which have Plaxton Pointer bodies; the oldest are late-1970s Atlanteans which are the backbone of the town's fleet. Between these extremes there are various generations of buses bought new – Dennis Dominators, followed by National 2s and Lynxes. The newest double-deckers are 1985 Dominators. Minibuses – 15 Alexander-bodied Renaults – play a minor role.

The Lewes fleet also has two 1980 Leopards with 1991 Willowbrook Warrior bodies, an unusual combination for a municipally-owned company. The chassis originated with Southend Transport and previously had Duple coach bodies which were scrapped after a short time in Brighton. Coaches are operated under the Brighton Coaches banner.

The Brighton & Hove Bus and Coach Co was formed by NBC in 1985 as part of the break-up of Southdown. In some ways this was a move which turned the clock back 15 years: in pre-NBC days there was a Tilling-owned Brighton Hove & District company. Southdown was owned by BET. The new Brighton & Hove business was bought from NBC by its management in 1987. The company is based in Hove. The older vehicles are, predictably, Leyland Nationals and VRTs which were taken over from Southdown. Some of the VRTs have two-door bodywork. On privatisation the company quickly established its own individual vehicle policy and now runs 30 East Lancs-bodied Scania double-deckers bought new between 1988 and 1990, along with four similar 1986 buses bought from Leicester Citybus in 1989.

Minibuses comprise three Mercedes L608D van conversions (by Alexander) taken over from Southdown, plus 19 Merc 811Ds with Wadham Stringer Wessex bodies which were new to Bournemouth Transport in 1989 and were purchased by Brighton & Hove the following year.

While Brighton Buses and Brighton & Hove have bus services in the area pretty well sewn up between them, there is competition from one small operator. Haven Bus started running in 1991 with a crew-operated service from Newhaven to Brighton. This is run by an odd collection of vehicles including Nationals and DMS Fleetlines – all at least third-hand but all originating with London.

Heading east along the Sussex coast, Eastbourne Buses is, like Brighton Buses, still running most of its services in its established operating area – but with some expansion out of the town on tendered services. Almost half of the Eastbourne fleet is of

Dennis manufacture. There are Dominators dating from 1981-82, although the newest double-deckers are 12 Northern Counties-bodied Olympians bought in 1988. More recent new purchases have been a mixed bag of Dennis products. First came Javelin buses bodied by Duple (1989/90), Plaxton (1991) and Wadham Stringer (1992) – there are seven in all. Next came the Dart of which there are five with Wadham Stringer Portsdown bodies, making Eastbourne the biggest user of the Dart/Wadham Stringer combination. The most recent additions have been Dennis Lances, also bodied by Wadham Stringer.

The oldest buses are the fairly uncommon combination of ECW bodywork on Atlantean chassis. Two are open-toppers, 1968 buses which were acquired from Ipswich in 1980. More recent additions, in 1990/91, have been P-registered closed-top examples from Colchester. Two East Lancs-bodied Atlanteans, once the fleet's standard bus, are still in operation.

Small operators in East Sussex include Autopoint of Herstmonceux, most of whose fleet carries AP registrations. Autopoint runs Mercedes minis and elderly Bedford and Ford coaches on services and contracts. On the coast there is the Bexhill Bus Co, standardised on ECW-bodied Bristol REs. The company's main service links Bexhill and Hastings. Hastings is also served by Coastal Coaches with two second-hand Nationals on a local service provided under contract to East Sussex county council. Between Hastings and Rye there is a service operated by Rambler of St Leonards, using assorted Bedfords. Rye Coaches also runs local bus services and contracts. It has two Nationals and an ex-South Yorkshire Roe-bodied Atlantean.

Top left: The most recent additions to the Brighton Borough Transport fleet are Plaxton-bodied Dennis Darts. Malcolm King

Centre left: Brighton & Hove's recent purchases have been Scanias but the previous generation of Brighton & Hove bus is the Bristol VRT. This one was inherited from Southdown and is comparatively unusual for a former NBC VRT in being of two-door layout. A Scania is visible behind. Graham Jones

Left: Recent deliveries to Eastbourne have been in the main Wadham Stringer-bodied Dennises. These have comprised Javelins, Darts and, shown here, Lances. Paul Gainsbury

This page: Bristol REs form the backbone of the Bexhill Bus Co fleet. This one was new to PMT in 1973. Paul Gainsbury

Rambler runs two unusual Wright TT-bodied Bedford YMTs. New in 1982 to Maidstone Borough Transport, they were bought by Rambler in 1992. Paul Gainsbury

Rye Coaches is one of the many operators to have benefited from South Yorkshire's withdrawal of comparatively modern Atlanteans. It runs two Roe-bodied examples. Paul Gainsbury

East Kent Road Car of Canterbury provides services in the far south-east corner of England with garages in Ashford, Dover, Folkestone, Herne Bay and Thanet. It was an NBC subsidiary until 1987 when it was taken over by its management. It was purchased by Stagecoach in summer 1993.

The East Kent fleet is a varied one. Its standard ECW-bodied VRTs are leavened by 19 with square-styled Willowbrook bodies, a rare combination for NBC companies and one specified only by East Kent, Maidstone & District and Northern General. East Kent's own Nationals – all Mark 1s – have over the years been joined by assorted second-hand specimens, most notably from London Country.

Since gaining its independence from NBC, East Kent has bought a variety of new double-deckers and minibuses. First came MCW Metrobuses, of which there are 22 Mark II models dating from 1988-89. These were accompanied by a pair of Alexander-bodied Scania N113s from dealer stock. Since 1990 the standard has been the Leyland Olympian with Northern Counties body. New minibuses have all been Iveco Dailys with a variety of bodies. They joined Dailys – and a few Transits and Sherpas – which were purchased in NBC days. The only single-deck buses bought new since 1987 are three Optare Deltas which are used on a park-and-ride service in Canterbury.

The coach fleet is worth a mention because it includes the country's biggest collection of single-deck MCW Metroliners. There are 12 bought new, plus four from Premier Travel and an ex-MCW demonstrator, making 17 in all. These include both the original short-lived flat-fronted design as well as the later model with a more conventional curved front end.

East Kent's territory hosts a few significant small operators. Thanet Bus concentrates on that part of Kent from which it takes its name, running mainly in the Margate and Ramsgate areas, although there is also a route to Canterbury. Thanet Bus runs an assortment of Leyland Nationals. Town & Around of Folkestone runs local services with Nationals, ex-SBG Fords with Alexander bus bodies, or a Leyland Swift which was bought new in 1991. Westbus of Ashford is owned by an Australian company and serves Hythe, Faversham and Folkestone with a smartly-liveried fleet which includes three Leyland Lynxes and a number of second-hand Nationals. Westbus also runs a 20-strong high-quality coach fleet.

Before the demise of MCW, the Mark II Metrobus was favoured by East Kent with 22 joining the fleet in 1988-89. In August 1993 Stagecoach announced a takeover bid for the East Kent company. Paul Gainsbury

Town & Around's two-tone blue and white livery is seen on its Leyland National, an ex-London Country example. Scott Tillbrook

Westbus runs a variety of single-deckers on service – Mark 1 and 2 Leyland Nationals and Leyland Lynxes. The Nationals came from a number of sources while the Lynxes were bought new. David Harman

To the west of East Kent lies Maidstone & District. M&D, bought by its management from NBC in 1986, is based in Chatham. Its busiest operations are in the Medway Towns on the north Kent coast but it has depots as far south as Tunbridge Wells (no doubt to the displeasure of that august town's most famous letter writer: 'Disgusted') and Hawkhurst.

The fleet is an interesting one. There is a dwindling number of Mark 1 Nationals, but the oldest single-deckers are 1972 Leopards with BET-style Marshall bodies which have proved to be remarkable survivors of a once common type. There are later Leopards with bodywork which marked the nadir of NBC's coach buying policies – the Willowbrook 003 and ECW B51 – as well as some with more respectable Duple and Plaxton bodywork. The newest coaches are mid-1980s Tigers. Many of M&D's coaches carry Invictaway names, the branding used for express services from Kent to London.

Other single-deck bus types are Dennis Darts with Plaxton Pointer bodies. Some are at Tenterden and Sittingbourne for Kent county council tendered services and there are others at Maidstone for park-and-ride operation. There are four Lynxes, taken over in 1991 when Shearings of Wigan pulled out of local bus services in Kent.

The real variety is in the double-deck fleet which has Bristol VRTs, Dennis Dominators, Leyland Atlanteans and Olympians and MCW Metrobuses. M&D was an early user of the Atlantean back in 1959, but during its 17 years as an NBC subsidiary had pretty well standardised on the VRT.

The Atlanteans comprise two MCW-bodied PDR1A/1s from the company's last large intake of the type, 20 delivered in 1972-73. One of these is an open-topper, used in Rochester in the summer. The other is kept immaculate at Gillingham depot and represents the company at many rallies. More recently it has bought second-hand examples with 15 of the ubiquitous ex-Greater Manchester standards arriving in 1987-88, followed by seven with NBC-specification Park Royal/Roe bodies from Luton & District in 1991-92. Most were new to London Country.

The 60 or so VRTs are pretty standard NBC machines, but M&D's Olympians are in the main long-wheelbase ECW-bodied coaches, bought for London commuter services, or post-privatisation standard-wheelbase models with Northern Counties bodies, of which there are now 20. In 1980 NBC decided to evaluate some of the new generation double-deck buses being launched and as part of this process M&D was allocated five MCW Metrobuses and six Dennis Dominators. The Metrobuses have gone (although there are still 10 Mark 2 versions delivered in 1984) but all six of the Dominators, with highbridge Willowbrook bodies, are still running.

While M&D may not have been sufficiently impressed with the Dominator to buy new ones, it has an interesting collection of second-hand examples which include three from Merseyside Transport, eight from East Staffordshire District

Council, and an unusual lowheight bus which has an Alexander body and was built for PMT, who ran it alongside a Foden-NC in another part of NBC's vehicle evaluation programme. The only other Dominator with this style of body (which has deeper windows upstairs than it has down, a reversal of accepted design practice) runs for Kelvin Central Buses in Scotland. Most of the M&D Fleetlines are ex-London DMSs with Leyland engines but there are also two former Greater Manchester buses.

Maidstone & District has 40 of these Rootes-bodied Mercedes L608Ds in its fleet, all purchased in deregulation year, 1986. This one is seen at work in Tunbridge Wells. Paul Gainsbury

M&D's double-deck fleet includes MCW Metrobuses, Dennis Dominators, Bristol VRTs and, as exemplified here, Leyland Olympians. Paul Gainsbury

M&D owns New Enterprise Coaches of Tonbridge and in 1992 took over the former Maidstone Boro'line operations around Maidstone when that municipally-owned fleet folded. It didn't take over any of the Boro'line fleet. Also serving Maidstone is Bygone Buses with a mixed fleet which includes ex-London DMSs, Bristol REs, a VRT (made to look like an AEC by the application of a triangular badge) and a Routemaster. The fleet livery is red. Farleigh Coaches run from Maidstone to Trottiscliffe, usually with an ex-London National although a more interesting reserve bus is an ex-East Kent Marshall-bodied AEC Swift.

Mercury Passenger Services operate in Maidstone and the Medway Towns with a small but varied fleet which ranges from Metrobuses through to a pair of Optare CityPacers. All are secondhand. Also operating out of Maidstone is Nu-Venture, with three Peugeot-Talbot minibuses as its front line vehicles.

Smith's of Sittingbourne operate in a distinctive black, grey and white livery using a fleet of second-hand Nationals. The company also runs an express service to London, often using a double-deck MCW Metroliner coach. Other noteworthy coaches in the 25-strong fleet are a Ward Dalesman (bought new in 1983), a Leyland Royal Tiger Doyen, and a 1937 Leyland Tiger TS8, which was new to East Kent. At Faversham, Donsway operates on Kent county council tendered services; the fleet includes a National and a CityPacer, both ex-London Buses, and assorted Bedford coaches.

Although primarily a London operator, Grey-Green run ex-Merthyr Tydfil Lynxes and ex-County Nationals on tendered routes around Maidstone and Tonbridge. They also run commuter coaches from north Kent to London.

New Enterprise has remained a separate operation since purchase by Maidstone & District. Its fleet mostly comprises coaches but there are a few buses including this Metrobus transferred from the main fleet. David Harman

A trio of tri-axle Peugeot-Talbot Pullmans is used by Nu-Venture for their bus services in the Maidstone area. David Harman

Bygone Buses have been competing in the Maidstone area with a varied assortment of second-hand buses. MBC

Fuggles of Benenden serve rural mid-Kent, mainly on tendered services. A pair of former East Kent Nationals share service duty with a trio of ageing Leopard buses. Fuggles, incidentally, as any real ale drinker will be sure to tell you, is a type of Kentish hop. Coach operator Warrens of Ticehurst is a recent convert to local bus operation with attractively-liveried Nationals and VRTs which carry polished wheel trims and graphically illustrate a lesson which many other small (and large) operators could usefully learn: old buses do not have to look scruffy. Warrens serve Hawkhurst, Wadhurst and Tunbridge Wells on tendered services. Wealden Beeline operates from Tunbridge Wells to Groombridge and to East Grinstead. There is a variety of Leopards in the Wealden Beeline operation, and a trio of unusual front-wheel-drive low-floor Omni minibuses. Pride of the fleet is a Wadham Stringer-bodied Dart. The East Grinstead service is run jointly with East Surrey, which also runs a Wadham Stringer-bodied Dart, making this the only operation in the country where it is possible to see two such buses owned by two different operators. East Surrey is based in South Godstone and its operations are covered by Optare StarRiders, CVE Omnis, and an assortment of Bedford and Ford buses with bodies by Duple, Plaxton, Wadham Stringer and Willowbrook. Despite the East Surrey name, the Omnis were provided with support from Kent county council and are used mainly on bus services around Edenbridge in Kent.

Despite high levels of car ownership the South East has seen its fair share of small operators come and go. Most have benefited from cutbacks by high-cost ex-NBC operators and in particular the former London Country companies, some of which have fared better than others.

With small operators coming and going fairly rapidly, this review has of necessity looked at the more interesting ones, but there are many others running infrequently, or concentrating on tendered services using second-hand minibuses or ageing coaches.

Fuggles run a mixture of Leopards and Nationals, all new in the 1970s, on local bus services. David Harman

Few small operators commission design consultants to develop their liveries. One who has, and to good effect, is Warrens of Ticehurst. The smart colour scheme devised by Best Impressions belies the age of the company's Nationals and VRTs. Paul Gainsbury

Wealden Beeline runs this one-time Midland Scottish Leyland Leopard. It came from Graham of Paisley in 1990 and has an Alexander Y-type body. T K Brookes

SOUTH WEST ENGLAND

A VRT in North Devon's South Western fleet is seen in Exeter. Graham Jones

The south-west of England conjures up a variety of images: Cotswold Hills with mellow villages and high-tech Swindon; graceful Bath and brash Weston; Dartmoor and the Devon coast. It's a vast area with no huge conurbations but instead a good spread of substantial towns and cities.

Bristol, with 372,000 inhabitants, is the biggest. It was also once the headquarters of one of Britain's biggest bus operators in the days when the Bristol Omnibus Company's tentacles stretched north to Tewkesbury and east to Oxford. In the early 1970s it ran 1,200 vehicles. Today the Bristol Omnibus Company trades as City Line, its fleet is under the 350 mark and its services are confined to the city from which it takes its name — but the neighbouring Badgerline, Cheltenham & Gloucester and Swindon & District fleets all still run vehicles of clear Bristol Omnibus ancestry.

In Tilling and NBC days Bristol was a fairly sombre company, with green buses which looked pretty much like anybody else's green buses. It's hard to square the old image with the 1990s City Line look in a yellow, red and blue livery which has to be one of the brightest around. Whatever way you look at them — even from the back — Bristol's buses look like fun.

The newest buses in Bristol are 30 Leyland Olympians with Northern Counties bodies, delivered to Bristol City Line in the winter of 1992/93 to replace Bristol VRTs. Malcolm King

Bristol VRTs in City Line's fleet have to some extent been ousted by new Olympians. Among survivors is this 1980 bus with dual-door ECW body. Alan Macfarlane

The company was privatised in 1987 in a deal between Midland Red West and Bristol's own management. Then in 1988 Badgerline Holdings stepped in, taking over both Midland Red West and Bristol City Line. Badgerline Holdings, at the risk of stating the obvious, owns Badgerline which had been the Bristol Omnibus country area until being split off as a separate company at the start of 1986.

The City Line fleet is a modern one. There are 62 Leyland Lynxes, delivered in two batches, and these were joined at the start of 1993 by 30 Northern Counties-bodied Leyland Olympians, a new choice of body on an established choice of chassis. These new buses have considerably reduced the numbers of Bristol VRTs but there are still around 30 in use, all with dual-door ECW bodywork. The only other

double-deckers are 46 Olympians from the company's NBC days, but unusual in that they have full-height Roe bodies, similar to those built for London Country, rather than the standard NBC ECW lowheight body. The older Olympians have Gardner engines; the new K-registered buses are powered by Cummins. The company has kept one Bristol Lodekka as a reminder of days past.

Bristol Omnibus runs a substantial network of minibus routes under the City Dart name. Most City Darts are Mercedes L608D van conversions dating back to 1986 but more recent additions to the fleet have been 48 Ivecos with Dormobile Routemaker bodies (new in 1988-89) to which have been added two dozen second-hand Ivecos bodied by Robin Hood.

The Leyland Lynx is the standard Bristol City Line single-decker, with two batches totalling 63 in operation. There are detail differences between the batches, the most obvious being the yellow strip between the windscreen and the destination display on the second delivery. Richard Eversden

The window is used for the Badgerline logo on this City Line Robin Hood-bodied Iveco. There are over 70 Iveco minibuses running for Bristol City Line; most carry the City Dart branding. Lee Turton

Badgerline is based at Weston-super-Mare and although it shares a common heritage with Bristol Omnibus, the two fleets now have few vehicle types in common. Badgerline has a few former Bristol Omnibus VRTs, but apart from two open-toppers these are all of single-door rather than two-door layout. It also has 11 Roe-bodied Olympians. And there the resemblance between the two companies ends. Badgerline's older minibuses are predominantly Ford Transits, with a small number of Ivecos. More recently it has switched to Mercedes, initially with Optare StarRider bodies (running mainly in Bristol) and then with Reeve Burgess/Plaxton Beaver bodywork.

Badgerline was privatised in a management buy-out in 1986 and in 1987 upgraded its fleet with 39 new Volvos, operated from a brand new depot and run under a contract maintenance agreement with the manufacturer. The Volvos had a mix of bodies — Alexander P-type bus bodies were fitted to 14, Alexander R-type double-deck bodies to 12, while the remaining 13 were Van Hool coaches, most of which were for National Express operation. Since then the company has bought seven new Lynx and ten Leyland-bodied Olympians.

It has also pulled in buses from other group fleets, such as three Alexander-bodied Citybuses from Western National, which sit more comfortably in the Badgerline fleet than in Western National where they were non-standard. There is a large fleet of VRTs from Thamesway, rendered redundant in the Essex company by new minibuses and the loss of some London tenders.

Other odd types include five MCW Metrobuses dating back to NBC days and based in Bath, and a pair of long-wheelbase Olympians with East Lancs coach bodies which started life in 1985 with Rhymney Valley and reached Badgerline in 1989 by way of G&G in Leamington. Eight Bristol REs remain in service, allocated to Wells. One wears a 1970s-style cream and green Bristol Omnibus livery.

Badgerline has a mixed open-top fleet, primarily to serve Bath (in conjunction with Guide Friday) and Weston-super-Mare.

Badgerline coaches reach as far north as Gloucester on service — usually Tigers with Duple Laser bodies. Gloucester is one of three main centres of operation of the Cheltenham & Gloucester Omnibus Company, which was split off from Bristol Omnibus as long ago as 1983. The company was privatised in a management buy-out in 1986 which set up Western Travel which owns not only C&G but later acquisitions, most notably Midland Red South and Red & White.

Although a decade has passed since the break with Bristol Omnibus, most of the company's big buses are the residue of those acquired from Bristol — VRTs, Olympians and Nationals. Many of the VRTs started life with two doors but have been rebuilt as single-door buses: they are identifiable by their centrally-located staircases. As in other Bristol-related fleets the Olympians have full-height Roe bodies. One odd Roe-bodied Olympian in Gloucester is an ex-West Yorkshire PTE bus, immediately identifiable by its flat glass windscreens.

Early purchases by Badgerline included 14 Alexander P bodied Volvo B10Ms. These are fitted with coach seats for use as dual-purpose vehicles. The Badger is becoming a Badgerline Holdings standard logo, appearing in other group fleets as well. Malcolm King

Minibuses carry a smart all green livery. This StarRider bodied Mercedes is one of 20 in the fleet. Malcolm King

There is still a sizeable fleet of Bristol VRTs in Badgerline ownership, including open-toppers in Bath where a city tour is operated in conjunction with Guide Friday. This 1976 bus started life as a closed-top Leyland 501-engined vehicle. It was fitted with a Gardner 6LXB engine in 1983 and converted to open-top in 1986. Allan Macfarlane

Since 1985 all of Cheltenham & Gloucester's new buses have been minis—Transits and Mercedes L608D van conversions in NBC days, followed by a batch of MCW Metroriders and, the newest in the fleet, six G-registered Merc 709Ds with PMT bodies. There are also some second-hand Transits, including elderly (by Ford minibus standards) B-registered buses from Go-Ahead Northern. The dearth of new big buses has been partially compensated for by the rebuilding of 13 Mark 1 Nationals with DAF engines and improved interior trim. These buses run in Gloucester and Cheltenham, wear a revised livery and carry National 3 badges.

Minibuses generally carry the fleetname Metro, with a silver livery relieved by red and blue stripes. Big buses carry one of three liveries: blue in Gloucester, red in Cheltenham and green in Stroud with, respectively, the fleetnames City of Gloucester, Cheltenham District and Stroud Valleys. All three liveries can be seen in in any one of the three centres of operation which are served by each of the three divisions. The livery carries a flash of contrasting relief colour which sweeps up on double-deckers but down on single-deckers.

Swindon & District was part of the Cheltenham & Gloucester company but has since the end of 1991 been a separate subsidiary of Western Travel, running 30 buses in and around Swindon. Its fleet includes Bristol Omnibus VRTs and Nationals. It also has the only double-deckers bought new by Western Travel, five long-wheelbase Alexander-bodied Olympians, delivered in 1990. These run alongside five one-time Greater Manchester Leyland Titan integrals, acquired from South Midland in 1990. Its newest buses are two Wright-bodied Mercedes minis, a popular type in the Western Travel empire. They entered service in 1993.

This dual-door VRT in the Cheltenham & Gloucester fleet dates back to 1976 and was originally owned by Bristol Omnibus. It is approaching the cross in Gloucester city centre. Stewart J Brown

Below: **Extensive rebuilding has seen Cheltenham & Gloucester produce what it calls National 3s – note the badge above the offside headlamp. These feature DAF engines and improved interiors. They have also been renumbered in a new 3xx series.** K R Crawley

The Stroud Valleys fleet carries a basically green livery. This 1980 National 2 was new to Bristol Omnibus as AAE647V and was re-registered by its current owner in 1993. It was photographed in Cheltenham. K R Crawley

Swindon & District was formerly part of Cheltenham & Gloucester but is now a separate Western Travel subsidiary. It runs Western Travel's only new double-deckers. These are five long-wheelbase Olympians with Gardner engines and 87-seat low-height Alexander bodies. The location is Swindon bus station. Malcolm King

Minibuses in the Cheltenham & Gloucester fleet operate under the Metro name and include Transits, Mercedes and Metroriders. A 1985 Transit/Alexander heads towards Gloucester bus station.
Stewart J Brown

This large area, embracing parts of Avon, Gloucestershire and Wiltshire, hosts a number of other operators, the biggest of which is Thamesdown Transport of Swindon. Thamesdown is the successor to Swindon Corporation and the bus fleet is still owned by the local authority. Services stretch far beyond the confines of the town boundary, running out to Newbury, Marlborough, Devizes and Cirencester.

The oldest buses are Fleetlines, bought both new and second-hand. Those purchased new all have ECW bodies (effectively a Thamesdown standard in the late 1970s) and the newest are 1980 V-registered buses. The oldest Fleetlines are second-hand buses from London and Manchester and most of these are now relegated to schools and contract work — an allocation denoted by a yellow diamond alongside the fleet number.

More recent purchases have been Dennises, a make of which there are 56 in the fleet embracing five models: Dominator, Lancet, Falcon, Javelin and Dart. There are Dominators bought new between 1982 and 1990, with both Northern Counties and East Lancs bodies. There are also second-hand Dominators, from Derby and East Staffordshire. Apart from 10 Darts with Plaxton Pointer bodies delivered in 1993, the Dennis single-deckers are all second-hand with seven handsome Duple-bodied Falcons from Leicester and five Wadham Stringer-bodied Lancets — all second or third hand. Lancets are a fairly rare type, and even more unusual in a major fleet.

Thamesdown runs a growing coach fleet and has a 50 per cent share in Kingston Coaches of Winterslow, Salisbury — the other half being owned by Southampton Citybus. Swindon's original growth was around the railway and this is recognised in the Thamesdown fleet which has named a few of its buses and coaches after famous locomotives run by the Great Western Railway or British Railways Western Region, or famous railway engineers. Evening Star, BR's last steam locomotive, was built in Swindon, and its name adorns a Northern Counties-bodied Dominator — which might just tempt unkind thoughts about the sublime and the ridiculous amongst readers with any passion for steam locomotives.

Thamesdown has been a good customer for Dennis products in recent times. This is one of 19 Northern Counties Dominators delivered new in 1982-85. Malcolm King

Thamesdown has the only Dennis Falcon fleet in the South West. There are seven, all with Duple Dominant bus bodies and all acquired from Leicester in 1987. This is a 1983 example. Malcolm King

The Pointer bodied Darts delivered to Thamesdown in 1993 carry an attractive new livery and Dartline branding. Malcolm King

Small operators running into Swindon include Fosseway of Chippenham, with ageing Transits on a local outer circle service and Regis Coaches of Faringdon, with an ex-London Fleetline on a service from Wantage. Services from Swindon to Malmesbury are operated by Andy James Coaches, normally with a Leopard coach. At Malmesbury there are usually connections with Fosseway for Chipping Sodbury and Yate. There is also a regular Malmesbury to Chippenham link, run by Anton Travel. Regis run a Sunday-only through service from Swindon to Bath, worked jointly with Clapton Coaches.

Since February 1993 Thamesdown buses have penetrated as far north as Gloucester on a twice daily extension of one of the Cirencester services. Gloucester attracts a number of small operators, as well as being served by Red & White buses working in from Wales and the Forest of Dean.

Cottrell's of Mitcheldean is an old-established business with services from the Forest of Dean to Gloucester. These are operated by a pair of former Greater Manchester Metrobuses which have now spent as long in Gloucestershire as they did in Manchester, a long-wheelbase Fleetline bought new in 1979, or one of the company's older Leopard or Tiger coaches. Also in the Forest of Dean is Dukes Travel, running locally in Coleford, and also to Ross-on-Wye and, on Saturdays, to Gloucester. Duke's have one new bus, a 1990 Dormobile-bodied Mercedes and one unusual second-hand bus, an ex-Ministry of Defence Leyland Leopard with Wadham Stringer Vanguard body. Leopard coaches are also used on service. Other small companies reaching Gloucester include Applegates of Berkeley and Newbury Coaches of Ledbury.

Swanbrook of Cheltenham takes its name from the founding partners, Messrs Swann and Brook. Swanbrook operate south from Gloucester to Quedgeley (often with one of a pair of a former Tyne & Wear Atlanteans which came by way of Colchester Borough Transport) and to Framilode, Frampton-on-Severn and Arlingham. A mixture of single-deckers is used ranging from a Willowbrook-rebodied Leopard and a pair of Plaxton bus-bodied Bedford YMTs to a solitary AEC Reliance coach (ex-Derby) or an ageing Bedford/Plaxton which bears testimony to the quality of Plaxton's paint finish with the legend 'Silver Jubilee coach' still visible on the rear. The Jubilee in question is the Queen's — in 1977. There are also six former London and West Midlands Fleetlines in the fleet.

Coaches are used on many local bus services in the South West. This Plaxton bodied Tiger with Dukes Travel dates from 1981. Stuart Jones

One of the regular performers on Cottrell's Gloucester service is this long Fleetline, an FE33ALR model, which was bought new in 1979. It has Northern Counties bodywork. Stewart J Brown

Most of Swanbrook's services are operated by Bedford YMTs. The newest are two with Plaxton Derwent bus bodies which were purchased in 1987. Stewart J Brown

Another Reliance operator running in to Gloucester is Mike's of Thornbury, with an immaculate Plaxton-bodied coach in blue, yellow and red. Local coach operator Bennett's runs a smart Duple bus-bodied Leopard on a service from Highnam. Circle Line of Gloucester, since 1992 part-owned by Western Travel, has a tidy fleet of green and cream double-deckers, mostly Bristol VRTs and former London DMSs and mostly on school contracts. Circle Line do run some infrequent tendered services to the south of the city, usually with a VRT or a former SBG Seddon Pennine 7.

In nearby Cheltenham, Castleways of Winchcombe serve the town and also run to Evesham and Broadway. Castleways use coaches for their services — Leopards with Plaxton bodies or Mercedes minis — and the fleet in its unusual black and dark grey livery is widely recognised as one of the smartest in the country. It operates from a small garage which is kept as clean and tidy as the company's vehicles. Pulham's of Bourton-on-the-Water link Cheltenham with Bourton and Moreton-in-Marsh. The company's 20 coaches range from a 1973 Leopard to a pair of 1991 Volvos, all bodied by Plaxton and most bought new. Services are in the hands of Leopards and Tigers.

Small operators are not highly visible in the Bristol area, where City Line's tight network has discouraged competition. ABUS runs a service from Keynsham, started in 1991. The fleetname is apt because 'a bus' is all that ABUS ran at first. The ABUS bus – an ex-Thamesdown Fleetline – has since been joined by an ex-Plymouth Atlantean. Somerbus, with eight vehicles, is one of the biggest small operators in Bristol since the collapse of Arrow Coaches in 1993. Somerbus owns two Leyland Nationals, a Bristol VRT and an ex-Greater Manchester Dodge S56 minibus. It also has coaches. Crown Coaches of Bristol run four former London Country VRTs on school contracts, alongside two elderly Atlanteans, an E-registered bus new to Aberdeen and a number of minibuses on tendered services into Bristol.

Ambassador Travel run a commercial service from Bristol city centre to the south of the city, using a green-painted Leyland National formerly with Arrow Coaches.

Bennetts of Gloucester, a high quality coach operator, runs this Duple-bodied Leyland Tiger on a service to Highnam. It was purchased from Thomas of Llandeilo in 1992. Bennetts also run equally smart double-deckers on contracts. Stewart J Brown

Circle Line of Gloucester operate a tendered service to Berkeley, normally using a Bristol VRT. Alan Simpkins

Somerbus have a number of contracts from Avon county council, on which their varied bus fleet is used. This Northern Counties bodied Dodge came from GM Buses. Neil Jennings

Durbin of Almondsbury operates VRTs and Sherpas on a small number of tendered and commercial services. Similarly Eagle of Bristol has Sherpas and a pair of Mercedes on tendered work.

Bakers of Weston-super-Mare, primarily a coach operator, maintain a fleet of six VRTs for contract work (including two former West Midlands PTE MCW-bodied examples) and have a pair of Carlyle-bodied Iveco 49.10s which are used on tendered services. Tendered services operated by Clapton Coaches of Radstock, near Bath, reach Weston-super-Mare as well as Swindon, Bristol and a number of smaller towns. The company's bus fleet is thus spread thinly. It includes Mercedes minis and two big buses in the shape of 1978 Leopards with 1992 Willowbrook Warrior bus bodies — vehicles which give Lynx-like looks for a fraction of the Lynx price.

In Bath itself, Ryan operate open-top VRTs, DMSs and an Atlantean on a city tour which competes with the joint Badgerline/Guide Friday venture. Ryan also has a small number of tenders for services from Bath, worked by coaches. Streamline Buses of Bath cover some off-peak country services which are otherwise operated by Badgerline. For this work they have a variety of Freight Rover Sherpa, Iveco and Ford Transit minibuses. Connor's of Calne serve Bath twice daily with trips in from Chippenham, a route served primarily by Badgerline.

The area to the south of Swindon is covered by Wilts & Dorset, based in Poole on the Dorset coast and running inland as far as Devizes, Marlborough, Swindon and Hungerford. The company was privatised in a management buy-out from NBC in 1987 and its livery is a stylish combination of red, white and black. The company has major centres of operation in Salisbury, Poole and Bournemouth. Although the present company dates back only as far as 1983, when it was formed on the division of Hants & Dorset (the division which also created Hampshire Bus), it is the successor to a much older

Wilts & Dorset operation which predated the creation of NBC and the subsequent amalgamation of the original company with Hants & Dorset.

From 1987 to 1992 all its new buses were Metroriders — built by both MCW and Optare. There are 108 bought new and a further 13 used examples, from Blackburn, Grimsby-Cleethorpes and Yorkshire Rider. The other major type is the standard NBC-specification Bristol VRT, of which there are 73. One VRT in the Poole area carries blue Verwood Transport livery, a memory of a four-bus company taken over in 1989.

Leyland Nationals play a small part in the fleet, as do Bristol LH buses. Some of the latter have cutaway front panels to improve the approach angle when using the Sandbanks Ferry on the route from Bournemouth to Swanage.

At privatisation there were seven Olympians in the Wilts & Dorset fleet. Judicious second-hand buying has increased that number to 27 with buses from the West Yorkshire PTE (Roe bodies), County Bus & Coach (also Roe, to London Country design), Crosville Wales (ECW) and, most unusually, Stevensons of Uttoxeter. The ex-Stevensons buses include three with East Lancs bodies which were new to Plymouth City Transport. They now operate in Poole. A number of Olympians can have their roofs removed for summer operation on the Isle of Purbeck (which, incidentally, breaks whatever section of the Trade Descriptions Act applies to islands: it is part of the mainland).

New double-deckers — the first for 10 years — appeared in 1993 with the arrival of 20 Optare Spectras. These are built to a low 13ft 8in overall height and the first 10 are allocated to the company's main trunk routes.

Above: **Wilts & Dorset have 121 Metroriders, easily the biggest fleet of the type in southern England outside London. These include both MCW and Optare versions, and a small number acquired from other operators. A 1992 Optare model is seen the New Forest.** Tony Wilson

Left: **Wilts & Dorset joined the select band of Spectra operators in 1993 when it took 20 into stock. This one is seen at Ringwood on one of the company's long-distance services.** Tony Wilson

Just along the Dorset coast lies Bournemouth—once in Hampshire, but now in Dorset. Here the major operator is Bournemouth Transport, which has shaken off its municipal image (but not its municipal ownership) by adopting the name Yellow Buses. Not long after deregulation the Bournemouth and Poole areas saw strong competition, in particular from Shamrock & Rambler trading as Charlie's Cars (owned by Drawlane, and primarily a coach operator) and Badger Vectis, a joint venture between Southern Vectis and Badgerline. Both were short-lived. Bournemouth Transport did go so far as to buy 20 Mercedes minis to help see off competition — and having done just that promptly sold them with all but one going along the coast to Brighton & Hove.

Now the Yellow Buses fleet is made up of double-deckers — just over 100 of them, and some coaches. Front-line coaches (Plaxton-bodied Leyland Tigers and DAF MBs) carry Yellow Coaches fleetnames. Five older Leopard coaches count as part of the bus fleet. There are also 16 Volvo B10Ms taken over with the Dorset Travel Services business in 1992 and operated on National Express contracts along with a few other coaches.

But back to the buses. Half of the double-deck fleet comprises Fleetlines, 54 all told, making Yellow Buses the biggest Fleetline operator south of West Midlands Travel. All have Alexander bodies and the P- and S-registered buses are convertible open toppers. Most are Leyland engined too, only the final deliveries having the more customary Fleetline power unit, a trusty Gardner.

The Fleetlines were followed by one batch of 20 Olympians, unique in having Marshall bodies. Then came two batches of Volvo Citybuses, one bodied by East Lancs, the other by Alexander, before a change of management saw a switch to Dennis Dominators. There are 18 Dominators running for Yellow Buses, all with East Lancs bodies based on the Alexander R-type design, and delivered between 1990 and 1992.

Competition re-appeared in Bournemouth in mid-1993 with the arrival of Bournemouth Heritage Transport using Routemasters and a few other elderly vehicles. In response, Yellow Buses set up a counter-competitive operation under the name White Bus.

Bournemouth's recent double-deck purchases have been of Alexander-lookalike East Lancs bodied Dominators. Tony Wilson

Bournemouth Transport operates Alexander-bodied Fleetlines, an unusual combination in the south of England. The body style specified is also unusual on a Fleetline, being more commonly associated with Atlanteans. This bus was new in 1974; the last of the type were delivered in 1981. Some of the older vehicles like this one were transferred in 1993 to the White Buses operation. Mike Harris

The White Buses operation was started in response to a competitive challenge from new operator Bournemouth Heritage Transport running three local routes (numbered 601/604/607), principally with RMs, in this attractive livery. Mike Harris

Rural Dorset and south Wiltshire support a number of small operators in what is broadly Wilts & Dorset operating territory. Beeline of Warminster operates a 20-strong fleet of Bedfords, including four with Duple Dominant bus bodies on tendered services. Beeline's tenders include a route to Salisbury. Maybury's of Cranborne also serve Salisbury, with a route from Fordingbridge, and reach Bournemouth and Poole on tendered services. The bus fleet comprises former London DMS Fleetlines, two similar buses which were new to South Yorkshire and a former South Midland VRT.

Inland from Poole the Blandford Bus Company serves Bere Regis and Dorchester. The company is a new one, set up in 1988, and its expansion has been funded partly by the Rural Transport Development Fund. It runs Bristols — two REs, three LHs and a Lodekka. Many of its services run on market days only. Blandford Forum is also the base for the associated businesses of Oakfield Travel and Stanbridge & Crichel. This company operates from depots in Blandford and Stanbridge, with services in Wimborne, Cranborne and down to Bournemouth. In a rather unlikely takeover at the end of 1992 it became a subsidiary of London Country South West who inherited a fleet which can most kindly be described as varied. It includes AEC Reliance and MAN SR280 coaches and an assortment of Bristol LHs and REs. The newest vehicle in the fleet, which is almost 30-strong, is a 1982 Bedford.

Much of the country to the west was served in NBC days by Western National, which in 1983 was split into four smaller companies — Southern National, North Devon, Devon General and a new slimmed-down Western National.

Southern National, based in Taunton, covers most of Somerset and parts of Dorset with 220 buses running from depots in Bridport, Bridgwater, Taunton, Weymouth and Yeovil. Southern National was privatised in a management buy-out in 1988.

Minibuses figure strongly in Southern National's operations with Ford Transits being the most common type in the fleet.

The big bus fleet includes VRTs and Nationals inherited from the NBC, and post-privatisation purchases of second-hand Olympians from Devon General and the West Yorkshire PTE. There are also 11 Bristol LHs with Plaxton coach bodies, some a Western National inheritance, others acquired from County of Atherington. Most are 7ft 6in wide, making them suitable for operation in rural lanes. Bristol RE buses survive, but only just, with four running for the associated Smiths of Portland operation. These were acquired from Western National in 1990 and are still in Western National's colours. New buses for Southern National since 1988 have all been Mercedes 709Ds, bodied by Carlyle, Marshall and Wright.

Vehicles operated by Oakfield Travel carry Guildford & West Surrey Buses legal lettering, and some even carry this as a fleetname, which looks rather out of place in Salisbury, where this AEC Reliance has travelled from Sturminster for market day. David Stewart

Above: **Southern National's older double-deckers are mainly NBC-style ECW-bodied VRTs. This one dates back to 1979.** Barry Spencer

Left: **Five Marshall-bodied Mercedes were added to the Southern National fleet in 1992. This 29-seat 709D shows clearly the body's Carlyle ancestry.** Barry Spencer

The neighbouring North Devon company was also privatised in a management buy-out, but with the involvement of Southern National. Both companies have common directors and their buses share a common series of fleet numbers. With fewer than 100 buses, North Devon is considerably smaller than Southern National and has depots at Barnstaple, Bideford and Ilfracombe. Its routes cover an area from Lynton to Bude and south to Tiverton and Exeter.

The company does not trade under the North Devon title. Instead most of its fleet runs under the Red Bus name — no prizes for guessing the livery but some are yellow — and there are other names too. South Western is carried on double-deckers in the Exeter area, Atlantic Blue (and a livery to match) on five Nationals running between Ilfracombe and Barnstaple, and Tiverton & District on nine buses, including some VRTs, in Tiverton.

The fleet is similar to that of its larger neighbour, from Transits and Ivecos, through LHs, Nationals and VRTs, to ex-Devon General Olympians. Odd recent acquisitions have been a pair of long-wheelbase Atlanteans from Blackpool, for South Western operations in Exeter, and new Dennis Darts — two in 1991 with Carlyle bodies, followed by one in 1992 with a Wright Handybus body.

Cawlett, the holding company formed to run both Southern National and North Devon also own Pearce, Darch and Wilcox of Martock which runs 20 coaches under the Comfy-Lux name.

Recent deliveries to North Devon have included 9.8m Dennis Darts. The first two, new in 1991, have 40-seat Carlyle bodies. Malcolm King

Atlantic Blue livery is carried on five of North Devon's Leyland Nationals. The most modern is this 1979 bus, seen leaving Ilfracombe bus station for Westward Ho! Ken Jubb

Tiverton & District is another of North Devon's identities, seen here in Old Village, Willand, on one of a pair of former London Leyland Nationals. Barry Spencer

Below left: **Unusual additions to the North Devon fleet in 1991 were its only Atlanteans, two long-wheelbase AN68/2s with 86-seat East Lancs bodies. They were new in 1978 and came from Blackpool Transport. Both carry South Western livery.** Barry Spencer

Below right: **Also carrying South Western colours is this 1992 Marshall-bodied 811D in Exeter. It is a 33-seater.** Barry Spencer

Competition for the Cawlett companies comes from a number of small operators. Wake's of Wincanton run from Shepton Mallet to Yeovil and from Castle Cary to Wincanton, as well as having a fine portfolio of tendered services with support from no fewer than three counties, Dorset, Somerset and Wiltshire. Most services are run by Bedford coaches, although there are also two Bedfords with Duple Dominant bus bodies as well as a number of more modern coaches.

Berry's Coaches of Taunton run under the Beaverbus name with services which provide links with Wellington, Tiverton and Bridgwater. These are worked by four ECW-bodied Bristol VRTs. Safeway Services of South Petherton is, like Berry's, an old-established company, but with a tradition of local bus operation which spans 75 years. The company's original service from Yeovil to Crewkerne is still operated and there are also routes from Yeovil to Ilminster and Taunton. The fleet is almost all Leyland, the exception being a 1949 Dennis Lancet III. The buses offer an interesting contrast in styles of Willowbrook-bodied Leopards. The two oldest are L-registered 1973 models with BET-style bodies, while the most-recent addition to the fleet is a 1985 Leopard with a 1992 Willowbrook Warrior body. There is also a Leopard with a Duple Dominant bus body.

Filer's of Ilfracombe introduced a service to Barnstaple in 1986 and now run to Bideford and Westward Ho!, with some services being provided under tender to Devon county council. Filer's blue and yellow bus fleet is made up of former London Fleetlines and a distinctive ex-Alder Valley Leyland Olympian coach. Leopards from the company's coach fleet are also used on service.

There are four ECW-bodied Bristol VRTs operated by Berrys of Taunton. This one was new to the Atomic Energy Research Establishment at Harwell. It carries promotional lettering for the Taunton to Wellington service and for the company's coaching activities. Graham Jones

The Safeway fleet is made up primarily of Leyland Leopards. This Willowbrook-bodied bus was new in 1976 to Trimdon Motor Services. Barry Spencer

The most unusual bus operated by Filer's is this Leyland-engined Olympian with ECW coach bodywork, seen leaving Barnstaple for Ilfracombe. It was new in 1985 to Alder Valley and came to Filer's in 1991. Barry Spencer

Kilmington Coaches, based just outside Axminster (of carpet fame), started running minibuses in 1988. It now runs 14 vehicles, the biggest of which is a 33-seat Wadham Stringer-bodied Ford R1115. The rest of the fleet contains a mixture of Transit, Sherpa and Dodge S56 minibuses, the Dodges including two with East Lancs bodies which were purchased from Ipswich Buses. Services, mainly under contract to Devon county council, reach as far north as Taunton and as far west as Exeter. Axminster is also served by Axe Valley Mini Travel, running in from the coastal towns of Seaton and Sidmouth. Axe Valley is based at Colyton, not far from the Seaton Tramway, and runs a collection of second-hand minibuses, including ex-Plymouth Dodges and a quaint Volkswagen LT50 bodied by Made-to-Measure (which seems a singularly inappropriate name for the builder of a most unusual-looking bus). There is one full-sized coach, a W-registered Bedford.

Clyst Honiton, on the River Clyst a few miles east of Exeter, is the home of Red Bus Services, running from Sidmouth to Ottery St Mary and Honiton, and from Ottery St Mary to Axminster. Red Bus Services' main claim to fame has to be the only Albion Nimbus in Britain still available for service, a delightful 1958 NS3N model with Willowbrook body, which was new to Devon General. The Nimbus, with a mid-mounted four-cylinder horizontal engine, was a midibus in the days before the term had been invented. More conventional workhorses in the Red Bus Services fleet include a Merc 811D bought new in 1991, three one-time SBG Seddon Pennine 7s with Alexander bodies and three VRTs. Interestingly the 811D, with 33 seats, can actually carry more than the Nimbus, a 31-seater.

Two of the company's buses run in the old Devon General livery, a flat-fronted VRT and a former Devon General Regent V. The latter operates an open-top service in Exeter.

Axe Valley Mini Travel's most modern buses are two 1986 Dodge S56s with Reeve Burgess bodies. They were new to Plymouth Citybus and joined Axe Valley in 1991. This one is seen in Beer. Barry Spencer

The Axe Valley fleet includes this oddly-styled Made-to-Measure body on a Volkswagen LT50. It is a 19-seater and was new in 1985. Axe Valley acquired it in 1988 from Golnia of Long Melford. Barry Spencer

Red Bus Services pays tribute to Devon General with the livery layout on this 1978 VRT which came from York City & District, but was new to West Yorkshire Road Car. It carries Devon county council's school bus signs as it passes through Sidford on a school run. Barry Spencer

Exeter is the headquarters of Transit Holdings, the country's leading exponent of the virtues of minibuses. Transit Holdings was formed as a holding company following a management buy-out of Devon General in 1986, which marked the first sale of an NBC bus operation. Transit Holdings has since spread the minibus gospel with varying degrees of success. It has had only one failure, Docklands Transit in London, which was a brave attempt to establish a commercial operation in the face of strong opposition. It has also had one last-minute change of heart, when Basingstoke Transit was abandoned within days of its launch. Its successes have been Thames Transit in Oxford, and Portsmouth Transit which metamorphosed into Blue Admiral and Red Admiral. And, of course, the Devon operations which it has fiercely defended from would-be opponents.

Rather than have a bus war on the streets of Exeter (which would lead to the risk of unquantifiable revenue losses), Devon General spent three years blocking an attempt by City of Oxford to introduce MetroRiders to the city by arguing in favour of the retention of a ban on buses over 20ft long in Exeter High Street. That was until the end of 1992, when Devon General wanted to introduce bigger Iveco minibuses and did a remarkable about-turn. Whatever Devon General may have argued before, longer buses were suddenly no longer a problem.

Minibuses were introduced to Exeter in NBC days, first replacing big buses on city services in 1984. Despite the reservations of many early users of small buses, the Transits which serve Exeter have proved remarkably long-lived. Over 30 A-registered buses are still in use, having operated for almost twice their initial maximum life expectancy of five years in busy stop-start bus operation. Transits — almost 150 of them and none newer than 1986 — provide all of the local bus services for the citizens of Exeter. They run in three liveries: in blue and silver as Exeter Bus Co, in green and gold as Exeter Nipper, and in red and yellow as Exeter Minibus. The Exeter Nipper name appeared in 1990 after City of Oxford announced it was going to launch its services in the city as Exeter City Nipper.

To the south in Torbay, the associated Bayline also runs a fleet made up largely of Transits. Those running in Teignmouth trade as Teignibus which is a sort of minibus pun, being pronounced 'teenybus'.

Longer distance services from Exeter, reaching as far inland as Okehampton and Taunton, are operated by Mercedes 709Ds with Reeve Burgess Beaver bodies. These are in cream and red and carry Devon General fleetnames. Bayline also has a few Mercs, including 12 with Carlyle bodies in the cream and blue livery of Brixham Coaches. There is only one bus in either of the two fleets with more than 33 seats, and that's a convertible open-top VRT which runs in Torbay in the summer, continuing a long-standing tradition of Devon General open toppers on the seafront. Farrar and Torbay Riviera also operate open-toppers in Torbay, the former operator running a replica of a London General B-type.

The Ford Transit typifies the older buses in Transit Holdings' fleets. This 1985 bus with 16-seat Carlyle body started life with Thames Transit in Oxford. It is now with Bayline. Barry Spencer

A Reeve Burgess-bodied Mercedes-Benz 709D from the Bayline fleet in Brixham. Mercs are used by Transit Holdings' subsidiaries on busy urban routes and on rural services. Barry Spencer

The newest buses in the Bayline fleet are Iveco Ford 59.12s delivered in 1983. They have bodywork by Mellor of Rochdale, a major supplier to Transit Holdings. Barry Spencer

The only double-decker operated by Bayline is a 1977 convertible open-top VRT. It runs in the Torbay area where there is competition from two other operators. Barry Spencer

Above and left: **Torbay Riviera run a veteran PDR1 Atlantean which was new to Maidstone & District in 1963 but was latterly with Badgerline. It has a Weymann body. The strangest open-topper in the area is run by Farrar of St Columb Road and is a Bedford VAM which has been fitted with a replica LGOC B-type body. Farrar runs another similar bus in Newquay.** Barry Spencer

The most southern and western of the one-time NBC companies is Western National, serving Cornwall and south-west Devon. It was privatised in 1987, being bought by a consortium which included Plympton Coachlines and Badgerline. It is now a wholly-owned Badgerline subsidiary. Western National runs 400 vehicles in a fleet which still includes a sizeable number of double-deckers. There are currently around 110 of which over 100 are Bristol VRTs with ECW bodies, and the balance are 1983 Olympians. Most of the VRTs were bought new, but since becoming part of Badgerline there has been an influx of second-hand specimens from sister companies in the group, notably Badgerline, South Wales and Thamesway. There are also some ex-Devon General examples, displaced as Western National's neighbour moved inexorably away from big bus operation. The former Badgerline buses include three highbridge models which were new to London Country.

The other common type is the Mercedes Benz L608D conversion, of which over 100 were taken into stock in the mid-1980s at the height of NBC's dash to small buses. Most of Western National's are Reeve Burgess conversions. The Bristol LH, for a long time a feature of the Western National fleet, has now gone.

A small number of coaches carry the Grenville name (a business acquired in 1988). Another small operator taken over in 1988 was Robert's Coaches of Plympton, and the Robert's name is carried on a few minibuses and on some small coaches.

Since privatisation Western National has bought small numbers of new buses. There are six Lynxes, five of which are in Plymouth. These are the only full-size single-deck buses in the fleet (Western National no longer has any Leyland Nationals). There were also three Volvo Citybus double-deckers, but these now run for Badgerline. Most new purchases since independence have, however, been Mercedes 811Ds. There are 26 with Carlyle bodies, delivered in 1990-91, and 13 with Plaxton Beaver bodies delivered in 1992. These have been joined by four with Optare StarRider bodies, transferred from Badgerline. Another 11 Beaver-bodied 811Ds arrived in 1993.

Western National's double-deckers are mainly ECW-bodied Bristol VRTs and the number has been swollen in recent times by the acquisition of buses from other Badgerline subsidiaries. This 1981 bus operating in Newquay is one of 14 transferred from Thamesway in 1991-92. Graham Jones

There are six Lynxes in the Western National fleet. This one in Torquay carries the latest livery with red and blue flags above the windows and a badger sitting at skirt level behind the rear wheels. Barry Spencer

Western National has been receiving some of the 241 Plaxton-bodied Mercedes-Benz on order for the Badgerline group in 1993-4. This is an 811D in Penzance. Barry Spencer

Plymouth is the biggest centre of population in the Western National area and is served primarily by local authority-owned Plymouth Citybus. Some 40 years of co-ordinated operation by the two companies came to an end with deregulation in 1986, which led to a brief intense bus war in the city. The situation has now stabilised, and the bulk of the Plymouth Citybus operations are within its traditional operating area around the city.

The fleet is gradually moving away from double-deckers. It has 50 — 46 Atlanteans, delivered between 1978 and 1981, and four Volvo Citybuses. Two of the latter were built as coaches in 1984 but are now conventional buses, while the other two are 78-seat East Lancs-bodied coaches delivered in 1991.

Plymouth embraced minibuses in a big way at deregulation, ordering 81 Dodge S56s with Reeve Burgess bodies — one of the largest single orders for coachbuilt bodies (as distinct from van conversions) in the history of the Reeve Burgess company. Replacement of these started in 1990 and after trying two Wadham Stringer-bodied Mercedes alongside two with Reeve Burgess Beaver bodies, the Beaver became the fleet's new standard. There are now 42 Beavers in use, all on Mercedes 709D chassis.

The success of the Beavers has seen Plymouth try midibuses, with nine Dennis Darts entering service in 1992. These have Plaxton Pointer bodies. More Darts and Mercs arrived in 1993.

The livery is an unusual combination of black, white and red, except on the Darts where grey is substituted for the black — to good effect. A modern coach fleet, mainly Plaxton-bodied Volvos, runs under the Plymouth Citycoach name.

Plymouth's displaced Dodges have found a number of ready buyers, including Brookside Travel Services in Relubbus who have four. These run alongside an N-registered LH which travelled north from Hants & Dorset to Teesside Motor Services before returning south to Brookside. There are also a few elderly coaches. Brookside runs from Relubbus to nearby Penzance, as well as to St Just (a few miles from Land's End), Truro and Falmouth.

Leyland Atlanteans form the backbone of the Plymouth Citybus double-deck fleet and most have dual-door East Lancs bodies. This one was new in 1979. Malc McDonald

Plymouth has joined the growing list of buyers for the Dennis Dart, adding its first in 1992. These have Plaxton Pointer bodies and a brighter livery with grey relief in place of the normal black. Malc McDonald

Truro is not only the headquarters of Western National, but the home of Truronian, owned since 1987 by former members of Western National's management. Truronian, in a red and silver livery, operates city services in Truro, and rural services which include some based on Helston. The double-deck fleet includes half a dozen ECW-bodied VRTs which originated with NBC companies Trent, Southdown and Yorkshire Traction. There are four Fleetlines — two London DMSs (the most south-westerly of the breed), a one-time Selnec Mancunian (a rare survivor in PSV use), and a former Burton-on-Trent bus. And there are two Atlanteans. One is an ex-Plymouth PDR2 while the other is a former Leyland experimental vehicle. It has an Alexander body built in the early 1970s to the rather odd style specified by the Merseyside PTE, but it was not registered until 1980 when it was sold by Leyland to Rennie of Dunfermline. Single-deck buses are an ECW-bodied Bristol LH and three LHSs, two of which were new to London Country and one to London Transport. The acquisition of Williams of St Agnes in 1993 included two Atlanteans and two Bedford coaches, plus their route to Truro.

From Truro, Hopley's serve Redruth and, on the north coast of Cornwall, St Agnes. This is normally covered by a 1975 Bedford YRT with 66-seat Duple Dominant bus bodywork. Further up the coast at Port Isaac, Prout Bros serve Wadebridge and also run school services. Available for service are two 1974 Willowbrook-bodied Bedford buses, as well as Bedford, Leyland Leopard or Volvo coaches.

Roselyn Coaches of Par operate to nearby Fowey and St Austell, but also get as far east as Plymouth, although not every day. Its front-line buses are a pair of mid-1970s Bedfords, one bodied by Duple and the other by Willowbrook. Both came from the Atomic Energy Research Establishment at Harwell. The AERE also supplied the oldest bus in the fleet, a 1962 Park Royal-bodied AEC Regent V, acquired in 1983. More conventional double-deckers are four Roe-bodied Fleetlines bought from Derby City Transport in 1989, one of which was new to Grimsby-Cleethorpes. The 'deckers are used on contract work. Roselyn also runs one of Plymouth's redundant Dodges, and a pair of Wadham Stringer-bodied Mercedes 709Ds one of which is registered J6EDE, Ede being the name of Roselyn Coaches' owner.

This Atlantean in the Truronian fleet was built as a development vehicle by Leyland who specified the Merseyside PTE-style Alexander bodywork. It was first registered in 1980 when it was sold to Rennie of Dunfermline. A British Leyland Mini grille adorns the front panel. Barry Spencer

The standard vehicle for Hopley's service to Truro is a 1975 Bedford YRT with Duple body. Three-plus-two seating is used to raise its capacity to 66 seats. Barry Spencer

Carrying its owners name – Ede – in the registration, this Mercedes 709D operated by Roselyn has 21-seat Wadham Stringer bodywork, an uncommon choice. It is seen in St Austell. Barry Spencer

Inland from Plymouth, Ford of Gunnislake (which is just inside Cornwall) operates tendered services in Devon in the Tavistock area. A Bedford YRQ with Duple Dominant bus body carries a livery to promote the route to Harrowbarrow. The fleet is made up primarily of assorted Leyland and Volvo coaches, and there are two ECW-bodied Atlanteans for school work. These were new to Northern General, but reached Ford by way of City of Oxford.

In the area which marks the overlap between Devon General and Western National, Tally Ho! (possibly the only British bus operator with an exclamation mark in its fleetname) of Kingsbridge operates thence to Salcombe and, on contract to Devon county council, from Dartmouth to Plymouth and Exeter. Tally Ho! runs a big fleet — about 40 vehicles — of which just over half are Bristols. There are no fewer than 13 former London LHs (bought over a 10 year period from 1982 to 1992), four REs and six VRTs. Three of the VRTs are standard ex-NBC machines bought from Devon General, but the other three are long-wheelbase Alexander-bodied buses, new in 1977 to Tayside Regional Transport. There are also three Dodge S56 minibuses, two of which are unusually early examples dating back to 1979. The S56 really only became popular as a bus (albeit briefly and selectively) with deregulation in 1986.

In Devon General country, a Dawlish town service is provided by Dawlish Coaches, who also run rural routes on contract to Devon county council. The bus fleet comprises three Fleetlines. Two are Roe-bodied buses from York Pullman; the third is a much travelled London Transport DMS. Another operator in the Devon General area is Devon Services, which has grown from nothing in 1985 to a 17-vehicle operation. Devon Services is based in Paignton and runs mainly around Totnes and Torbay with an odd assortment of 1970s second-hand buses. These include a Willowbrook-bodied Ford R192, a type once popular with small operators but now nearing extinction, an ex-SBG Alexander-bodied Leopard, and a variety of Bristol LHs which includes buses new to London Transport, London Country and Greater Manchester Transport. Fleet livery is white and blue.

In an area as vast as south-west England there are many other small operators running mainly on tendered services, which often change operators when they come up for renewal.

ECW-bodied Bristols feature prominently in the Tally Ho! fleet. Most are LHs which originated with London Transport. This example is seen in Torquay. Barry Spencer

The three double-deckers (all Fleetlines) in the Dawlish Coaches fleet were repainted in a restrained all-over blue livery in 1992. This Roe bodied bus is seen in Exminster. Graham Jones

Devon Services have seven Bristol LHs. This one, a 1973 LHS6L, was new to London Country Bus Services. It has a 37-seat ECW body and is seen in Exeter. Graham Jones

WALES

With the Great Orme as a backdrop, a Crosville Mercedes minibus is seen in Llandudno. John Jones

The bulk of Welsh bus activity is in the south, with major operators serving the industrial belt through which the M4 motorway runs, and the tightly-packed valleys which lie to the north. It is an area which has prospered — and declined — on coal. Head north and there are few major centres of population apart from Aberystwyth until you reach the north coast with the university town of Bangor, and the resorts at Llandudno, Rhyl and Colwyn Bay.

The bus industry in South Wales has seen rapid and dramatic changes since deregulation. The municipally-operated fleets at Rhymney Valley (Inter Valley Link), Merthyr Tydfil, Taff Ely and Cynon Valley have gone, largely victims of National Welsh rapacity. National Welsh was the subject of a management buy-out from NBC and could claim as late as 1990 to be the biggest bus company in Wales, with 626 buses and coaches. Within two years it had vanished. It had competed and expanded with some aggression — and failed. Its failure in 1992 created opportunities for other operators and parts of what was once National Welsh live on, most obviously in the Red & White and Rhondda fleets.

First, there are the three surviving South Wales municipal fleets — Cardiff, Newport and Islwyn.

Cardiff City Transport Services, with almost 300 vehicles, is one of the biggest bus companies in South Wales. It runs east to Newport and north to Tredegar and, taking advantage of National Welsh's failure, is now the major operator in Barry, once a National Welsh town. Back in the 1970s Cardiff was the first major operator in Wales to use fleetnames in both Welsh and English. This practice continues with Cardiff Bus on the nearside and Bws Caerdydd on the offside of big buses. Small buses run as Cardiff Clipper Bus — in English only.

Before the watershed of deregulation the fleet was predominantly double-decked. It still is, but since 1987 a growing number of MetroRider minibuses has been put into operation, built by both MCW and Optare, and there are now approaching 70 in use. Services in Barry are operated almost exclusively by MetroRiders. The Cardiff small bus fleet also includes 10 ex-Plymouth Dodge S56s with Reeve Burgess bodies.

The late 1970s standard in Cardiff was the Bristol VRT with Alexander body, an unusual combination bought only by Cardiff, Northampton and Tayside. Around 70 are in operation, making them the most numerous of Cardiff's big buses. The early 1980s saw a change of direction and orders were divided between front-engined Ailsas with Northern Counties bodies and rear-engined Olympians with East Lancs bodies. There are 36 of each. Cardiff was the only Welsh operator to buy new Ailsas.

More recent big bus purchases have seen Leylands and Scanias join the fleet. There are 41 Lynxes (including 12 Lynx IIs) which were delivered between 1989 and 1991. The Scanias are 23 N113s — 10 with Alexander double-deck bodies and 13 with Plaxton Verde single-deck bodies. The Verdes were purchased from dealer stock in 1992 when buses were needed at short notice as National Welsh started to disappear.

Ailsas are uncommon in Wales, with Cardiff City Transport being the only operator to have ordered the model. It runs 36, all with Northern Counties bodywork. Stewart J Brown

The first Scanias for the Welsh capital were seven N113s with Alexander R-type bodies, taken into stock in 1990. Cardiff also runs an earlier generation of Alexander bodywork with AL-type bodies on a fleet of Bristol VRTs. John Jones

Newport Transport runs just over 90 buses. These reach Cardiff and also run north to Cwmbran new town, but the bulk of operations are concentrated in Newport. The oldest buses in regular use are 1980 MCW Metrobuses. There are eight Metrobuses in the fleet, delivered at the same time as Newport's first Scanias, 11 W-registered 1981 BR112 models with double-deck Marshall bodies. These were the first Scania buses in Britain (if you allow that the Metro-Scania was an Anglo-Swedish hybrid) and set the scene for future big bus purchases, with a further batch of Marshall-bodied 'deckers which were followed in 1983 by nine BR112s with Wadham Stringer Vanguard bodies, a combination not to be found anywhere else.

From 1984 all of the new Scanias were double-deckers with bodies by East Lancs and Alexander — but that changed in 1993 with the arrival of six N113s with Alexander's new Strider single-deck body. Deregulation brought minibuses — Newport Nippers — into the fleet. Some spectacularly unattractive East Lancs-bodied Dodges have come and gone, and now all 14 of Newport's small buses are MetroRiders, the first two built by MCW, the remainder by Optare.

Two elderly buses are retained. There is a 1972 Metro-Scania single-decker, marking an earlier generation of Swedish-inspired buses, and a 1958 Leyland Titan PD2 with Longwell Green bodywork. There is also a fleet of four Leyland Tiger coaches.

Islwyn Borough Transport, formed in 1974 to succeed the grandly titled West Monmouthshire Omnibus Board, is the sole survivor of the five local authority bus fleets which served the valley townships when deregulation came in 1986. It has not only survived but has grown, increasing its fleet from 30 to 40 vehicles principally by diversifying into the coach business. Its routes are centred around Blackwood but reach north to Tredegar, south to Cardiff and west to Pontypridd. The standard bus in the 1970s was Leyland's trusty Leopard, and 13 are still in use, delivered between 1972 and 1981 and fitted with BET-style bus bodies by Willowbrook and Marshall. Since the demise of the Leopard, Islwyn has only bought three batches of new buses. Three East Lancs-bodied Tigers were delivered in 1986, followed by three more in 1987. More unusual, and the last new purchases, are six Dodge GO8 midibuses with 25-seat East Lancs bodies, a combination unique to Islwyn. The GO8 is a light truck chassis but has proved remarkably reliable as a small bus.

Since 1988 the only additions to the bus fleet have been former Inter Valley Link Leopards (two are in use) and second-hand Sherpas and the company has instead been buying coaches. These have ranged from 1978 Leopards to a 1985 Mercedes-Benz O303 integral. The Mercedes was acquired with the business of Paul Diaper Eurotours in 1991. Two coaches retain the Diaper name, and five run under the Kingfisher Travel banner in a pink, light blue and mid-blue livery which replaces the previous maroon scheme. The bus fleet is two-tone blue and white.

Newport's oldest buses are MCW Metrobuses which were new in 1981. John Jones

The first full-size single-deckers for Newport Transport for 10 years arrived in 1993. These were six Scania N113s with Alexander's new Strider bodywork. John Jones

Below: **Islwyn Borough Transport introduced a simplified version of its blue and white livery in 1993. A freshly repainted Tiger is seen in Cardiff at the start of a journey of some thirty miles to Tredegar. This 1986 East Lancs bodied bus is one of six similar vehicles in the fleet.** John Jones

Red & White Services, based in Cwmbran, was the first part of the National Welsh empire to be sold. Red & White was a trading name for the eastern part of National Welsh and is a name which can be traced back to 1929. It was reformed as a company in 1991 and purchased by Western Travel, which owns the neighbouring Cheltenham & Gloucester business just across the border in England. Gloucester is the eastern limit of Red & White operations. Services reach Cardiff in the south and extend north to Abergavenny, Brecon, Hereford and Ross-on-Wye.

The big bus fleet is ageing and comprises in the main Leyland Nationals and Bristol VRTs to standard NBC specifications. VRT variety is provided by four former Tayside long-wheelbase buses with Alexander bodies. The newest big buses in the fleet were, until 1992, W-registered VRTs. The change in 1992 came with the take-over of Cynon Valley's services in Aberdare. With them came an assortment of Cynon Valley buses including ECW-bodied REs, Leyland Nationals and five former Merthyr Tydfil Leyland Lynxes. Some of these buses are now in Red & White livery while a few still retain Cynon Valley's cream, green and orange. The former Cynon Valley services are run by the Aberdare Bus Co, another Western Travel subsidiary which shares Red & White's livery and fleet numbering series. Another similar Red & White sister company is The Valleys Bus Company, based in Pengam and running in the Rhymney and Merthyr Valleys.

Red & White runs a large number of Freight Rover Sherpas – nearly 50 – but has more recently been buying new Mercedes minis with bodywork by Alexander and Wright, along with second-hand Dodges and Ford Transits. The Mercedes have generally been replacing old Nationals and many operate on quite long routes, such as Newport to Brecon. Further examples, with Marshall bodies, are on order. Red & White's livery is red, white and grey — but in a variety of shades and applications.

Rhondda Buses has taken over the Porth depot and part of the Caerphilly Busways operation of National Welsh and runs some 80 buses in a dark maroon and cream livery. It is owned by a consortium which includes directors from Stevensons of Uttoxeter and Midland Fox. There are Leyland Nationals, Bristol VRTs and Leyland Olympians in the fleet, along with MCW Metroriders which originated with Inter Valley Link and London Buses. The Inter Valley Link inheritance is also seen in five Tigers with East Lancs bus bodies. Although only formed in 1992, Rhondda Buses has been quick to buy new vehicles and has introduced the Dennis Dart to South Wales with examples bodied by Plaxton and Wright. It has also added second-hand Transits and a pair of Rolls-Royce-engined Metrobuses and this influx of new and used buses has almost eliminated Sherpas and Ivecos from the fleet. In June 1993 Rhondda expanded with the takeover of the bus operations and 15 buses run by Cyril Evans of Senghenydd. The Cyril Evans services are being amalgamated with Rhondda's Caerphilly Busways operation using a modified version of the cream and red Cyril Evans livery.

Red & White acquired three operational Bristol REs from Cynon Valley which seem secure for a while yet as they are receiving fleet livery. One of these lively machines is seen at Abercynon in August 1993. John Jones

New deliveries to Red & White have been Mercedes-Benz minibuses with bodywork by Alexander and, as seen here in Pontypool, Wright. Stewart J Brown

Below: **Rhondda has been investing in new Dennis Darts, taking examples with both Plaxton Pointer and Wright Handybus bodies. This is a Plaxton in Bridgend.** John Jones

South Wales has seen the rapid growth of small fleets since deregulation. Phil Anslow of Pontypool is now the main operator around that town, and operates through three companies — Phil Anslow Travel (in green and yellow), Cwmbran Mini Link (blue and grey) and Gwent Omnibus Company (white). Services reach Newport, Cwmbran and Chepstow with extensions in 1993 to Hereford, Monmouth and Abergavenny. Second-hand Freight Rover Sherpa minibuses, around 25 of them, form the bulk of the fleet.

Henley's of Abertillery is one of the longer established bus operators in the area. The business dates back to the early post-war years and the pattern of operation has changed very little. The fleet, once an AEC stronghold, is now more varied but there remain two AECs in use – a Willowbrook dating from 1961 and a Plaxton from 1973. The livery is two-tone green and white.

Glyn Williams of Pontllanfraith, who also controls Crosskeys Coach Hire, operates around Blackwood, Risca, Newbridge and Newport, largely in association with Red & White, with services also extending as far as Brynmawr and Ebbw Vale. These are operated by a mixture of Leyland Nationals, all bought second-hand, and Mercedes-Benz minibuses, most of which were bought new. The livery is green and white.

Operators in the Rhymney Valley include Harris Coaches of Fleur de Lis, which has been running bus services in the Blackwood and Bargoed areas since 1988 and has a fleet of 13 Sherpas, four Mercedes plus three Nationals and a couple of Transits. Services are operated in competition with Islwyn and reach out to Caerphilly and Gelligaer.

Thomas Motors has been operating between Barry Island and Cardiff for many years and these days Leyland Nationals are normally used. One which originated with Eastern National is seen at the Mill Lane terminus in the Welsh capital. John Jones

Anslow's E69SUH is a former Bebb Optare Citypacer bodied Volkswagen, the only such vehicle remaining in the fleet. It is seen in Pontypool whilst operating a local service. John Jones

The Henley's fleet still contains two AEC Reliances, the real gem amongst them being this 1961 Willowbrook bodied vehicle which is still going strong. New to Western Welsh as a 'semi-coach', it has long since been fitted with bus seats, and is seen leaving Abertillery town centre. John Jones

One of the biggest of the post-deregulation bus companies is Parfitt's of Rhymney Bridge, a coach operator now running 20 former London Buses Nationals on services centred on Merthyr Tydfil. All of the Nationals have been rebuilt as single-door buses; 14 have been re-trimmed and seven have alternative power units — six with Volvo engines and one with a DAF engine. Amongst the other vehicles used on bus work are eight ex-London Metroriders for lightly-loaded services, five former Merthyr Tydfil Duple-bodied Leopard buses and one bus-bodied Tiger which came from Hill's of Tredegar, an old-established company which closed down in 1992. The most unusual bus in the fleet is the Renault PR100 which was operated by London Buses. It was acquired in 1993. Fleet livery is cream and red.

Silverline of Merthyr Tydfil started in 1986 with three Optare CityPacers. It bought a fourth in 1987 and followed that with three Leyland Swifts. All of these were bought new. One CityPacer and the three Swifts are still in use, along with a fourth Swift, a Leyland demonstrator which had been running for Jersey Motor Transport. A new Dennis Javelin with Wadham Stringer Vanguard body arrived in August 1993. Services operate north to Brecon, north-west to Llandovery and west to Swansea.

A small operator in Merthyr Tydfil is John's Transport with a pair of Sherpas running to Heolgerrig. A former Greater London Ford school bus is also used.

Services in Pontypridd are now mainly provided by Alison Jones, running as Shamrock Shoppa. The company operates as far afield as Bridgend and Cardiff. There are over 100 buses in the fleet, mostly minibuses (with a wide variety of bodywork). Mercs predominate – there are 49, all but two bought new. Unusual vehicles are four rare front-wheel-drive CVE Omnis, used mainly on South Glamorgan county council's Village Bus tendered operation. The Village Bus network serves Bridgend, Talbot Green, Cowbridge, Llantwit Major and Barry.

Harris Coaches of Fleur de Lis operates minibuses and three ex-London Buses Nationals. John Jones

Parfitts serve Merthyr Tydfil with ex-London Nationals and this Renault PR100 from the same source. Steve Warburton

There are four Leyland Swifts in the Silverline fleet. A Wadham Stringer-bodied bus loads at Merthyr Tydfil station for Brecon. Malc McDonald

Among the more unusual vehicles in the Alison Jones Shamrock Shoppa fleet are four CVE Omnis. The Omni has front-wheel-drive and a low floor – but also an unusually high driving position. The Shamrock buses are 23-seaters. John Jones

In Llantwit Fardre, to the south of Pontypridd, old-established coach operator Bebb runs a number of local bus services, including the company's original Beddau to Pontypridd route. Services are operated by five Optare StarRiders, four Freight Rover Sherpas, two CityPacers and two Ivecos, all bought new. Busier services are handled by unusual Leyland Tigers with Plaxton 321 coach bodies. The 321 was a Plaxton-built version of the Duple 320, using Duple's jigs and parts. Only 25 were built, of which 15 went to Bebb: five of these remain in the fleet. Bebb also provides coaches for National Express operation.

Golden Coaches of Llandow was formed in 1988 and runs several routes in the Vale of Glamorgan as well as its original service between Llantwit Major and Cardiff. These are run by a variety of vehicles including a former Cynon Valley Bristol RE, three Nationals and two Sherpas from National Welsh, an ECW-bodied LH and a Mercedes 608D. Thomas Motors of Barry runs to Cardiff and has done so since 1921. Three Leyland Nationals are currently used.

Other small fleets include Burrows of Ogmore Vale, running two VRTs, one Leopard and three former SBG Nationals on two services to Bridgend. Also running from Porthcawl is the Porthcawl Omnibus Co. Its bus fleet includes two 1973 Fleetlines from Nottingham, and an MCW-bodied VRT which was new to the West Midlands PTE. Among the single-deck fleet, made up mainly of Leopard coaches, there is an ex-Western Scottish Leopard/Alexander bus and a Volvo with Jonckheere Bermuda coach body which is used regularly on service to Cardiff.

Other operators in Bridgend include Pathfinder, running second-hand minibuses.

Bebb's Optare StarRiders add a touch of style to the streets of Pontypridd. This is one of five bought new in 1991. Malcolm King

The varied Golden Coaches fleet includes two Bristol service buses, an RE and an LH. Both have ECW bodies. One of Cardiff's Plaxton Verde bodied Scanias is overtaking in this view. Alan Simpkins

One of the relatively uncommon full-height ECW bodied VRTs was acquired by Burrows in the spring of 1993 from Brewers. It has been repainted in a revised livery which abandons the blue relief previously used. John Jones

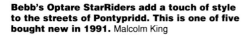

Westwards from Bridgend lies South Wales Transport territory. SWT was privatised in a management buy-out from NBC in 1987 and in the following year purchased Brewers Motor Services of Maesteg and the Swansea operations of Cleverly of Cwmbran. In 1990 SWT and its associated companies were sold to Badgerline and in 1992 Badgerline reorganised the operation by expanding the Brewers fleet and reducing the size of SWT. Brewers now run not only from Maesteg, but also from what was the SWT depot at Port Talbot (now Brewers' headquarters) and from the former United Welsh Coaches depot at Gorseinon.

At the start of 1992 there were 20 vehicles running for Brewers. Twelve months later this had risen to 120, with a corresponding reduction in the SWT fleet which now numbers around the 240 mark. The recent expansion of Brewers makes it a colourful fleet. The livery was blue and white, but is being changed to red. Many buses retain South Wales Transport's green. There are in addition vehicles transferred from other Badgerline subsidiaries which retain their previous liveries including ex-Bristol City Line VRTs and Nationals.

The bus fleet consists mainly of VRTs, Nationals and Mercedes minis. Five Lynx IIs were delivered in 1992, two J-registered Volvo-engined ex-demonstrators and three new K-registered Cummins-powered buses. But apart from these the newest big bus in the fleet is an X-registered ex-Thamesway VRT. Dual-purpose Leopards are used for some inter-town services and three former Thamesway Tigers with Alexander TE bodies wear a promotional livery for the X3 Maesteg to Swansea limited stop service.

United Welsh Coaches was primarily a coach operation, and a fleet of DAFs, Leopards, Tigers and Royal Tigers carry the United Welsh name. The Royal Tigers include a comparatively rare Plaxton-bodied coach which was acquired from Grey-Green of London. The majority of Royal Tigers were Doyen integrals, built completely by Leyland.

The Brewers fleet has seen considerable expansion in recent times largely due to the transfer of vehicles from South Wales Transport and United Welsh. However some new vehicles have also been received including ten Plaxton bodied Mercedes-Benz 811Ds, one of which is seen at Bridgend in July 1993. John Jones

The new Brewers livery has been applied to many older vehicles in the fleet. This VRT, as yet without the badger, was new in 1981 to Eastern National. John Jones

A former Volvo-Leyland Lynx II demonstrator in the Brewers fleet is seen in Bridgend. Keith Grimes

South Wales Transport is based in Swansea; its most westerly depot is in Haverfordwest. Mercedes minibuses feature prominently throughout SWT's territory. There are early L608D van conversions by Robin Hood, followed by batches of 709Ds and 811Ds bodied by Reeve Burgess, Robin Hood and Phoenix. SWT's most recent Mercedes — F-registered buses onwards — are of the more powerful 140bhp 814D variety. Most operators settle for the more common 110bhp 811D. There are also 26 MCW Metroriders based in Swansea. Most Swansea local services are minibus operated, many with unusual (and ungainly) roof-mounted advertising displays.

The small double-deck fleet comprises 21 VRTs plus nine Olympians. Of the latter, seven are standard NBC-style buses while two are long-wheelbase coaches which were new to Eastern National but came to SWT from Thamesway. They are allocated to the Swansea to Cardiff limited stop operation and are named after two famous Welshmen, Dylan Thomas and Sir Harry Secombe. Another odd vehicle with Eastern National connections is SWT's only open-topper, a 1953 Bristol KSW5G which provides a summer service in Swansea. It moved from Essex to Wales in 1974.

Although roof mounted advertisement boards are a feature of South Wales Transport's early Mercedes-Benz minibuses, they are also to be found on this MCW Metrorider. It is one of 25 Metroriders purchased in 1987 which, unusually, are fitted with manual transmission. John Jones

SWT now runs only 31 double-deckers, 21 of which are VRTs. This 1980 vehicle in Swansea shows the recently introduced colour-coded destination display. John Jones

Only around 20 Leyland Nationals remain in the South Wales Transport fleet when at one time well over 100 were owned. A 1979 example is seen in Swansea city centre returning from Townhill, an area once served by vehicles specially adapted to cope with a very steep hill on the route. John Jones

City Connection, operated by Hawkes Coaches of Waunarlwydd, runs into Swansea from Gorseinon, using a pair of ex-Clydeside Scottish Seddon Pennine 7s with Alexander bodies, an Alexander-bodied Bedford YRT which was new to Edinburgh Corporation Transport, and a former Southern Vectis Bristol RE. In nearby Neath, another SWT stronghold, Merlyn's Coaches of Skewen operates a service to Birchgrove, normally using a 1981 Leopard with Duple Dominant bus body which came from the Merthyr Tydfil Transport fleet in 1989. It carries the same livery as the company's coaches, white and turquoise with bright red and yellow relief.

Brian Isaac Coaches of Swansea has for many years operated a free Tesco bus service. In 1992 it took over the Neath service of Jenkins of Skewen. Jenkins was owned by Shearings who were divesting themselves of local bus operations throughout the country. Two one-time Central Scottish Mercedes Benz L608Ds are used alongside two Sherpas.

Beyond Swansea and Llanelli, Wales becomes more rural. It is an area which supports some large and long-established independent operators. D Coaches of Morriston, just outside Swansea, runs 70 vehicles. The company has expanded by acquisition, taking over West Wales in 1984 and Rees & Williams in 1987. Both names are carried on buses, while minibuses run as Dyfed Diamonds. D Coaches run between Swansea and Llandeilo and also serve Ammanford, Carmarthen and Llanelli. Many of the services are operated as part of the county's Bws Dyfed scheme. Second-hand Leopards dominate the fleet, but more modern vehicles bought for specific tendered services are four Optare CityPacers acquired from Bebb of Llantwit Fardre, and three Dennis Darts with Plaxton Pointer bodies bought new in 1992. A fourth Dart, with Alexander Dash body, followed later in 1992. There are also two second-hand Nationals, but these see little use. A large double-deck fleet with a number of one-time Glasgow and Edinburgh Atlanteans and former London Fleetlines is maintained, primarily for schools services.

There are few Seddons in Wales. Hawkes Coaches runs two former SBG Pennine 7s with Alexander Y-type bodies. New to Western SMT in 1977, they came to Hawkes in 1987 and 1988. John Jones

D Coaches run four Dennis Darts. Three have Reeve Burgess Pointer bodies. The R&W lettering is a reference to Rees & Williams, taken over in 1987. The trading name is still used for part of D Coaches' operations. John Jones

Although twenty years old, Rees & Williams liveried WTH338M is still a regular performer on the Swansea – Llandeilo service. This Plaxton Derwent bodied Leyland Leopard is seen turning into Kingsway, Swansea as it leaves for the small Dyfed town. John Jones

Llandeilo is the home of Thomas Bros, who serve Carmarthen and Llandovery. Their most modern bus is a Dennis Lancet with Duple Dominant body which was built as a Motor Show exhibit in 1986 when it carried the livery of Northumbria Motor Services. Dennis and Duple were hoping to convince Northumbria that the Lancet could replace its fleet of LHs. It is unusual (and possibly unique) for a Lancet in having a Cummins engine and it was one of the last Lancets with one of the last Duple Dominant bodies to be built. Older Thomas Bros buses, all second-hand, include ECW-bodied Bristol LHs and a 1975 Leopard with a 1989 Willowbrook Warrior body.

Davies Bros are particularly strong in the Llanelli and Carmarthen areas and run 80 buses and coaches. Bus services are largely in the hands of Leyland Leopards and Tigers with a mixture of bodywork. There are contrasting styles of Willowbrook bodies with some Leopards running with 1970s BET-style bodies while others have been rebodied with new square-looking Warrior bodies. There are some unusual Tigers too, including a rare 10m model with East Lancs bodywork which came from National Welsh (but was new to Rhymney Valley), and a former Leyland demonstration chassis built in 1984 with left-hand drive but not bodied until 1990 after being purchased by Davies Bros and converted to right-hand drive. It has a Willowbrook Warrior body. Three second-hand Fleetline 'deckers are used for school contracts, the oldest being a J-registered ECW-bodied bus which was new to Alexander (Midland). Five Mercedes minibuses are also run.

Ffoshelig of Newchurch serves Carmarthen with a network of routes, operated by a variety of buses in a smart cream and brown livery. It runs two second-hand Leopard buses, one with a Duple Dominant body, the other bodied by Willowbrook. There are also a couple of ECW-bodied LHs and two minibuses in the shape of a Mercedes 609D and an ex-Greater Manchester Buses Dodge S56 with Northern Counties body. Jones of Login keeps four Leopards with Duple bus bodies in what is primarily a coach fleet. These are for operation on schools and market day services.

Edwards of Tiers Cross runs town services in Haverfordwest and Milford Haven, normally with a minibus. Silcox of Pembroke Dock maintains a fleet of 70 vehicles which includes a number of buses bought new. These are four Leopards and, unusually for a private sector company, two Bristol LHs which have Duple Dominant bus bodies, a rare combination. Bought in 1976 they were Silcox's last new Bristols, a make with which the company was long associated. Recent new buses have been Dormobile-bodied Mercs, while used purchases have included a pair of Alexander-bodied Leopards new to Western Scottish, two similar buses new to the Tyne & Wear PTE and a one-time Central SMT bus. There are also three Leopards with Willowbrook Warrior bodies which were purchased from Glyn Williams of Pontllanfraith in 1992. Many of Silcox's older Leopard coaches were built to bus grant specification and are also still used on service.

A former Nottingham Leopard operated by Thomas of Llandeilo shows both English and Welsh versions of the fleet name. The chassis was new in 1975, the Willowbrook Warrior body in 1989. *John Jones*

This Willowbrook-bodied Leopard operated by Ffoshelig since 1990 was previously owned by Davies of Pencader. It was new in 1978. *Malcolm King*

The Silcox fleet was well-known for its Bristols, although these are now reduced to a few LHs and VRTs while an assortment of new and second-hand Leopards have taken over most of the company's services. *John Jones*

Richards Bros (or Brodyr Richards if you look at the offside of the firm's buses) is based in Cardigan and operates south to Haverfordwest and north to Aberystwyth. The company's standard bus is the combination of Bedford Y-series chassis and Duple Dominant bus body, a type of which it has 18 dating from between 1975 and 1983 and of varying ancestry, including some bought new. There are older Willowbrook-bodied Bedfords, including three SB5s now demoted to contract work. More recent vehicles in the fleet include two Optare Deltas out of only five in Wales, and a Carlyle-bodied Dennis Dart, which was delivered in 1991 and was among the first in the Principality.

Midway Motors runs to Cardigan from its home town of Crymych, usually with a Ford R-series, an increasingly uncommon model. The normal vehicle is a former Highland Scottish example with a Duple Dominant coach body fitted from new with bus seats, the Dominant E.

Inland from Aberaeron, James Brothers of Llangeitho run two Reeve Burgess-bodied Mercedes on a tendered service between Lampeter and Pontrhydfendigaid. Other Dyfed tenders are held and are operated by smaller Mercedes or Bedford coaches.

Eastward lies Powys, the largest and least densely populated county in Wales, and here Browns of Builth operates tendered services which take its vehicles, mainly Bedford coaches, to Aberystwyth,

Abergavenny, Newtown and Llandrindod Wells. Cross Gates Coaches of Llandrindod Wells runs locally with a fleet of predominantly Bedford coaches, although there is also a Plaxton-bodied LHS and three Plaxton-bodied Reliances. Cross Gates also runs to Cardiff three times a week, normally with a Van Hool-bodied Scania or Bedford YNV coach.

The newest vehicle operated by Richards Bros is a 1991 Carlyle-bodied Dart. Note the use of bilingual fleetnames. Malcolm King

Mercedes-Benz minibuses are used on the Bws Dyfed services operated by James Brothers.

Aberystwyth, on the west coast, has the southernmost Crosville Wales depot, although there are outstations further south at New Quay, Llanrhystyd and Tregaron. Crosville Wales was created in 1986 when the Chester-based Crosville company, once one of NBC's biggest, was split in two in readiness for privatisation and deregulation. The English Crosville company has effectively disappeared, being reduced to a fleetname on PMT buses. But Crosville Wales is still going strong, although its business has been slimmed down since it was privatised in a management buy-out in 1987.

Ownership has changed too. In 1988 the company was bought by National Express but is now owned by British Bus (formerly Drawlane). There have been cuts at Wrexham following severe industrial relations problems and, reflecting the Drawlane involvement, operations in Oswestry were transferred to Midland Red North (also a Drawlane subsidiary) at the end of 1991. The company has also lost some tendered services, although recent contract gains have reversed the downward trend.

One of the delights of Crosville is its fleet numbering system, a rare survivor from the days before computerisation which ultimately made most operators abandon easily-understood letter codes in favour of numbers which computers could cope with. Most vehicles have a three letter prefix with the letters indicating vehicle type (double-deck, single-deck, minibus, coach), chassis make or type and engine make. Thus CTL indicates Coach Tiger Leyland and DOG stands for Double-deck Olympian Gardner. It all makes a lot of sense.

The Crosville Wales headquarters is in Llandudno Junction and it has other depots throughout North Wales at Mold, Bangor, Blaenau Ffestiniog and Rhyl, with numerous outstations besides. The full-size single-deck fleet is made up primarily of B-series Leyland Nationals delivered in 1978-79. The B-series was offered as a low-cost option by Leyland with conventional underseat heating in place of the overhead pod of the original model. East Lancs National Greenway rebuilds are being delivered in 1993. Older Leopard and Tiger coaches are used on long-distance services. The only new big buses delivered to Crosville Wales since its privatisation are two Optare Deltas. These were delivered in 1989 and were the first in Wales. They are based at Dolgellau and run between Wrexham and Barmouth.

Double-deckers are mainly VRTs. But there are 10 Olympians, five of which have coach-type seats and are allocated to the Coastliner express service which runs to Chester. Five of the VRTs are open-toppers (three permanent, two convertible) and there are other open-toppers too: six ex-Southdown and two ex-Southend Fleetlines, one former London DMS, an Atlantean which was new to Plymouth and a Bristol Lodekka FS6G. These operate mainly along the north coast from Llandudno and carry Happy Dragon fleetnames. A closed-top FS6G is available when the weather is bad. Other reminders of Crosville's heritage are two 1957 Bristol SCs which carry period Tilling green livery.

As in many other fleets, the late 1980s saw Crosville Wales invest in minibuses. It inherited Mercedes L608Ds and Freight Rover Sherpas from NBC and to these it has added second-hand L608Ds and new 709Ds and Iveco 49.10s. The L608Ds are van conversions; the other types have coachbuilt bodies by Reeve Burgess, Robin Hood, Carlyle and Phoenix. Four Wright bodied Mercedes 811Ds – the first new buses for four years – joined the fleet in August 1993.

The Crosville Wales livery is an attractive bright green and white. On tendered services in Gwynedd, a red front is added, to meet the requirements of Gwynedd county council.

Not only Crosville Wales is affected. A number of smaller operators in the county also have red-fronted buses which sport Bws Gwynedd names. On the principle of he who pays for the piper calling the tune, this is a move which cannot be argued with. Indeed, it is surprising that more tendering authorities have not forced the issue. Would London's route network make more sense to visitors if all buses had red fronts?

Crosville Wales operates 45 Leyland Nationals, all Mark 1 B-series variants with no roof pods. These are now being joined by East Lancs National Greenway rebuilds, with five due in 1993. This bus is a rebuild of a former London Country vehicle. Malcolm King

Many vehicles running on services supported by Gwynedd county council have red fronts and Bws Gwynedd names, though these also appear on other services, which may defeat the object. Robin Hood bodywork is fitted to this 1988 Crosville Wales Iveco Ford 49.10 in Bangor. Stewart J Brown

Be that as it may, there are red-fronted buses in most of the fleets operating Gwynedd services. Notable exceptions to the red front rule are KMP and Purple Motors.

Cambrian Coast of Tywyn operates around Dolgellau and along the coast to Barmouth, as well as running services inland. The fleet comprises a National and two Freight Rover Sherpas.

The Clynnog & Trefor Motor Company runs from Pwllheli, on the Lleyn Peninsula, to Caernarfon, serving on the way the two villages from which it takes its name. An ex-London Fleetline shares the work with a former Chester Fleetline. There is also a Duple Dominant-bodied Leopard which was new to PMT and has been fitted with bus seats and four ECW-bodied Bristol VRTs for contracts. The service from Pwllheli to Llithfaen is run by Williams of Llithfaen, normally with a Duple bus-bodied Bedford YMQ. There is also a Willowbrook-bodied YRQ and, for a school service, a 1982 Bedford VAS5.

Express Motors of Bontnewydd operates to Caernarfon, Bangor, Blaenau Ffestiniog, Dolgellau and Porthmadog among other places. The 30-vehicle fleet is varied, ranging from G-registered Bristol REs (from United Counties) to an ex-demonstration Leyland Swift with Wadham Stringer body. Between these extremes there is an assortment of Leopard coaches, Nationals, Bristol VRTs, a Willowbrook Warrior bodied Leopard, Mercedes minibuses and even a former West Midlands PTE Ailsa.

Silver Star of Upper Llandwrog also operates into Caernarfon from Cesarea and Carmel. Most Silver Star buses are ECW-bodied LHs, including some former London examples. In 1992 a new bus was added to the fleet – a Plaxton-bodied Dart.

KMP of Llanberis operates to Caernarfon, normally with an ex-Crosville National in an attractive two-tone blue livery. The KMP name comes from the initials of the owner's children, Karen, Maldwyn and Petula.

Clynnog & Trefor operates two Fleetlines, the newer of which is this ex-Chester bus with lowheight Northern Counties bodywork. It is a 1978 FE30AGR model. Malc McDonald

Williams of Llithfaen runs two Bedford Y-series buses. The older is a 1970 YRQ with Willowbrook body. John Jones

Silver Star's first new vehicle for many years arrived in 1992. It is a Dennis Dart with Plaxton Pointer body and is seen leaving Caernarfon. It shares the scene with Crosville and Express Motors. Malc McDonald

Another operator who was based in Llanberis is Padarn, which takes its name from a nearby lake. Padarn now operate from Caernarfon and run from Bangor to Llanrug, and across the Menai Bridge to Llangefni on Anglesey. The Llangefni route is normally served by two Dennis Darts bought new in 1991. These have Carlyle bodies finished in London Buses red. There are also second-hand Sherpas, an LH and an Iveco Ford Daily.

On Anglesey there are a number of small operators including Lewis y Llan from Llanerchymedd running two Optare StarRiders between Holyhead and Amlwch. The fleet also includes an ex-West Midlands Fleetline and a former Eastern Scottish Alexander-bodied Bedford YRT. Ellis of Llangefni has six Bristol VRTs and one RE, used on school contracts, and Iveco Ford minibuses for local services, one of which is ex-London Buses.

Purple Motors run from Bethesda to Bangor via two routes using an interesting collection of buses. There is one 'decker (an Ailsa from Tayside), three Leopards with Duple bus bodies and a fourth Leopard rebodied with a Willowbrook Warrior body. Services from Bangor to Dinorwig and Llanberis are operated by Ieuan Williams of Deiniolen with two Leyland Nationals and a VRT - all second-hand, of course.

D&G of Llanllechid, near Bethesda, run between Gerlan and Bangor using a rare PMT Knype-bodied Leyland Swift. An Alexander Y-type bodied Seddon is also owned and recent acquisitions are two Duple Dominant bodied Leopards from Red & White.

Alpine of Llandudno operate from Conwy to Llysfaen and Llanrwst to Rhyl for Clwyd county council, while also running a Conwy local service and to Penmaenmawr for Gwynedd. A variety of vehicles is used ranging from Ivecos with Robin Hood bodies bought new to second-hand Leyland Nationals including two Volvo re-engined examples from Tame Valley. These also appear on school contracts, along with Fleetlines which came from Chester City Transport and Camm of Nottingham, ex-Chester Dodge minibuses and a pair of former Maidstone Wadham Stringer-bodied Bedfords. Alpine also run a sizeable coach fleet using the Creams and Royal Red fleetnames.

At Bagillt on the Dee estuary, Lloyd operate local services including routes from Holywell to Mostyn and Shotton. Of interest is Lloyd's collection of second-hand Fleetlines which are used on schools and works contracts. These include buses which were new to SBG, West Midlands PTE and Nottingham City Transport. There are now 11, all immaculately turned out in cream and red.

Wrexham is the headquarters of The Wright Company, a substantial local operator. The Wright business has grown since deregulation, partly at the expense of Crosville Wales. As well as local services around Wrexham, Wright run through to Chester and as far south as Oswestry. The fleet is a fascinating mixture. The front-line buses are an Optare Delta and four Leyland Lynxes, all bought new. There were two Deltas, but one has been sold. There is also one double-decker bought new, a 1985 East Lancs-bodied Volvo Citybus.

London red livery, complete with grey skirt, is worn by a pair of Dennis Darts in the Padarn fleet. Both were bought new in 1991 and have Carlyle bodies. *Stewart J Brown*

Large Volvo letters on the grille leave no doubt about the parentage of this Scottish-built Ailsa operated by Purple Motors of Bethesda, seen leaving Bangor. It has an Alexander body and was new to Tayside in 1976. It is Purple Motors' only double-decker and has been operated since 1988. *Stewart J Brown*

The sizeable Alpine fleet contains several minibuses acquired new for stage carriage work. This Fiat 49-10 with Phoenix bodywork was new in 1990 and is seen in a sunny Colwyn Bay. *John Jones*

Wright's older single-deckers include second-hand Nationals. There is also an assortment of small buses with the most numerous type being Carlyle-bodied Sherpas. Wright runs around two dozen vehicles. Before deregulation it had eight.

Chaloner's of Wrexham for many years operated a local service with a Bedford SB. That, sadly, has vanished and it's a sign of the times that its replacement is nothing more interesting than a Mercedes 811D with Reeve Burgess Beaver body. Bought new in 1990, it is Chaloner's only bus and, uniquely for a vehicle of its size, is crew-operated. Somewhat bigger than Chaloner's is Edwards with six coaches and one bus. The bus, a Duple-bodied Bedford YMT, links Wrexham with Minera, a few miles to the west and close to Edwards' base in Bwlchgwyn.

Jones of Ponciau provides local services around Wrexham with a fleet of four Duple Dominant buses. Three are on conventional Bedford Y-series chassis, the fourth is on a front-engined Leyland Cub, one of 16 bought by Lothian Region Transport in 1981. It joined the Jones fleet in 1991. Other noteworthy buses are two Dennis Lancets with Wadham Stringer bodies. Also in Ponciau is Williams, an old-established operator running south from Wrexham to Rhosllanerchrugog. The Williams bus fleet is made up of a Plaxton-bodied Ford, and two Bedford Y-series, one bodied by Plaxton, the other by Duple.

Eagles & Crawford in Mold operate coaches and five VRTs, primarily on school services. Phillips of Holywell run in to Mold and on tendered services in the area. The mainstay of the fleet are four 1975 Bristol LHs, bought from Crosville in 1983 and still in regular use. There are also two second-hand Sherpas and a former SBG Alexander-bodied Seddon Pennine 7. Llangollen, to the south of Wrexham, is the home of Bryn Melyn Motor Services who run three Mercedes minibuses on local services and on routes to Wrexham and Oswestry.

Devaway Travel is only just in Wales, being based in Bretton which is barely a mile from the English border. It was started in 1987 by two former Crosville employees. The company's main Welsh operation is a frequent service from Mold to Chester. A number of services are provided under contract to Cheshire county council and some of these are operated from a base at Ellesmere Port. The fleet has expanded quickly and now numbers over 30 buses. Around half are Mark 1 Leyland Nationals from a variety of sources. There are also four ex-Halton East Lancs-bodied Bristol REs, five Freight Rover Sherpa minibuses, half a dozen Leopard dual-purpose coaches and one double-decker, a former West Riding VRT. The livery is cream and red.

The fleet of Wrights of Wrexham has a generally modern profile and includes four Leyland Lynxes. A Mark 1 version is seen at Chester. Ken Jubb

Jones of Ponciau operates into Wrexham. The fleet includes three 1981 Bedford YMQs with Duple Dominant bus bodies. This one came from Davies of Carmarthen. John Jones

Much of Devaway's service work is operated by Leyland Nationals such as NEN 952R, seen here passing through Sealand in June 1993. New to Greater Manchester PTE, it was acquired from Scarborough and District in 1988. John Jones

Badgerline Holdings
Badgerline
A E & F R Brewer
Bristol Omnibus Co
Eastern National
Midland Red West
South Wales Transport
Thamesway
Wessex Coaches
Western National

Blazefield Holdings
Blazefield Buses
Cambridge Coach Services
Harrogate & District Travel
Harrogate Independent Travel
Keighley & District Travel
Sovereign Bus & Coach Co
Welwyn Hatfield Line
Yorkshire Coastliner

British Bus
Bee Line Buzz Co
C-Line Bus Co
Express Travel Services
Guildford & West Surrey Buses
London & Country
Midland Fox
Midland Red North
North Western Road Car Co
Southend Transport
East Lancashire Coach Builders

Caldaire Holdings
Selby & District Bus Co
West Riding Automobile Co
Yorkshire Woollen District Transport Co

Cambus Holdings
Buckinghamshire Road Car Co
Cambus
Johnsons
Milton Keynes City Bus
Premier Travel Services
Viscount Bus & Coach Co

EYMS Group
Cherry Coaches
East Yorkshire Motor Services
Finglands
Hull & District Motor Services
Primrose Valley Coaches
Scarborough & District Motor Services

Go-Ahead Northern
Gateshead & District Omnibus Co (Go Ahead Gateshead)
Langley Park Motor Co (Gypsy Queen)
Low Fell Coaches
Northern General Transport Co
Northern National Transport Co
Sunderland & District Omnibus Co (Wear Buses)
Tynemouth & District Omnibus Co (Coastline)
Tyneside Omnibus Co (VFM Buses)

GRT Holdings
Grampian Transport
Kirkpatrick of Deeside
Mairs Coaches
Midland Bluebird
Oban & District (part)

London Buses
CentreWest London Buses
East London Bus & Coach Co
Leaside Bus Co
London Central Bus Co
London General Transport Services
London Northern Bus Co
London United
Metroline Travel
South East London & Kent Bus Co
South London Transport
Stanwell Buses

Luton & District
Clydeside 2000 (part)
Derby City Transport (part)

Proudmutual
Kentish Bus & Coach Co
Moordale Coaches
Northumbria Motor Services

Stagecoach Holdings
Bluebird Buses
Cumberland Motor Services
East Kent Road Car Co Ltd
East Midland Motor Services
Fife Scottish Omnibuses
Hampshire Bus Co
Ribble Motor Services
South Coast Buses
Stagecoach Scotland
Stagecoach South
Sussex Coastline
United Counties Omnibus Co

Transit Holdings
Bayline Minibus
Blue Admiral
Devon General
Red Admiral
Thames Transit

Western Travel
Cheltenham & Gloucester Omnibus Co
Circle Line (part)
G&G Travel
Midland Red South
Red & White
Swindon & District
Vanguard Coaches

Yorkshire Traction
Barnsley & District Traction Co
Lincolnshire Road Car Co
Strathtay Scottish Omnibuses
Yorkshire Traction